OUT FOR BLOOD

OUT FOR BLOOD

A Cultural History of Carrie *the Musical*

Chris Adams

methuen | drama

LONDON • NEW YORK • OXFORD • NEW DELHI • SYDNEY

METHUEN DRAMA
Bloomsbury Publishing Plc
50 Bedford Square, London, WC1B 3DP, UK
1385 Broadway, New York, NY 10018, USA
29 Earlsfort Terrace, Dublin 2, Ireland

BLOOMSBURY, METHUEN DRAMA and the Methuen Drama logo are trademarks
of Bloomsbury Publishing Plc

First published in Great Britain 2023

Cover images (clockwise from top left): Linzi Hateley on stage as Carrie, 1988 (ArenaPAL);
the Virginia Theatre in May 1988 (Mary Ann Hermansen); dance rehearsal in Stratford, 1988
(Kenny Linden); Linzi Hateley and Sally Ann Triplett in rehearsal, 1988 (Kenny Linden); Sally
Ann Triplett in rehearsal, 1988 (Kenny Linden); the cast in front of a branded Carrie bus in
Stratford, 1988 (Mary Anne Hermansen); Marin Mazzie and Molly Ranson on stage as
Margaret and Carrie, off-Broadway, 2012 (Joan Marcus) a ticket for Carrie on Broadway
(courtesy of Gil Benbrook); Barbara Cook and Linzi Hateley in rehearsal, 1988
(Kenny Linden); Emily Lopez as Carrie, LA, 2015 (Jason Niedle)

A catalogue record for this book is available from the British Library.

A catalog record for this book is available from the Library of Congress.

ISBN: HB: 978-1-3503-2054-3
       PB: 978-1-3503-2053-6
       ePDF: 978-1-3503-2055-0
       eBook: 978-1-3503-2056-7

Typeset by RefineCatch Limited, Bungay, Suffolk
Printed and bound in Great Britain

To find out more about our authors and books visit www.bloomsbury.com
and sign up for our newsletters.

I like to think of it now
as the most successful
flop on Broadway.

**LINZI HATELEY, 'CARRIE WHITE',
STRATFORD AND BROADWAY**

CONTENTS

PLATES AND IMAGES

Plates

Images

CAST OF CHARACTERS

Adams, Kevin	Lighting Designer, off-Broadway, 2012
Altomare, Christy	Sue Snell, off-Broadway, 2012
Argent, Philip	Audience member, Stratford, 1988
Arima, Stafford	Director, off-Broadway, 2012
Bailey, Mark	Assistant to Scenic Designer Ralph Koltai, Stratford and Broadway, 1988
Benbrook, Gil	Audience member, Broadway, 1988
Berg, Michael	Audience member, Stratford, 1988
Besterman, Doug	Orchestrator, off-Broadway, 2012
Borowski, Mike	*Carrie* fan and *TheatreWeek* intern, 1991
Briefer, Scott	Audience member, Broadway, 1988
Buckley, Betty	Margaret White, Broadway, 1988
Callaway, Liz	Chris Hargensen, Workshop, 1984
Campbell, Mary-Mitchell	Musical Director, off-Broadway, 2012
Cerda, David	Creator, *S'Carrie*, 1998/2005
Clayton, Paul	Audience member, Stratford, 1988
Cleary, Vivienne	Margaret White, Stagedoor Manor, 1999
Coffey, Catherine	Ensemble, Stratford and Broadway, 1988
Cohen, Lawrence D.	Book writer/screenwriter of *Carrie* movie
Cohen, Julie	Ensemble, Workshop, 1984
Criswell, Kim	Auditionee/audience member, Broadway, 1988, Margaret White, London, 2015
Cusack, Carmen	Miss Gardner, off-Broadway, 2012
D'Amboise, Charlotte	Chris Hargensen, Stratford and Broadway, 1988
De Waal, Jeanna	Chris Hargensen, off-Broadway, 2012
Dean, Laura	Sue Snell, Workshop, 1984
Dolginoff, Stephen	Audience member, Broadway, 1988
Donahue, Jimmy	*TheaterWeek* magazine staff
Du Verney, Michèle	Ensemble, Stratford and Broadway, 1988
Edwards, John Owen	Musical Director, Stratford rehearsals, 1988
Eljas, Anders	Orchestrator, Stratford, 1988
Gilliom, Eric	Ensemble, Stratford and Broadway, 1988
Golden, Annie	Carrie White, Workshop, 1984
Gore, Michael	Composer
Graff, Todd	Tommy Ross, Workshop, 1984, audience member, Stratford, 1988

Hateley, Linzi	Carrie White, Stratford and Broadway, 1988
Hepworth, Craig	*Carrie* fan
Hodgson, Michelle 'Shelley'	Ensemble, Stratford and Broadway, 1988
Hoskins, Evelyn	Carrie White, London, 2015
Iconis, Joe	*Carrie* fan
Jackson, Erik	Writer, *Carrie* (play), 2006
Jackson, Rosemary	Ensemble, Stratford and Broadway, 1988
Kleiner, Julie	Carrie White, Stagedoor Manor, 1999
Klena, Derek	Tommy Ross, off-Broadway, 2012
Lavine, Audrey	Cover Margaret White, Broadway, 1988
Levan, Martin	Sound Designer, Broadway, 1988
Linden, Kenny	Ensemble, Stratford and Broadway, 1988
Littlefield, Kelly	Ensemble, Stratford and Broadway, 1988
Lloyd, Gary	Director and Choreographer, London, 2015
Lopez, Emily	Carrie White, La Mirada / Los Angeles, 2015
Lupone, Bob	Co-Artistic Director, MCC Theater
Marino, Peter Michael	Audience member, Broadway, 1988
McKintosh, Peter	Theatre student, Stratford, 1988
McKneely, Joey	Ensemble, Stratford and Broadway, 1988
Milazzo, AnnMarie	Vocal Designer, off-Broadway, 2012
Murphy, Jeffrey	Director, Stagedoor Manor, 1999
Nelson, Michelle	Ensemble, Stratford and Broadway, 1988
Noone, James	Audience member, Broadway, 1988
Oedy, Mary Ann	Ensemble, Stratford and Broadway, 1988
Opie, Simon	Production Manager, Stratford and Broadway, 1988
Ortel, Sven	Projections Designer, off-Broadway, 2012
Otterson, Georgia	Assistant to Barbara Cook, Stratford, 1988
Parker, Kayla	Sue Snell, La Mirada / Los Angeles, 2015
Pitchford, Dean	Lyricist
Putman, Jon	*Carrie* fan
Ranson, Molly	Carrie White, off-Broadway, 2012
Rich, Steve	Audience member, Stratford, 1988
Rosenzweig, Josh	Director, *Carrie* (play), 2006
Rozelle, Robbie	Webmaster, unofficial *Carrie* fan site
Santoro, Mark	Ensemble, Stratford and Broadway, 1988
Schwartz, Paul	Musical Director, Stratford and Broadway, 1988
Schwind, Brady	Director, La Mirada / Los Angeles, 2015
Sembiante, Bob	Audience member, Broadway, 1988
Shenton, Mark	Theatre journalist
Silver, Mark	Audience member, Broadway, 1988
Smith, Kaily	Chris Hargensen, Stagedoor Manor, 1999
Starobin, Michael	Orchestrator, Stratford, 1988
Sturt, Jeremy	Deputy Stage Manager, Stratford and Broadway, 1988
Telsey, Berney	Casting Director, off-Broadway, 2012 and co-Artistic Director, MCC Theater
Thomas, Suzanne	Ensemble, Stratford and Broadway, 1988
Triplett, Sally Ann	Sue Snell, Stratford and Broadway, 1988

Vincent, Bev	Author, *Stephen King: A Complete Exploration of His Work, Life, and Influences*
Vine, Sherry	Carrie White, *Carrie* (play), 2006
Wachter, Adam	Assistant Musical Director, off-Broadway, 2012
Whittaker, Keaton	Carrie White, Seattle, 2013
Williams, Matthew	Choreographer, off-Broadway, 2012
Wise, Scott	Ensemble, Stratford and Broadway, 1988
Wolf, Matt	Theatre journalist
Zinn, David	Scenic Designer, off-Broadway, 2012

A note on interviews

Unless stated in the footnotes, interviews with the above participants were conducted in person, via webcam or via email between July 2020 and September 2022, either for the express purpose of inclusion in this book or as part of the podcast *Out for Blood*, and have been reproduced with permission. Oral interviews were transcribed and, for clarity, have had hesitations, repetitions and asides edited out, with responses occasionally re-ordered as appropriate to the chronology of the story. Betty Buckley's interview was adapted from various sources with edits authorized by Buckley. Interviewee names reflect the subject's professional name at the time of their involvement with the show.

Opinions expressed and recollections made are those of the interviewee only, and do not necessarily reflect the opinions of the author, publisher or any other individual. Where an individual has mentioned another party or occurrence in their interview, every effort has been made to reach the other party or verify the occurrence. However, some individuals declined to be interviewed or were unreachable.

PREFACE AND ACKNOWLEDGEMENTS

t is hard to be specific about who or what caused the original *Carrie* – the infamous musical 'flop' which had a short, tumultuous life back in 1988 – to collapse so spectacularly and gain such notoriety. Ask anyone involved who or what was to blame and they'll give you a different answer – whether it be internal stakeholder or external force – and those myriad factors contributed to the enduring legacy of this notorious show.

For every hazy account of an on-stage near-decapitation or blurry photograph of a perplexing, seemingly out-of-place costume, there are plenty more oft-repeated anecdotes of other bewildering incidents, staging choices and dubious decisions which may have contributed to its demise.

Telling the story of a short-lived musical that ended abruptly thirty-five years ago has not been easy: there is certainly no central repository where the truth about *Carrie* can be quickly uncovered, and the hastiness of its closure (in the pre-digital era) meant that few records or testimonies were preserved. Understandably, it is unlikely that anyone at the time was considering the needs of a researcher keen to sift through the wreckage of this strange episode in Broadway history at some point in the distant future. Of course, a sort of 'top-line', apocryphal version of the *Carrie* story formed over the years: a mishmash of urban legends, smudgy newspaper cuttings and hearsay presented as fact. But – much like the surviving 'bootleg' videos of the show that have circulated for decades – that version of the tale is blurry and disorienting, and offers a primarily external perspective.

In this book, I try to patch together the real story of *Carrie*'s creation, downfall and ultimate reinvention with the help of people who were actually there, both on- and off-stage. Doing so has been a bit like putting together an enormous jigsaw puzzle without really knowing if all the pieces are there, or even what the final picture is supposed to look like. Those jigsaw pieces are the memories of the 80+ contributors I have tracked down, and the scrappy bundles of reviews, articles, documents, tapes and photographs now scattered across dusty archives, personal collections and ancient, obsolete websites. So, my thanks go out to everybody from the *Carrie* multiverse who contributed their time, memories and ephemera to help piece together the jigsaw as completely as possible. Their opinions, recollections and memories are presented throughout in 'oral history' style with additional context gleaned from press articles and other contemporaneous sources. There are too many contributors to thank individually, but you will find them listed in the Cast of Characters, which I hope will also act as a handy guide to the role of each speaker as they appear.

I would particularly like to thank the show's lyricist Dean Pitchford, not only for his contribution from the perspective as one of the musical's key personnel from its earliest days, but for his advice as a writer. It is not often you receive tips from someone who has won an Oscar and a Golden Globe for their prowess with words, so I am very grateful for his assistance.

I owe enormous thanks to my friend Holly Morgan. Around 2006, we watched one of those video tapes of *Carrie*. We found it captivating, and the very idea that this bizarre show existed stoked an unusual fixation. In 2020, together with her husband Tom Moores, we created the podcast *Out for Blood: The Story of Carrie the Musical*, and this book is based on the arc of that podcast. Those grainy, distant figures we had glimpsed on a tiny TV screen years before had become legends to Holly and I, so to meet them and hear their memories first-hand was an extraordinary experience that our younger selves could never have dreamed of. This book would not have been possible without the many hours that the three of us shared interviewing, recording and laughing ... thank you both.

As we released the podcast episodes week by week, more and more people involved in the show came forward with their stories, or suggested someone who knew someone else who had a great anecdote to share. It soon became clear that we had merely scratched the surface of the story, and that there was a much more detailed tale to be told about the musical's creation, staging and reinvention. So, with access to dusty archives restored after the pandemic and armed with a list of potential further interviewees, I approached Dom O'Hanlon at Methuen Drama about the possibility of writing this book. Luckily, he had devoured the podcast and could see the value of an even deeper dive into *Carrie* within a wider cultural context. I am extremely grateful for Dom's invaluable advice, patience and expansive musical theatre knowledge.

Many other people helped me to shape this book. Particular thanks go to Jon Putnam for his dedicated assistance in tracking down cast members, fact-checking and even translating some material from German, and to Charles Arrowsmith, who has the most grammatically correct mind I know. Additional thanks to the staff at the Shakespeare Birthplace Trust, the British Film Institute (BFI) Reuben Library, Alexandra Finlay, Jane V. Grater, Thomas Kohut, Sam Nicholls, Fiona Pearce, Adam Pirani, Rebecca Pitt, Blake Ross and everyone involved in the Sedos production of *Carrie*.

Finally, my thanks go to my husband Richard Hawkins, for everything, and to my parents, Ralph and Susan Adams, for supporting me in all I have done.

INTRODUCTION: THE SOUND OF DISTANT THUNDER

Horror show

It had so much going for it.

It was a balmy Friday afternoon in August 1984. As producers and Broadway bigwigs buzzed around a folding table at the back of a rehearsal studio to claim a cool glass of white wine, there was excitement in the air. These potential investors, producers and theatre owners had come out to enjoy a semi-staged presentation of the first half of a much-anticipated new musical, and now they chatted with the young, excited writers and performers about what might lie ahead. Little did the assembled crowd know that they had witnessed the earliest incarnation of what would become known as one of Broadway's most notorious disasters, and that decades later it would still be generating regular magazine headlines like 'Is *Carrie* the worst musical of all time?'[1]

Carrie had a stellar creative team comprising Oscar-winning composer and lyricist duo Michael Gore and Dean Pitchford, fresh off the back of *Fame*, and lauded screenwriter Lawrence D. Cohen, who had written the script for Brian de Palma's critically acclaimed 1976 movie adaptation of Stephen King's best-selling debut novel. And, perhaps somewhat incongruously, it would soon have the backing of the Royal Shakespeare Company – one of the world's most recognizable and respected stage companies, and its Olivier-winning, Tony-nominated artistic director, Terry Hands.

---

[1]Michael Schulman, 'Is "Carrie" the Worst Musical of All Time?', *The New Yorker*, 27 January 2012, available online: https://www.newyorker.com/culture/culture-desk/is-carrie-the-worst-musical-of-all-time (accessed 5 May 2022).

It was certainly not traditional Broadway fare. The unlikely tale of a teenager with telekinetic powers triggered by her first period. A high-school horror in which almost everyone is dead by the final curtain. Not unlike the bloodbath which ends the show, *Carrie* would itself be met with some of the most savage reviews in critical history.

That response would lend *Carrie* an almost mythical status in popular culture and make it a byword for theatrical disasters. Even as recently as November 2021, after a critical panning following the arrival of *Diana: The Musical* on Netflix, the *Broadway News* blog asked if the show was 'the "Carrie" *de nos jours*?'[2] (that show closed a few weeks after its Covid-delayed Broadway opening). For many years, it had the dubious honour of not only being Broadway's most infamous flop but its most expensive, losing an unheard-of investment somewhere in the region of $8 million (equivalent to about $20 million as of writing). For scale, a modern Broadway flop like 2010's *Spider-Man: Turn Off the Dark* doesn't get out of bed for less than $60 million.

Carrie – in one of many head-scratching twists in the tale – opened in Stratford-upon-Avon, the sleepy birthplace of William Shakespeare and home of the RSC. It was a location that felt geographically and culturally about as far from the show's typical American high school setting as one could get. As unlikely as the pairing of material and producer may have been, the company was not unfamiliar with creating new 'megamusicals', having co-produced *Les Misérables* a couple of years earlier. That show, although somewhat of a departure from the company's core work, was at least closer to its traditional output: an epic, period adaptation of classic literature. It also premiered in London rather than Stratford, arguably a safer testing ground for major new musicals. Reaction to the news that the country's premier theatrical troupe would be taking on what many regarded as a pulpy horror novel with menstruation at the centre of its plot would cause quite the stir. The British critics would soon trash almost every aspect of the show, declaring that the company had sold its soul to commercial Broadway producers and lost its way.

After a long, strained rehearsal process and a tumultuous three weeks onstage in the British heartlands, *Carrie* would, doggedly and largely unchanged (other than the high-profile replacement of a leading lady), make the leap to Broadway. All eyes would be on this strange new show after whispers about its more unusual components had made their way across the pre-internet Atlantic. A new, vulturous batch of critics hovered; rumours swirled that it may not make it past opening night.

It did – barely. After sixteen previews and five regular performances, *Carrie* closed suddenly, its dream of Broadway success snatched away like Carrie White's own glimpse of acceptance at the Prom.

---

[2]Charles Isherwood, 'Review: "Diana," a Musical So Bad that It Must Be Seen', *Broadway News*, 17 November 2021, available online: http://broadwaynews.com/2021/11/17/review-diana-a-musical-so-bad-that-it-must-be-seen/ (accessed 11 November 2022).

That might have been where this tale ends, but something unusual happened. *Carrie* quickly became legendary in theatrical circles, and, in the years that followed, the curious tale of this peculiar episode in Broadway history spread far and wide. In the face of steely silence from those involved in its creation, and without an official cast album for fans to consult, urban legends soon grew around the show, its songs, its questionable design aesthetic and its turbulent creation. These tales were propagated by the steady appearance of illicitly recorded audio and video tapes, which not only painted a picture of a troubled show in perpetual flux, but also fed fans tasters of songs both soaring and silly; with an outright block on new productions of the show, they provided the only samples of a show that would remain perpetually just out of reach. They also presented primary evidence of the infamous audience response, which seemed to oscillate wildly between show-stopping standing ovations one moment and guffaws of disbelief the next. Stoking the mystique, Ken Mandelbaum's seminal 1991 book on musical flops, *Not Since Carrie*, cemented the show as the byword for theatrical turkeys, and the show has regularly topped the charts in articles about famous follies in the years since.

With the emergence of online message boards and, eventually, video-sharing sites, new generations of theatre kids discovered the show and delved into its lore, perhaps attracted by its surprisingly powerful tale of an underdog rising up to defeat her tormentors. Some 'Friends of Carrie' went a step further, producing their own show merchandise or even staging unauthorized productions. Eventually came *Carrie*'s redemption, as, two decades after the doomed original, the authors agreed to a rewrite and revival.

Now, *Carrie* is one of the most-produced shows in colleges and community groups, and its 2012 cast recording has racked up millions of streams and downloads. It has won awards and has been translated into several different languages. This much-maligned musical was even the inspiration for a musical episode of teen drama series *Riverdale*, exposing it to a league of new, mainstream viewers. All the attention on the 'new' *Carrie* has revitalized interest in the original production and, in some arenas, prompted serious critical reappraisal of it.

Carrie did as all good horror heroines should: she came back from the dead.

Carrie in context

For a so-called disaster, *Carrie* is spoken about more passionately than any other musical flop. Where are the books, podcasts and online forums dedicated to, for example, the space epic *Via Galactica* (1972, seven performances), featuring stage-mounted trampolines to simulate interplanetary weightlessness, and whose plot was so complex that printed synopses were slipped into the Playbills? Why doesn't anybody obsess over bootleg recordings of, say, *Roza* (1987, thirty-two performances), the unlikely tale of a former sex worker and concentration camp survivor set to music? Then there's the special club of shows which lasted only a single performance: spare a thought for the Broadway productions of *Glory Days* (2008), *Take Me Along* (1985), the curious-sounding *Cleavage* (1982), *Home Sweet Homer* (1974), *Heathen!* (1972) and numerous others. Perhaps only *Moose Murders* (1983), an infamous hot mess of a Broadway mystery play which opened and closed on the same night comes close to reaching the dizzy heights of *Carrie* as a byword for stage bombs, described by the famously savage *New York Times* critic Frank Rich as 'the worst play I've ever seen on a Broadway stage.'[3] One-night flops are not exclusive to Broadway; West End luvvies still speak in hushed tones of the zero-star clanger *Oscar Wilde: The Musical*, which shuttered after a single chaotic performance in October 2004 ('you begin to wonder whether the sound system is being affected by the hefty rumbling of Oscar Wilde turning in his grave'[4] – the *Guardian*). At least those shows closed before having to deal with the tricky problem of balancing the critics' snark with the need to sell tickets.

Clearly, there is something about *Carrie* that captured the imagination and led to its long-term notoriety.

Schadenfreude

Mandelbaum's book (1991) makes it clear that keen 'flop collectors' have always existed, but it could be argued that *Carrie*'s infamy kick-started a new wave of interest in curiously unsuccessful shows. 'I think that *Carrie* became a kind of lead car in the train of people who maybe take perverse pleasure in seeing something that's bad,' Stephen Purdy, author of *Flop Musicals of the Twenty-First Century* (2020), explained to me. 'I think there's a reason Mandelbaum called the book *Not Since Carrie*. I think that it's probably not the most audacious musical, although it's one of them. But it's certainly the most audacious flop.'

Never before have we, as audiences, been so invested in the world of entertainment. Thanks to the internet, we can find out instantly what's hot and what's not in our preferred area of interest, be it movies, music, literature or theatre. Reviews and audience comments tell us what media we should be bingeing within hours of a new release.

On the other hand, we love to hear about an epic failure. There is something about the mishaps or poor judgement of others that appeals to our primitive need to reassure ourselves that we're not the biggest loser in the room. Websites showing us the plastic surgery errors of celebrities, the downfall of reality television stars or the sordid misdeeds of politicians and CEOs attract millions of eyeballs every day.

---

[3]Frank Rich, *Hot Seat: Theater Criticism for* The New York Times, *1980–1993* (New York: Random House, 1998), 973.
[4]Elizabeth Mahoney, 'Oscar Wilde', review, *The Guardian*, 21 October 2004, available online: https://www.theguardian.com/stage/2004/oct/21/theatre (accessed 15 October 2022).

Algorithms maximize advertising revenue by prioritizing 'epic fails' in our news feeds and encouraging us in our endless 'doom scrolling'. So, whilst we like to be told what entertainment products are the best, we also want to revel in the responses to the worst.

A musical closing early rarely makes the news, but occasionally, the sheer chutzpah of a Broadway flop will receive mainstream attention. If there is a star name attached – even that of a well-known superhero – so much the better; a January 2011 cover of the *New Yorker* gleefully featured a hospital ward full of bandaged-up Spider-men following multiple reports of injuries during rehearsals for that particular folly. The New York transfer of the Boy George bio-musical *Taboo* (2002), considered a success in its scrappier, off-West End life before being reworked and glammed up for Broadway, shone an unwelcome spotlight on celebrity producer Rosie O'Donnell, who reportedly lost her personal investment of $10 million in the show after its critical panning and tales of backstage rows hit the front pages of gossip magazines. In the 2018 Broadway season, audiences steered clear of *The Cher Show* and *King Kong* despite their big-name subjects – both closed a few months after opening, only just scraping past the measure of 250 performances used by Mandelbaum to define a flop, but losing a fortune nonetheless.

The financial disaster

As the costs of mounting a new musical rocket, putting on a Broadway show has become increasingly unsustainable without sky-high ticket prices. Producers need to find unique selling points – a celebrity name, popular source material, a zeitgeisty topic – to persuade people to splash enough cash to keep the show running long enough to become self-sufficient. Often shows rely on an expensive gimmick to generate word-of-mouth and a focus for reviewers. The big 'megamusical'[5] imports of the 80s all had their iconic setpieces – the rotating barricades in *Les Mis*, *Phantom*'s falling chandelier, the roller-skating trains of *Starlight Express*. *Carrie* tried its luck with a spectacular and enormously expensive finale, surprising audiences after utilizing fairly unassuming scenery for a couple of hours – though, in this case, it clearly didn't save the show. That finale was part of Terry Hands' unusual aesthetic and directorial approach to the material which will be explored here in (much) further depth.

How do Broadway shows – presumably carefully budgeted – go so far off par? Of course, someone has to foot the bill and keep an eye on spending. That's the producer – these days, there can be many – and if they don't have the experience

---

[5] A term popularized by Jessica Sternfeld in her book *The Megamusical* (Bloomington, IN: University of Indiana Press).

or gumption needed to step in and call time when spending gets out of hand (an accusation levelled at those in charge of *Carrie*'s books, as we shall see), a musical can find itself financially doomed before it even opens.

Indeed, big budget losses make the snappiest headlines. Our friendly neighbourhood superhero musical, perhaps the most notorious flop of the new millennium thus far, was all over the news when it closed and reportedly failed to break even on its eight-figure outlay. In the minds of the public, losses in the tens of millions appeal not only to our sense of *schadenfreude* but provoke disbelief, even disgust. How could someone allow that much money to be wasted? Why did nobody put a stop to it? The level of funding ploughed into a single *Spider-Man: Turn Off the Dark* could build a good-sized hospital – or revolutionize access to Broadway shows for those who can't afford even the cheap seats, the cost of which are now rarely below three figures. 'I don't want to get preachy,' says Purdy, 'but think of the things that we could do in terms of cultivating audiences and introducing theatre to those who can't afford it or who don't know about it.'

In the case of *Carrie*, the RSC – a publicly funded organization – had been attacked by the British press for mounting the show, despite the Thatcher government urging companies like it to become more self-sufficient and less reliant on 'handouts'. Hands, director of the show as well as the company's leader, was adamant that the show fell within the RSC's remit, and insisted that it was protected from financial risk by the involvement of a commercial co-producer. As long as the show sold well in the UK (which it did, in its limited run), the risk on Broadway would fall at the feet of the other stakeholders. But reputational damage is something altogether different to financial loss, and the RSC – its leader in particular – was haunted by *Carrie* for years to come, as we shall learn.

The artistic mess

Often there is a very clear line from a show's critical mauling to its premature closure, particularly on Broadway, where a scathing critique from the *New York Times* often precedes the death of a show by mere days. A badly received show in the West End, where costs are lower and audiences are arguably less sensitive to negative reviews, can coast along for months before quietly departing, particularly with a wealthy backer at the helm. Andrew Lloyd Webber's *Stephen Ward* (2013), a 'flaccid'[6] show based on the Profumo Affair that was bogged down by political exposition and unmemorable songs, dragged on for months despite an entirely mediocre response from critics. More recently, his *Cinderella* (2021) struggled on

---

[6]David Benedict, 'West End Review: Andrew Lloyd Webber's *Stephen Ward*', *Variety*, (19 December 2019, available online: https://variety.com/2013/legit/reviews/west-end-review-andrew-lloyd-webbers-stephen-ward-1200977286/ (accessed 9 November 2022).

for a year between numerous Covid-19 suspensions. Some decent reviews were overshadowed by disappointment from audience members and rumours of backstage unrest. Instead of turning up to the final performance, the composer provided a letter that was read aloud by the director, thanking the company before calling the decision to open during the pandemic 'a costly mistake' – a comment met by resounding boos from the audience and eye rolls from the gathered cast.[7]

Critical mass

Prominent critics like the *New York Times*' so-called 'Butcher of Broadway' Frank Rich have long argued that critics don't have the power to close a show, only a producer does. Many people involved in *Carrie* would disagree. So would the backers of hundreds of other flops, including the doomed *Marilyn: An American Fable* (1983, fifty-one performances), which Rich called 'incoherent to the point of being loony.'[8] Not a quote for the poster. Of the thousands of shows Rich reviewed across his career, *Carrie* appears in his list of Top 5 'Fabulous Flops: The Most Unforgettable Disasters'.[9]

Of course, reviews are subjective, and there are plenty of examples of shows receiving mediocre reviews only to go on to wide success (bonjour, *Les Mis*). Others, like 2012's West End Spice Girls vehicle *Viva Forever!* try to capitalize on poor notices, attempting to suggest that the critics simply don't know what they're talking about. Desperate producers assembled ads lining up five one-star ratings in a column with the somewhat hopeless strapline 'The critics may not have been dancing in the aisles, but the audiences at the Piccadilly Theatre certainly are!' Presumably they hoped that flop curators would flock to catch the so-bad-it's-good show before it disappeared . . . forever. The show duly closed soon after with a reported £5 million loss.[10]

It was the reaction of the audience which made headlines around the London production of Ernest Hemingway bio-musical *Too Close to the Sun*. Snarkily redubbed *Ernie Get Your Gun* by internet wags after our hero, in a move straight from Chekhov, made a fuss about leaving a gun on the fireplace in the opening scene, it was its sheer laughability that guaranteed its failure. Hysterical witnesses to this bizarre four-hander – which somehow made it to the West End during a quiet summer period in 2009 thanks to funding from its aerospace engineer-cum-writer – recalled on social

---

[7]In October 2022, Lloyd Webber announced he would be reviving the show on Broadway with a new name: *Bad Cinderella*.
[8]Rich, *Hot Seat*, 271.
[9]Ibid., 993.
[10]Andy Sherwin, 'Viva Forever? Not Exactly – Spice Girls Musical Closes after Six Months Leaving Backers with £5m Loss', *The Independent*, 2 May 2013, available online: https://www.independent.co.uk/arts-entertainment/theatre-dance/news/viva-forever-not-exactly-spice-girls-musical-closes-after-six-months-leaving-backers-with-ps5m-loss-8600424.html (accessed 15 October 2022).

media waves of giggles, walk-outs and even shrieks of laughter in response to some of the characters' more dramatic lines ('Enough of this bullshit!'). Audience members' accounts of collapsing onstage furniture, a constant flow of people through the exit doors and the furious faces of the reluctant cast during the curtain call swiftly made it into the mainstream papers. *Too Close to the Sun* closed soon after.

In its UK run, *Carrie* received a critical flogging whilst actual ticket-buyers were, by all accounts, quite taken with it. Their loud cheers led Hands to consider it structurally sound and to dismiss much of the critics' reaction, trimming lines which had led to ripples of laughter, and inadvertently making the plot gradually more incomprehensible to the casual viewer with each round of edits. But, with all respect, Stratford-upon-Avon may not have been the ideal testing ground for a major Broadway musical. The somewhat more particular and diverse New York audience had heard all about *Carrie*, and many were primed to see a show they had already heard was a car crash. *Carrie* lyricist Dean Pitchford speaks about the importance of carefully choosing your out-of-town try-out venue: 'In America, there are cities that you can go to if you are previewing a show. You can go to Boston, where you get feedback which is about on par with what you're going to get in New York. So that's a smart city to preview, because you get helpful input. In Stratford, we stood in the back of the audience going 'no no no, you're sending all the wrong signals!''

Many blamed the scathing reviews for *Carrie*'s untimely closure just days after opening. While they were certainly a contributing factor, as we shall learn, there is much more to the story of this particular 'disaster'.

Queen of flops

Whereas shows like *Moose Murders* or *Oscar Wilde* were declared to be artistic messes as well as losing millions, *Carrie*'s position is not so clear cut. Yes, it was most certainly a financial disaster for its commercial producers, but the RSC escaped relatively unscathed. According to most critics, what was presented on stage was an overarching mess, but similarly, almost all of the reviews highlight at least one stellar performance or a particularly moving or impressive moment; certainly, the show's reinvention suggests a core of material worthy of appreciation, and fans would argue that there is plenty about *Carrie* to love.

Carrie is a special kind of failure: its lofty position in the Flops Hall of Fame has been shored up substantially by years of urban myths and oft-repeated stories about its chaotic journey to the stage. By using this unfortunate but beloved show as a case study and unpacking these tales, we can understand the complex processes involved in putting together a new Broadway show.

Through the *Carrie* lens, we can learn the importance of the mix of people involved, and of their visions, specialities and processes, as well as how their experience (or lack thereof) can influence the success of a show. We can examine how misunderstandings and seemingly innocuous decisions can change a show's fate in an instant, and we can try to pinpoint the red flags that determine whether a show will flourish or flop. We can consider the external factors and stakeholders who play a part in determining whether a show lives or dies. And, in *Carrie*'s case, we can – quite uniquely – see how a show written off as a disaster can be reinvented and prosper decades later.

The original *Carrie* is the Prom Queen of musical calamities, but she could have been anything but. As its poster strapline read, 'There's never been a musical like her.' To understand why, we must go back to the very early days.

PART ONE

THE CREATION

1 PAGE TO STAGE

Pig blood for a pig

It's an image so well known it has become a pop culture cliché: the betrayed Prom Queen, hair and dress slick with blood, walking wide-eyed and vengeful through the burning school gym. Even those unfamiliar with Stephen King's 1974 debut novel, Brian De Palma's 1976 big-screen adaptation or the subsequent plethora of remakes, sequels and spin-offs have an inclination as to the fate of the iconic Carrie White.

The creation of *Carrie* is literary lore in itself. King, a cash-strapped high school teacher, snatched any spare time he could find to work on his writing, supplementing his wife Tabitha's income from her part-time doughnut store job by submitting stories to the fiction pages of men's magazines. *Carrie* started life as one of many such attempts to tide the couple over until the next month's pay cheque.

Bev Vincent (author, *Stephen King: A Complete Exploration of His Work, Life, and Influences*, 2022)   But as he started working on it, he realized this thing needed a longer build-up. He didn't think that he had the knowledge of what teenage girls experienced to really do it justice, or the time to devote to a novel, given that he'd already had two rejected previously. So, after he had four or five pages of the story written, he threw the pages away. Famously, his wife found them in the trash can, read them, and encouraged him to continue with the story.[1]

And the rest, as they say, is history. King completed the story and submitted it to publishing house Doubleday, who bought the hardback rights for $2,500. The first edition of *Carrie* sold 13,000 copies.[2] The paperback rights were snapped up

---

[1]The dedication in the first and subsequent editions of *Carrie* is: 'This is for Tabby, who got me into it – and then bailed me out of it.'
[2]George Beahm (ed.), *The Stephen King Companion* (London: Macdonald, 1989), 10.

by New American Library for $400,000, with that edition selling over four million.[3] King's decades-long residency at the top of the bestseller lists had begun.

The titular *Carrie* is Carrietta N. White, a shy, teenage misfit, 'a frog among swans',[4] bullied by her peers and abused by her God-fearing mother, Margaret.

The inspiration for Carrie's character and her plight came from an amalgamation of two of King's students. One had a similarly devout mother, and another was ridiculed by her peers for wearing the same clothes to school every day; saving up her meagre pocket money to buy a fashionable outfit, she was mocked even more for her desperate attempt to fit in.

For the fictional Carrie, things come to a head in the showers after gym class. Never having had the facts of life explained to her, she suffers a traumatizing panic attack after experiencing her first period. Her classmates, led by chief bully Christine 'Chris' Hargensen, set about pelting her with sanitary pads, chanting cruelly as she cowers under the running water, diluted blood pooling round the drain. In the mayhem, as Carrie's terror climaxes, an overhead light bulb shatters.

> **Vincent**   The interesting thing about Carrie is that she has some latent telekinetic abilities that emerge when she comes into her adolescence, and that is one of the crucial triggers in the book. And so, she discovers that she can move things with her mind . . .

Told in a series of flashbacks, we hear about her violent home life, where – amongst other tyrannical acts – Margaret frequently locks her daughter in a closet, forcing her to pray for forgiveness for a litany of perceived sins. Carrie begins to use her telekinesis to fight off some of the more hostile behaviour, which only goes to further convince Margaret that her daughter is under the thumb of Satan, and therefore must be sacrificed. Of course, Carrie's major demonstration of her power is held back until the big event of the high school season: the Senior Prom.

In an act of attempted redemption for the attack in the showers, Hargensen's friend Sue Snell has convinced her boyfriend Tommy Ross to invite Carrie as his date, giving her a taste of normality. Hargensen, banned from attending by gym teacher Miss Desjardin for refusing to apologize for her antics in the locker room, vows to stage a triumphant final humiliation of Carrie by dumping a bucket of pigs' blood ('Pig blood for a pig')[5] on her as she steps up to take her place as Prom Queen – after a rigged vote, of course.

As the blood slops down, coating Carrie's home-made dress . . .

> **Vincent**   She goes full-blown telekinetic, and wreaks havoc on the Prom.

---

[3]Carol Lawson, 'Behind the Bestsellers: Stephen King', *New York Times*, 23 September 1979.
[4]Stephen King, *Carrie*, 19th edn (London: New English Library, 1974), 10.
[5]Ibid., 107.

Immediately convinced the whole evening was a set-up from the start, Carrie uses her powers to trap her classmates and teachers in the school as it's engulfed in flames, casually dispatching everyone present in deliciously creative ways. Making her way back through town to her humble home, she destroys everything in her wake. There, meeting her deranged mother, Carrie is literally stabbed in the back by the one person supposed to protect her. Carrie *flexes* her powers one final time to stop Margaret's heart, before eventually flipping Chris and boyfriend Billy's car into a wall, and dying in Sue's arms.

Which all seems like perfect material for a Broadway musical.

Hollywood

Lawrence D. Cohen (Book writer)   After graduating college in 1969, I moved to New York and did freelance writing on film and theatre for several major periodicals. I was then hired to review Broadway and off-Broadway opening nights as a critic for the *Hollywood Reporter*. It was a dream gig, but it only paid a meagre $5 per review, and I desperately needed a better salaried job to help make my rent. Out of the blue, I was offered a position as a reader to assess unpublished manuscripts and film scripts for the veteran TV and movie producer, David Susskind. I returned from lunch one day in 1973 to find a typed, advanced publication copy of a manuscript of a short novel waiting to be read. The cover page bore just a single one-word title, *CARRIE*, and the author's name: Stephen King, then unknown. It was only 199 pages, more of a novella than a novel. After reading the first few pages, I was immediately hooked and read the book in one sitting. This author, this 'Stephen King', had me at 'hello'.

Impressed, Cohen embarked on a crusade to persuade his producer boss to option the rights, but to no avail. He then received rejections from numerous studios scared off by the dark material, but was doubtful they had actually read more than the first few pages. To his disappointment, none of the Hollywood studios expressed interest.

Cohen   A year later, I moved to Los Angeles and was introduced to the Hollywood producer Paul Monash, who had just signed a development deal at 20th Century Fox. He was looking to hire a story reader, so we had a meeting in which he told me about the projects he had in development, none of which interested me. I was out the door and halfway down the hall when Paul called out to me to say that he'd forgotten to mention an additional piece of material he'd recently optioned. It was a short, first novel that he was sure I'd never heard of. It was *Carrie*. Without a beat, I turned around and said 'yes' to the job offer.

When the first script he had commissioned didn't work out, Monash gave Cohen the chance to adapt King's book himself. Still, the predominantly male Fox studio execs were squeamish about the material, and – only two days after Cohen submitted his screenplay – they put the project into 'turnaround', effectively leaving it without a studio (or funding) attached. Eventually, United Artists came to the rescue with a deal, signing Brian De Palma to direct.

Cohen   We faced nothing but uphill battles. The studio insisted on cutting down what was already a very low budget, causing a stalemate that came perilously close to the film being cancelled. Along the way, they actually asked us to change the title to *Pray for Carrie*! Even after the film was completed, the studio President expressed major reservations; he confessed he just didn't get it, until – eventually – his teenage daughter explained it to him. At the eleventh hour, the studio decided to do a midnight sneak preview on Halloween at over 350 cinemas across the country, to test the film and see what they had. The screenings received an insanely vocal response from audiences, followed by predominantly rave reviews, and terrific Box Office that grew weekly.

In De Palma's movie, Sissy Spacek plays a hauntingly withdrawn Carrie White – all pale and bony, unlike the plump, clumsy character described in the novel – with an unrestrained Piper Laurie playing her mother Margaret. Betty Buckley, later to star in the stage musical as the mother, played Carrie's gym teacher and mentor, Miss Collins.[6]

The movie, with its combination of supernatural creepiness, jump scares and high-camp turns was a critical and commercial success, grossing $35 million against its $1.8 million budget.[7] Both Spacek and Laurie received Oscar nominations. King was a fan of the adaptation, calling it 'terrific' and 'far more stylish than my book'.[8]

The workshop

In late 1980, Cohen and his partner, the composer Michael Gore, attended a performance of Alban Berg's *Lulu* at the Metropolitan Opera. Gore had recently found great success with the movie *Fame*, released in May that year, having written some of the songs with lyricist Dean Pitchford; the duo would shortly win both an Academy Award and a Golden Globe for the title song. Gore, additionally

---

[6]The name changed from Desjardin, presumably to make it easier to pronounce. In the musical, she becomes the anglicized Miss Gardner.
[7]Neil Mitchell, *Devil's Advocates: Carrie* (Leighton Buzzard: Auteur, 2013), 12.
[8]Beahm, *Stephen King Companion*, 27.

nominated for the song 'Out Here on My Own' with his sister Lesley, would also win the Oscar for Best Original Score.[9]

Michael Gore (Composer)   The material in *Lulu* was anything but conventional; it was dark, subversive, ferocious, sexy and concluded, unforgettably, with its title character being killed by Jack the Ripper. After the show, Larry and I were heading down the Met stairs when I turned to him and said, 'You know, if Alban Berg were alive today and writing for the Met, he'd be doing *Carrie* as an opera.' It was like being struck by lightning. The more we talked, late into the night and over the next few days, the more we came to believe it was perfect material, not as an opera but as a musical.

Cohen   There were one or two tonally dark Broadway shows that offered clues as to how what we had in mind might work, most prominently Sondheim and Wheeler's *Sweeney Todd* and Lloyd Webber's *Evita*. We looked at what a lot of Broadway musicals had become: very expensive spectacles, light revues, pieces like *Cats* and *Starlight Express* – all enormously enjoyable, but we had grown up with *West Side Story*, *Gypsy*, Rodgers and Hammerstein's classics … we missed the emotion and depth from those pieces. *Carrie* had two unforgettable lead characters, whose mother–daughter scenes were already fiercely operatic and duet-ready star turns. It also had a young high school setting that offered a pop side to balance the drama, and the chance to become original commercial theatre. It had a beginning, middle and end, and a terrific story.

Cohen and Gore called King at his home in Maine, and pitched the notion of *Carrie* as a musical.

Cohen   We explained what we had in mind, and there was utter silence on the other end of the phone. At first, we thought he'd hung up on us. Then he said, 'Well, if they can make a musical about a dictator in Argentina and a show about a barber who kills his clients and turns them into meat pies, why the hell not?'

They formed a plan. Gore would set about composing songs, and Cohen would revisit the novel and adapt it – as well as write new material – for the show's scenes.[10] And they would approach Gore's writing partner, Pitchford, to write lyrics, reviving their award-winning partnership. For Pitchford, it would be a return to a world he knew and loved.

---

[9]*Fame* won the Golden Globe Award for Best Original Song (for the title song) in January 1981 and the Academy Award for Best Original Score and Best Original Song (for the title song) in March 1981.
[10]The 'book', in musical parlance.

Dean Pitchford (Lyricist)   I had been a Broadway baby. I grew up in Honolulu, but I was raised on the cast albums that my mother collected. I left Hawaii and I went to Yale, because I wanted to be the next Anthony Newley. I did *Godspell* in New York before I even got out of college. I went into *Pippin* on Broadway[11] and did *The Umbrellas of Cherbourg* at the Public Theatre. Broadway was in my blood.

Gore and Cohen invited Pitchford for drinks and a proposal.

Pitchford   They sat me down and said, 'What do you think?' I thought it was a fantastic idea. I always loved the book and the movie, but I also loved the premise of these two worlds: Carrie and her mother in one world, Carrie trying her best to fit in at school in the other. At the centre of it are these two wacko women belting at the tops of their ranges over, you know, matters of life and death. Sign me up!

Cohen   It was a cross-country and years-long collaboration. We would periodically meet up in person on both coasts, but for the most part, we worked by long-distance phone calls until we'd gotten a draft of the first act together that we were pleased with.

Pitchford   I was living in Los Angeles, but I carved out time every two or three months to go back to New York and work with Michael and Larry [Cohen], and periodically they'd come out to me in LA. It wasn't like we were sitting on our hands; we were all torn in many different directions. So, it took us about three years to put together Act One.

In August 1984, they took the leap to self-fund an exploratory two-week workshop in New York City, giving them the chance to hear their Act One material performed for the first time.

Maureen McGovern, whose career had transitioned in the early 1980s from singing Oscar-winning songs on movie soundtracks to starry stage roles including *The Pirates of Penzance* (1981) and *Nine* (1982), would sing the role of Margaret White. 'The musical, which is somewhat tamer [than the movie], is moving into the workshop stage,' she said in an interview published in 1984. 'If it does well in the workshop, we hope it goes to Broadway.'[12]

Laurie Beechman, taking the role of Miss Gardner, had originated the Broadway role of the Narrator in *Joseph and the Amazing Technicolor Dreamcoat* (1982) and was the first Grizabella in the US tour of *Cats*.[13] Liz Callaway, nominated for a Tony Award in 1984 for *Baby*, would play bitchy Chris Hargensen, alongside *Fame*

---

[11]Pitchford starred as the title role in the 1975 replacement cast of *Pippin* alongside Betty Buckley as Catherine.

[12]Carl Apone, 'Maureen McGovern has Big Heart for CLO', *The Pittsburgh Press*, 12 August 1984, 93.

[13]She also replaced Betty Buckley in the role on Broadway, performing it for over four years.

alumna Laura Dean as good-girl Sue Snell. Todd Graff – who would go on to create the cult musical movie *Camp*[14] – would play her boyfriend Tommy Ross, and the small Ensemble included future two-time Tony winner Donna Murphy, and Julie Cohen, another *Fame* graduate.

Annie Golden, lead singer of punk band The Shirts, was offered the title role.

Annie Golden ('Carrie White', 1984 workshop)   They said, 'We're doing a musical of *Carrie*.' Right away, I was my bubbly, enthusiastic self and said, 'Oh, I love that movie!' I never thought about the lead role. I just thought, yeah, sure, I'd love to be one of the teenagers. Then they said, 'We'd like you to be Carrie!'

Golden was only two years younger than her on-stage mother, McGovern.

Golden   I'd been passing for younger for a long time in my career. I had done an off-Broadway revue called *Leader of the Pack*, the Ellie Greenwich story.[15] I came from CBGBs,[16] and Ellie kind of discovered me. I think Michael Gore and Dean Pitchford came to see the musical, so I was on their radar.

Laura Dean ('Sue Snell', 1984 workshop)   I don't think I auditioned for the workshop. It was just a meeting, because Dean and Michael knew me and my voice [from *Fame* the movie].

Dean was surprised by her casting.

Dean   For much of my young adult years, I appeared in a lot of after-school specials . . . TV mini-movies that were full of important life lessons! And I always played the conniving bitch in those! But they [Gore and Pitchford] hired me to play the nice girl, Sue – the character Amy Irving played in the movie. Liz Callaway – who is always playing innocent young women – got chosen to be the nasty one!

Liz Callaway ('Chris Hargensen', 1984 workshop)   I played Chris, the bitch! I remember thinking it was a terrific score. I did the workshop shortly after *Baby* closed on Broadway, and my *Baby* castmate, Todd Graff, was in it too.

Todd Graff ('Tommy Ross', 1984 workshop)   I had left *Baby* early to do a movie, so I was out of the country. I came back for the Tony Awards, because I was nominated, and I just kind of shoe-horned in the *Carrie* workshop. In the

---

[14]Graff's involvement in the workshop led to a lifelong friendship with Michael Gore, who contributed an original song to *Camp*. It's set at a musical theatre summer camp inspired by Stagedoor Manor, which plays a later role in the *Carrie* story . . .

[15]*Leader of the Pack* also starred Peter Neptune – Chris's bad boy boyfriend Billy Nolan in the *Carrie* workshop – and Darlene Love, who would eventually play Miss Gardner in the show.

[16]The legendary punk rock and new wave venue in New York's East Village – geographically close to but a million miles away from Broadway . . .

movie, Tommy is the William Katt character, all-American, you know, the blonde-haired, blue-eyed, muscly guy ... which I certainly wasn't then and clearly am not now! I was this skinny character, but for whatever reason – I think because I had had somewhat of a success with *Baby* and Michael and Larry saw that show – they approached me to see if I wanted to do it.

Pitchford   On the Saturday midway between our two weeks of rehearsal for the workshop, the 1984 Summer Olympics opened in Los Angeles. Marvin Hamlisch and I had been asked to write the convocation for the Opening Ceremony, and I didn't want to miss that! So that Friday afternoon, after week one of *Carrie* rehearsals, I grabbed a cab to a heliport on the East Side of Manhattan, took a helicopter to Kennedy Airport and then flew to LA. The next day, Marvin and I were sitting together at the Los Angeles Coliseum when a choir of 1,000 sang our song 'Welcome'. It was thrilling! And then Sunday morning, I returned to New York and was back in the rehearsal studio on Monday for the start of our second week.

Golden and fellow cast member Julie Cohen also had a side project during rehearsals.

Julie Cohen (Ensemble, 1984 workshop)   We were playing hookers together in a B-movie called *Streetwalkin'*. We were filming together at night while we were doing the *Carrie* workshop during the day. She played one called Phoebe and mine was Trisha! So, we were working very long days, but we wanted to do both projects, and we managed to stay up all night![17]

Golden   I was so tired!

J. Cohen   The memory of those nights is really vivid to me. I loved bonding with Annie. We'd share a cab from the shoot at eight in the morning, go over to the studios and have coffee before rehearsal.

Dean   I did a lot of workshops in the 1980s, and lots of times the writers would come in with no material, and basically, the actors would write the show. Not with *Carrie*. They had music and lyrics ready. They came in prepared.

Golden   The first day is always a marathon of music. The chairs are set up with music stands around the piano, and that's when you get excited, because you hear everybody's voices together for the first time.

Pitchford   I had a room filled with some of the most extraordinary talent, extraordinary voices.

Golden   We worked 10 am to 6 pm every day. I remember my voice would go and go until it couldn't go any more.

---

[17]Please do search online for the *Streetwalkin'* trailer: it's quite something.

The workshops were held downtown at 890 Broadway, a former shirt factory converted into a complex of rehearsal rooms and dance studios owned by Michael Bennett, the director of *A Chorus Line*.

Cohen   I'd worked for Michael as an assistant director and dramaturg on two Broadway shows, and he gave us the rehearsal space.

Dean   I remember *Cats* was rehearsing down one hallway, and *The Rink* with Chita Rivera was rehearsing down the other. It was like *the* Broadway rehearsal place.

The team workshopped the first act of the show for ten days. Pleased with the results and eager to see how it would be received, they mounted two so-called 'backers' auditions' – rough, script-in-hand readings designed to give potential investors and stakeholders a taste of the show – on 3 August 1984.

Cohen   We invited the 'Who's Who' of theatre owners, producers and directors.

Pitchford   Every chair was filled. People crowded in, standing around the edges of the room.

J. Cohen   I remember thinking that if a bomb had fallen on 890 Studios that day, musical theatre as we know it would cease to exist! When Tommy Tune walked in, I thought I'd have a heart attack. You can't miss him, he's like seven and a half feet tall.[18]

Golden   It was a packed room. And in a sense, I was carrying it, which I tried not to give too much weight to.

Graff   We held scripts and sat on chairs at one end of the room. The room wasn't very big, and there was only piano accompaniment from Michael. When we were in a scene, or sang a song, we got up and came forward. No props. No mics.

A grainy audio recording of the workshop was later leaked and traded amongst fans, an early example of *Carrie* 'bootlegs' making their way into the public domain. On it, we hear the writers introduce the presentation, and explain the 'single act' premise. 'What you're about to see and hear today will require your imagination,' Pitchford teases. 'There are a lot of special effects in our show, thanks to Carrie's very strange gift. Lights explode, objects levitate, windows slam, lasers come out of Carrie's fingers … you get the idea!' The writers explain that the choreography – though not present in the workshop – will be done in a 'very 80s, very MTV style'.

---

[18]Ten-time Tony Award winner Tommy Tune is actually 6'6½" tall.

Occasionally, there is an audible cut in the tape: presumably edits made by the authors, keen to include their preferred performance of each song from one of the two showcases.

The presentation begins with a musical setting of 'The Lord's Prayer', sung by Carrie, followed by the energetic 'Ain't It a Bitch', sung by the high school girls during gym class. The action moves to the showers, where the girls share their innermost (albeit, superficial) desires in 'Dream On'.

The following scene, in which Carrie bleeds and is attacked by the other girls, is narrated. On her way home, Carrie desperately shares her feelings and fears in the melancholy 'I Can Hear My Heart'. On arriving, she is met by her mother, who sings 'Open Your Heart' along with a gospel choir on the radio. Upon receiving a phone call from Carrie's gym teacher, Miss Gardner,[19] about the shower incident, the tone changes. Margaret's violent punishment of her daughter is portrayed in 'And Eve Was Weak', at the end of which Margaret hurls Carrie into her 'prayer closet' and locks the door.

The narration soon diverts us to the local movie drive-in, where the sound of sexual moaning emanates from a row of cars, kicking off 'Don't Waste the Moon', in which Chris, Billy, Sue and Tommy trade sexual innuendos. The action returns to the White home, where Carrie – still locked in her closet – and Margaret each begin to sing their 'Evening Prayers'. During the course of the number, Margaret releases her daughter, and they each apologize for their actions, plead for each other's forgiveness, and declare their undying love. We are told that Carrie starts to control her newfound power, levitating a candelabra to illuminate a portrait of Jesus.

The next day, in English class, Tommy reluctantly reads out his poem 'Dreamer in Disguise', captivating Carrie in the process.

In the gym scene that follows, Miss Gardner demands that each girl apologize to Carrie. Refusing to do so, a furious Chris is banned from the Prom.

That night, at the Cavalier, 'an after-school hangout', Chris and Sue beg their boyfriends to 'Do Me a Favor'. Sue's request is that, to atone for her cruelty in the showers, Tommy invites Carrie to the Prom in her place. Chris, still seething from her banishment, cajoles Billy into helping her exact revenge on Carrie.

At school, Tommy – as promised – asks Carrie to be his date, but she assumes she is being tricked and runs away. She bumps into Miss Gardner, who reassures her that 'It Only Has to Happen Once' – she is certain that Carrie will find someone to love her.

Tommy turns up at Carrie's house, and she reluctantly accepts his invitation before being called inside by her mother. At the dinner table, when Carrie nervously but excitedly reveals her Prom plans, Margaret flies into a rage in the Act One finale 'I Remember How Those Boys Could Dance', demanding that Carrie says 'no' to Tommy. But Carrie will not back down, using her powers to

---

[19]For those keeping track of the gym teacher's ever-evolving name, she introduces herself here as 'Suzanne Gardner'.

slam the windows shut, as the now-terrified Margaret screams 'Witch!' Carrie exits, leaving her mother alone in the darkness, as the curtain falls.

On the recording, we hear rapturous applause, then each performer's name is called out as they take a bow. There is a low murmur of laughter as Cohen reminds the audience that Carrie does, indeed, get to go to the Prom. 'Carrie becomes Cinderella, alright,' he says, 'Cinderella with a vengeance.' A final round of applause, and the promise of a glass of wine at the back.

As quickly as they were assembled, the first cast of *Carrie* disbanded after their fleetingly brief project.

J. Cohen   You all work together, you make something magic, you bond, and then you split. But we'll always have that moment of magic that we shared.

Taking part in a workshop is no guarantee of being cast in any eventual production: time passes, alternative concepts are shaped and participants get other jobs. McGovern seems to have held out hopes of continuing in her role, referring to it in articles throughout the following year. She told one interviewer, 'I hope the play is produced, because I know I'd have a great time playing the lunatic mother.'[20]

Golden   I knew that I was going to age out by the time they got it together. I was OK with that. You don't want to be Baby Jane![21]

Callaway   At one point I was actually going to play Sue in the British production, but then they ended up needing to use someone from the UK.[22] Maybe it was decided that I was more believable as a nice girl!

Graff   I was clearly not going to be in the show, and rightly so, considering how insanely miscast I would have been! But I knew a lot about it, and I was kind of a 'friend of the court'.

Dean   I do feel proud to have been part of the creative process. I remember thinking, 'Wow, this is really special,' because even though it seems odd to put music to a horror film, they were really trying to hone in on the characters.

J. Cohen   Any time someone mentions *Carrie*, I drop in, 'Hey, I was in the first ever workshop of that!' Usually, people say, 'There was a *Carrie* musical?' And I sing 'Silver lace, with a blue-grey bodice …!'[23]

Graff   It was a great thing to be a part of, and I seem to remember it going over well – especially Annie and Maureen's scenes and songs. There was a sense that this was going to be their [the writers'] next big thing.

---

[20]Andy Clearfield, 'Maureen McGovern has a "Morning After"', *Camden New Jersey Courier-Post*, 26 October 1984, 51.

[21]The fictional ageing former child star, iconically played by Bette Davis in *What Ever Happened to Baby Jane?* (1962).

[22]More on the reasons for this later …

[23]Cohen recalls and sings these lyrics from the song 'Dream On' after thirty-seven years …

'All the producers came, the Shuberts and Nederlanders were there,' Cohen proudly informed *Newsday* soon after the presentations. 'We got a good response.'[24]

Cohen   Many of the people in attendance expressed immediate, enthusiastic interest beyond our wildest dreams. Little did we know that this would be the last time that we would see our show the way we'd initially intended ...

The impresarios

Hopes for a full-scale production were raised. Fortuitous, because the workshop had been self-funded to the tune of $93,536 by White Cap Productions, the business entity of Cohen and Gore, according to a memorandum for potential investors detailed in *Variety*.[25] The recent creation of White Cap would formalize the pair's role in the production of the show, and was intended to act as a platform for the creation of other musicals based on movies in the future: 'We want to bring about a synthesis between Broadway and Hollywood,' Gore told the *New York Times*.[26]

Pitchford   We were very fortunate to sign a deal with Barry and Fran Weissler, the husband-and-wife producing team responsible for, amongst other things, *Chicago* and *Waitress*, and Fred Zollo, who went on to an estimable career producing shows and movies. Very smart, very enthusiastic people.

Zollo would focus on the logistics of getting the production up and running, whilst the Weisslers would raise funds. By November 1985, the producing team were, according to the *New York Times*, 'at the starting gate,'[27] with the show expected to begin rehearsals in Spring 1986 and a Broadway opening pencilled in for the Autumn.

Progress was not as rapid as first hoped, with the team struggling to attract further investors to provide the necessary funds. 'Somehow,' Zollo later told *Telegraph* magazine, 'the idea of a musical based on a young girl experiencing menstruation didn't appeal.'[28]

Generally, it was becoming harder and harder to attract investors to Broadway shows – even those without periods or supernatural powers at their core. 'The public is demanding so much more in terms of production value, and giving them that kind of spectacle has added a whole new level of costs,'[29] theatre lawyer John

---

[24] Drew Fetherston, 'Broadway Goes for Blood', *Newsday*, 8 May 1988, 72.
[25] Richard Hummler, 'Weisslers, Zollo in on "Carrie" for Percentage of Gross, Profits', *Variety*, 11 May 11 1988, 129,136.
[26] Enid Nemy, 'Broadway' column, *New York Times*, 30 August 1985, 44.
[27] Mel Gussow, 'Chilling "Carrie" in Vengeful Return – as a Musical', *New York Times*, 29 November 1985, 62.
[28] Christopher Tookey, 'Flop!', *Telegraph* magazine, 3 December 1988, 16.
[29] Mervyn Rothstein, 'On Broadway, Spectacle Raises the Stakes', *New York Times*, 8 January 1989.

Breglio said in a *New York Times* piece about the spiralling costs of mounting and maintaining a show; investors were increasingly forced to wait longer to see a return on their money, if it came at all.

Pitchford   It started to dawn on the producers that the material didn't appeal to the typical Broadway theatre-goer at that time, and they would have to think creatively. We had this show that was filled with young people and their problems. The idea of creating theatre for a younger audience – which is all the rage these days – just wasn't a 'thing' then.

Interestingly, the desire to attract a younger audience to Broadway was one of the project's attractions for Zollo: he had been involved in the lobbying of legislators in Massachusetts to provide funding to send school students to the theatre. 'The Broadway audience is in serious jeopardy,' he told the *New York Times* in April 1986. 'The only way we can rebuild the audience is to start from the ground up.'[30]

To demonstrate that unusual subjects could be successful on Broadway, the writers and producers reminded potential investors of another unusual but successful show.

Pitchford   The only vaguely comparable thing was *Sweeney Todd*. But that was written by Stephen Sondheim, it was directed by Harold Prince, and it starred Angela Lansbury. Big names. It was much easier for people to comprehend how that show could be a success. We were newcomers to Broadway. We didn't have a cast yet. We didn't have a director. All we had was a tape of the songs.

To assist with the pitches, the trio had recorded demo versions of six songs, with Gore playing piano, Cohen reading a brief introduction to each number, and Pitchford singing (sometimes layered against multiple tracks of his own voice). They included 'In' (a reworked version of 'Ain't It a Bitch' from the workshop), 'Unsuspecting Hearts' (replacing 'It Only Has to Happen Once') and four songs destined for the second act of the show, 'Crackerjack', 'Once I Loved a Boy', 'Heaven' and 'Carrie (Lullaby/Finale)'.

Debbie does dancing

All three writers were close friends with Debbie Allen, primarily through her work on the 1980 *Fame* motion picture and its television spin-off, which aired from 1982 to 1987.

---

[30]Samuel G. Freedman, 'Putting it Together: A Producer's Week on Broadway', *New York Times*, 6 April 1986, 93.

As a performer, Allen had won Tony Awards for her star turns in the Broadway revivals of *West Side Story* (1980) and *Sweet Charity* (1986), as well as the 1983 Golden Globe Award for Best Actress (Television Series Musical or Comedy) for her role as Lydia Grant in *Fame* (Image 1.1). She also received the Primetime Emmy Award for Outstanding Choreography for *Fame* for two years running, in 1982 and 1983.

Pitchford   When it came time to find a choreographer who knew how to make kids move and had experience with high school settings, Debbie was the obvious choice. She had an incredible profile, mad chops as a choreographer, and – thanks to *Fame* – she had become a superstar.

It seems safe to assume that the writers had Allen's signature dance style in mind as they shaped up the show. Given the plot, the writers also 'felt that it was important to have a woman on board, to give it a woman's perspective.'[31]

IMAGE 1.1 Debbie Allen in the *Fame* TV series. Everett Collection Inc. / Alamy Stock Photo.

---

[31]Timothy Harper, 'STAGE: Horrors! The Royal Shakespeare Stages "Carrie"', *Los Angeles Times*, 27 March 1988, 51.

'When they told me it was based on Stephen King's novel *Carrie*, I said, "It's based on *whaaaat*?"'[32] she told the *Los Angeles Times*. Attempting to describe the show to CNN, Allen said: 'You could call it *Fame* with a macabre ending. Or you could say it was *Sweeney Todd* for children! There's certainly a comparison [to *Fame*] because it's high school, it's young kids, it's high energy, it's a lot of high-energy dancing. I'm sure it's reminiscent in many ways of *Fame*, but there's some things you can do in the theatre that you can't do on television.'[33]

Much ado about nothing

With Allen on board, Gore, Pitchford and Cohen continued to search for a director to bring their vision to life on a Broadway stage.

Cohen   Legendary New York agent Sam Cohn, from ICM, took a passionate interest in our show, and organized a series of meetings in New York with his A-list director clients. We sat down and went through the script and score with Mike Nichols, who loved the piece but really, _really_ didn't want Carrie to go to the Prom, as well as Bob Fosse, who also loved it, but was concerned it was too 'rangey' for dancers.[34] Jerome Robbins invited us to come out to his house in the Hamptons to hear it, Tom O'Horgan, who staged *Hair* and *Jesus Christ Superstar* on Broadway, came up to our apartment . . . you name it, we met our theatre idols. Extraordinary, once-in-a-lifetime experiences.

According to an interview in the *Telegraph* magazine, they also met with Adrian Noble, a director at the Royal Shakespeare Company.[35] Noble was tempted by the offer of his first Broadway musical, but turned it down. 'I couldn't find a way, myself, of taking the *Carrie* material and making it non-sexist,'[36] he said.
Soon, the name of another prominent British director came to the fore.

Pitchford   Sam [Cohn] had signed Terry Hands, the Artistic Director of the Royal Shakespeare Company, as a client. Terry had already brought to Broadway a couple of RSC productions that had made him very popular. He did a gorgeous *Cyrano de Bergerac* alternating with *Much Ado About Nothing* in repertory.[37] We all saw them and were impressed.

---

[32]Ibid.

[33]CNN news footage archived at: https://youtu.be/ITiAa_WFFwY (accessed 5 May 2022), original broadcast date unknown.

[34]As in, it would be a struggle for them to sing the notes whilst dancing his signature choreography style.

[35]Noble would go on to succeed Terry Hands as the RSC's Artistic Director in 1990.

[36]Tookey, 'Flop!', 16.

[37]Hands' *Cyrano de Bergerac* and *Much Ado About Nothing* had shared an engagement at the Gershwin Theatre between October 1984 and January 1985.

In good hands

Terry Hands (Image 1.2), an extremely well-respected director of classical and Shakespearean plays, had co-run the RSC with Trevor Nunn since 1978. Nunn had co-directed the company's successful commercial co-production of *Les Misérables* (1985) with John Caird, but had also found success as a freelance director with shows including *Cats* (1981) and *Starlight Express* (1984). When he departed the RSC in 1986 to focus on his own projects, Hands continued to run the company as the sole Artistic Director.

Hands 'came to epitomize the idea of the theatre director: enigmatic, European-minded, habitually dressed in black . . . he marched with an arrogant swagger across

IMAGE 1.2 Terry Hands in 1988. Roy Jones / ArenaPAL.

the biggest stages',[38] according to Simon Trowbidge in *The Rise and Fall of the Royal Shakespeare Company.* His productions were known for their scale and dynamism, and his detailed knowledge of lighting design – Hands often lit his own productions – infused his work with bold, expressionistic effects. He was interested in a total theatre[39] approach with minimal stage clutter, cutting through to the core themes of a play. Known for his experimental, avant-garde productions, Hands had won numerous awards during his time at the RSC, including Olivier Awards for *Henry VI* and *Cyrano de Bergerac.*

However, Hands had little experience of directing musical theatre, let alone the process of developing a musical from scratch. His one prior experience with the genre had been with *Poppy* (1982), a musical satire by Peter Nichols and Monty Norman about the Opium Wars, styled as a pastiche of traditional British pantomime. Reports suggested that tensions between Hands and Nichols on that production were rife, with the playwright even refusing to attend the opening night. Nichols described Hands as 'a wayward, self-destructive genius'. Hands fired back that Nichols had been 'over-sensitive'.[40]

Cohen   To be frank, Michael and I had seen *Poppy* in London and left at intermission. We weren't the least bit keen on him as a choice based on his work directing a musical, but Sam pleaded with us to at least meet with him, so we did. He came to the apartment, smoking non-stop and downing two pots of black coffee.

Hands listened to the songs, sharing his admiration for the Stephen King novel.

Cohen   When our hour-long presentation was over, he told us that when he agreed to meet with us, he had no idea what a musical of *Carrie* could possibly be. He proceeded to sell us our own show for the next hour in the most incredibly articulate and persuasive way.

'I thought they must be out of their minds,' Hands recalled. 'But . . . I loved the music and got on with the creative boys. I said I would work on it as long as it could be done in a great epic style'.[41]

Cohen   Against all our prior instincts that his prior musical work didn't persuade us that he was a match, we said yes; his two productions of classics

---

[38]Simon Trowbridge, *The Rise and Fall of the Royal Shakespeare Company* (Oxford: Editions Albert Creed, 2013), 97.
[39]A theatrical style fusing all the resources of the stage, including sound, light, song, dance, projection and other theatre technology.
[40]Nick Smurthwaite, 'The Odd Man In', *The Stage*, 8 September 1988, 12.
[41]Michael Owen, '"Carrie on Terry"/"Two in Tune"', *Evening Standard*, 8 January 1988, 24.

PAGE TO STAGE   **29**

on Broadway were undeniably brilliant, and we asked ourselves . . . who in their right mind could turn down [the Artistic Director of] the Royal Shakespeare Company? Talk about famous last words!

Hands was intrigued by the possibilities of staging the story as a sort of modern myth. Despite being a contemporary tale, he saw resonances in biblical stories and the great tragedies of Ancient Greece: an epic tale in which the underdog acquires mystical powers and takes vengeance against her enemies, after having her dream cruelly snatched away. 'She was too young to control it [her power], it is something that destroys everybody, including herself. There should be the classical inevitability of a tragedy,' he said. 'What makes it unusual as a musical is that it is not a musical comedy, but a musical tragedy.'[42]

He described a desire to dispose of a realistic setting and naturalism, and to apply the style and structure of the classical plays he was famous for staging: 'Classically, you can move space and time whenever you wish, and you can also build towards the kind of climax, or anti-climax, that the classical theatre delights in . . . to allow music, dance and iconography to tell the story.'[43]

If Hands' proclamations about ancient myths and classical allusions came across as somewhat ostentatious in the context of a musical based on a Stephen King story, the writers were clearly reassured by his passion, credentials, and the fact he had given the project so much serious thought. 'When Terry came into the picture,' an enthusiastic Pitchford told the New York Times, 'he completely shook up our thinking. It was as though we had been locked in a room together for a very long time, and he threw open all the doors and windows.'[44] 'They loved the idea,' Hands said. 'That [the staging concept] was an area of experience which I was able to bring, as their experience was in terms of their music and their lyrics.'[45]

As it would turn out, Hands' classical overlay was more than an obscure concept: he would literally and liberally apply the aesthetics and practises of classical theatre to all aspects of the production, from design to direction. The writers had found their visionary director, but the way that this particular vision would manifest itself was certainly not what they had imagined.

Hands planned to take a leave of absence from the RSC to direct *Carrie* in an independent capacity.[46] Having witnessed the success of other directors who had turned their hands to commercial musical theatre – not least his former RSC colleague Nunn, whose productions were being rapidly replicated around the world – it was no doubt an appealing prospect.

---

[42] *Theatre Craft*/Pirani interview tapes.
[43] Ibid.
[44] Mervyn Rothstein, 'After Seven Years and $7 Million, 'Carrie''s a Kinetic Memory', *New York Times*, 17 May 1988, 61.
[45] *Theatre Craft*/Pirani interview tapes.
[46] Fetherston, 'Broadway Goes for Blood', 72.

Jeremy Sturt (Deputy Stage Manager, Stratford and Broadway)   He had an absolute itch to do it, not only because he loved the classical references in the work but also because he was not involved in *Les Mis* at all. I think he was probably quite jealous of its success, and wanted to put on something that would encapsulate that, and work in other markets.

Making progress

With a Director and Choreographer on board, production forged ahead. 'Mr Zollo and his co-producers … want to put the musical into rehearsal in August and open on Broadway on Halloween,' the *New York Times*' noted in April 1986.

Casting began in earnest, despite the ongoing search for financial backers. Dance calls were announced, to take place at the Minskoff Rehearsal Studio complex in New York City.

Mark Santoro (Ensemble, Stratford and Broadway)   My first audition was in the summer of 1986.

Rosemary Jackson (Ensemble/Understudy 'Carrie White', Stratford and Broadway)   I had been a huge fan of Debbie Allen since the beginning of time. I was a college student, and somehow I convinced my mom to let me go to New York to audition and take classes. I got on an elevator going to a class, and Debbie got on right after me. I was absolutely speechless. She got off and the door closed after her, and I thought, 'Oh my God, I can't believe I didn't say anything.' So, I went back down and kind of weaved around until I found out where she was. I slid a horrible picture and a resumé full of lies under the door! A guy opened the door and said, 'Is this yours?' and I said, 'Yes, could you please give that to Ms. Allen?' I stood there for a minute and nothing happened. As I was walking away, the man came back and said, 'We're in a meeting right now, but she wants you to come to an audition.' It was happening in, like, four days, and it was for *Carrie*. I didn't even know what that was. I didn't even care, but I was going to show up to that audition.

Kelly Littlefield (Ensemble, Stratford and Broadway)   I flew in from Boston. I was eighteen at the time. I had never done a musical before. There were well over 500 girls at the open call.[47] From what I was told, there were almost as many at the Equity call that was held the day before. We were brought in to dance, forty to fifty people at a time. Debbie was at the table, with a big floppy

---

[47]An audition open to anyone interested in trying out for the role, sometimes called a non-Equity call, as opposed to invited auditions for Union members.

hat on. She had us line up across the back of the room. She said, 'I want you to come to the centre of the room, state your name, age and where you're from.'

Mary Ann Oedy (Ensemble, Stratford and Broadway)   I had been in a couple of episodes of *Fame* but Debbie had left the show by that point, so she didn't know me, and I really had to prove myself to her. I was up for the role of Chris.[48] All of my auditions were focused on that.

Allen had a challenging routine for the hopefuls to perform.

Littlefield 'Do a double pirouette to the right, double to the left, battements right and left, a layout and fouetté turns . . . go!' Most of the girls before me weren't very good at fouetté turns – in fact, the girl right before me ended up facing the back. So, when it came to me, I conveniently skipped the layout (since I had never had a flexible back) and went straight into fouetté turns and ended with a quad. Debbie slapped the table and said, 'Thank God someone can do them! Get back in line!' She only kept six of us, and then taught us a jump combo that we did to a lone drummer in the corner. I still remember the combo. From there the remaining dancers learned a jazz combination to 'Sing, Sing, Sing' from the amazing Adrian Rosario.[49]

Oedy   In the audition, I remember Debbie was eating sushi, and she was looking down a lot as she ate it. I was like, 'No, please look up! Give me a shot!'

Those who survived the movement audition were asked to stay for a singing session.

Santoro   I made it through all of the cuts and even sang well.

Littlefield   I was so nervous! I handed over my headshot and resumé, which I had put in an old-fashioned sticky photo page and trimmed off the fringe. I started singing next to the piano, then Dean Pitchford asked if I knew the lyrics by heart. I said yes and he asked me to come to the centre of the room and sing the chorus. I did, and he asked me to sing it again louder. He said, 'I like your headshot, it must be expensive to laminate your pictures and resumés like this!' I said, 'No, that's my only one.' He asked if I would like it back, and I told him, 'That's okay, my mom can type me another one!' I was so green! They said they would contact us for callbacks. I went home to Massachusetts, as I was scheduled to have my tonsils out the following week. A few days after getting home I received the callback. I had to cancel my surgery. I went to the callback where we did the jump-and-jazz combos again.

---

[48]Oedy would eventually end up understudying the role.
[49]A dancer from *Fame* who had also appeared in *West Side Story* and *Sweet Charity* with Allen.

About ten girls and ten guys were kept till the end. Dean taught the girls 'In', the opening song, and each of us had a turn to sing it alone.

Jackson   Everything went well. Then I didn't hear anything for, like, two years.

'Make it like Greece!'

Meanwhile, preparations for the physical production got underway. How would the dual worlds of Carrie's traumatic life be represented on stage in Hands' abstract interpretation?

Pitchford   American high school, which is the vernacular of our show, did not – in 1988 at least – have an equivalent in English, and so Terry and his design team struggled to interpret everything we described about this story's setting. Instead, he shoehorned the story into a framework that he *did* understand, which was classical Greek theatre.

A popular and oft-repeated[50] urban legend about the show states that one of the producers encouraged Hands to think about popular high school-set musicals for inspiration: to 'make it like *Grease!*'

Cohen   Terry misunderstood and thought that she meant 'Greece', which he was very familiar with, having directed Greek plays as part of the RSC repertory.

The apparent misunderstanding is said to have led to the surprise appearance of all sorts of Hellenic references in the show, from togas to temples. An alternative version of the tale flips the responsible party, with Hands explaining to Allen that he was working on a *Greece* concept, with the choreographer, naturally, assuming he had meant *Grease* . . .[51]

Cohen   It was a tonally catastrophic misunderstanding from which the production never recovered.

Broadway's very own 'Greek myth' eventually became one of the most well-known elements of *Carrie*'s lore, and is often laughed about in theatrical circles. Indeed, it appears as fact in many publications, however unlikely it may sound.

Of course, nothing ends up on a Broadway stage 'by mistake' – months of discussions and many rounds of designs would have exposed such a misunderstanding long before a troupe of dancers turned up to the dress rehearsal

---

[50]Probably two-thirds of the people interviewed for this project referenced the *Grease*/Greece legend!
[51]It is unlikely Hands' classical references were lost on Allen, who majored in Greek literature, Theatre and Speech at Howard University. Indeed, in a January 1988 *Daily Mail* article, she claims it was her idea to bring on Hands because 'this is classic stuff and we needed someone who could understand it'.

in Athenian garb. We know that Hands signed up for the project with an 'epic' classical interpretation in mind, and pitched his vision as such to the writers and producers. And contrary to the much-repeated myth, nobody actually appears in a toga: the costumes are not strictly classical Greek, but inspired by its aesthetic, and 'tend towards the futuristic or universal'.[52]

Whatever the origin of the anecdote, Hands ploughed ahead with his plans. He set about briefing his RSC design associates Ralph Koltai (Set) and Alexander Reid (Costume) to get started on building set models and drawing up costume sketches inspired by the aesthetics of ancient Greece and the tropes of classical theatre. He wanted a stark, temple-like set and simple, symbolic costumes. Put simply, Hands' *Carrie* would not be set in a lifelike American high school or home, but in a representative space in which his 'musical drama' could play out uninhibited by the limitations of realism.

Designing *Carrie*

Mark Bailey (Assistant to Set Designer Ralph Koltai[53])   I was Ralph's assistant for about five years, from late 1984 until 1989. During that time, we worked together on about a dozen productions, both in the UK and Europe. I was very lucky, in that Ralph used his assistant as a sort of PA, so as well as working with him in the studio on the designs and models, I also accompanied him to rehearsals, workshop visits, fit-ups and stage rehearsals in the theatre.

Koltai had been one of the RSC's long-term associates, and one of the earliest contributors to its repertoire of plays. In a retrospective of his work, Trevor Nunn described him as 'one of the best stage designers in the world ... [his] *curriculum vitae* reads like a history of the developments of the last forty years of theatre in this country'.[54]

In a diary piece written for *The Listener*, Koltai recalls Hands approaching him about the show in January 1986. 'I'm always open-minded about things because I distrust my own snap judgments,' he said. 'Even so, a musical about a girl having her first period?'[55]

Bailey   At the time, Ralph and Terry had been working together for about ten years. They had a close relationship, both professionally and personally.

---

[52] *Theatre Craft*/Pirani interview tapes.
[53] Koltai passed away in 2018.
[54] Sylvia Backemeye (ed.), *Ralph Koltai Designer for the Stage*, rev. edn (London: Nick Hern Books, 2003), 13.
[55] Nick Smurthwaite, '"Carrie" from Behind the Scenes', *The Listener*, 11 February 1988.

They had had several big successes including the famous award-winning *Much Ado* and *Cyrano* productions that went to Broadway, and had known each other as friends for a long time.

'I respect and trust his judgement,' Koltai said, 'and that's what sways me. He has found a classical resonance in the story that I find appealing.' He described Hands drawing some simple sketches as inspiration. 'I don't respond too well to over-intellectualization, so he feeds me just enough information to get me going.'[56]

Bailey   Ralph didn't respond well to being given a 'brief', and liked to find his own solution and present that to the director. Once he had an initial 'concept' to present, there were many meetings with the director to develop the design.

Hands likened his working partnership with Koltai to a marriage, 'where you develop a shorthand over the years . . . feeding things in, getting things back. Some things from him affect the production, some things from me affect the design. It's very difficult to put a knife between it, it's a team.'[57]

Koltai's designs for the stage were strikingly bold and non-realistic, with expanses of colour, defined lines and angles. He embraced the emerging mechanization of theatrical sets, often using machinery and automation at a time when many regarded these advancements as suspicious or inauthentic, and experimented with industrial materials such as metal, plastics and mirrors.

Bailey   In essence, he was not interested in a pictorial, illustrative approach to design. He aimed to find the essence of the piece and to present that on stage. He tried to find one image or idea that would sum up the play, ballet or opera and to present that. Ralph always worked sculpturally in the model box, he never sketched a design, to my knowledge. We would explore options and create 'sketches' in 3D with pieces of card or materials Ralph had collected in the studio, and gradually a design would come together. Ralph was famous for saying that all good design happened by accident, and the skill was in recognizing the moment when the accident happened and the design emerged. He always gave the impression that his design just happened, but in reality he spent a lot of time looking at images, books of photography and other visual material.

For *Carrie*, Koltai created a stark, multi-functional playing space to act as an 'envelope' for all of the settings of the play.

---

[56]Ibid.
[57]*Theatre Craft/Pirani* interview tapes.

Simon Opie (Production Manager, Stratford and Broadway)   In essence, it was a simple idea – a box with walls and a ceiling that could be white, black or mirrored.

Bailey   Sections in the side walls were able to open to allow other pieces of scenery through.

When empty, the 'box' would represent the gymnasium of Carrie's school – the scene of much of her humiliation throughout the show. The basic space would then 'transform' into representative sets for the other locations in the story.

'[The school gym] is an environment you'd associate with teenagers – naturalistic, recognizable. Then we transform that space into the subsequent settings, and it becomes less naturalistic each time, as Carrie's powers take hold,'[58] Koltai explained in an interview.

The walls of the 'box' were made up of 'an intriguingly stylized array of translucent and opaque panels, which flip over and come together to suggest various locations'.[59] The reverse of each 11-foot, tall, glossy white panel was covered by a mirror. Additionally, each could be covered by a matte or glossy black panel, offering four potential finishes for the walls of the set, depending on the supposed location and Hands' desired lighting effects.

The set also had a ceiling, which 'doesn't change colour, it's white ... well, it's white at the moment, it may change. Terry is worried about it reflecting too much light, but by the time he's got all his lighting gear on it, I don't think you'll see the white ceiling.' The closed ceiling generally presented problems for the lighting equipment: Hands requested Koltai add three metal 'trusses' to the set to disguise the array of lanterns in use and retain the clean lines of the box.[60]

Koltai was no doubt aware that the sophistication of his set designs might be an appealing asset for investors and, ultimately, the theatre critics. 'One has to find a way to give the show a certain elegance,' he explained –

People, having read the book or seen the film, they think realistically. Only artists see things unrealistically, the ordinary businessman who gives the money sees things realistically. So, when you read that horror story, if you think of it as a musical in realistic terms ... people think about sanitary towels flying about the stage, they think, 'Oh, no, that's disgusting, I don't want anything to do with it, I'll put my million dollars somewhere else'. It wasn't a problem for me because I'm accustomed to thinking in stylised terms, abstract terms and thinking in

---

[58]Ibid.
[59]Matthew Wolf, 'The Horror of "Carrie" was Getting it Staged', *The Chicago Tribune*, 26 February 1988, 51.
[60]*Theatre Craft*/Pirani interview tapes.

metaphors . . . so, the result is a show which I think will be stylish, elegant and totally inoffensive.[61]

The critics would certainly be impressed: in an otherwise damning review of the show, the *Guardian* would say that Koltai's set, 'as if aware of the show's defects . . . acts the musical off the stage'.[62] It may have been impressive, but it was certainly not cheap: unnamed sources 'involved in financing the project' estimated that the show's design elements cost 'nearly $4 million, including about $1 million each for costumes, sound and the set'.[63]

Like Koltai, costume designer Alexander Reid had worked with Hands for several years, teaming up on *Much Ado* and *Cyrano*, as well as creating the flamboyant, satirical costumes required for *Poppy*.

In an interview, he said that Hands asked him to work on a new show soon after the first performance of their production of *The Winter's Tale* in April 1986. 'I expected it to be a Shakespeare and he said, "Oh, it's *Carrie*." I said, "Oh, are you sure you've got the right person for this? Because I'm not a modern designer, I'm not into modern clothes!". . . He said, "Yes, but the reason why I'm asking you is because we want to do it differently, we don't want to do jeans and sweaters and t-shirts, we want to approach it in a different way . . ."'[64]

Hands, Koltai and Reid agreed on a colour scheme that was largely black, white and silver with red accents. 'I wanted, conceptually, a world which emphasised the people, and therefore by disciplining the world around it, the people would stand out against it,' said Hands.[65]

By July 1986, with set and costume designs in progress, Hands and Koltai headed to New York City to meet with the Weisslers. Koltai recalled that they seemed pleased with the ten model boxes he showed them, but was nervous of their nonchalance around the potential cost. 'I spend a lot of time hearing how there is no problem with the show, which arouses my suspicions,' he said. 'I've learned to be wary of certain phrases like, "That's no problem," and, "One thing you don't have to worry about is the money."'[66]

The team toured various theatres, seemingly concluding that the Majestic on 44th Street was a strong contender to house the show. 'I designed the show before there was a theatre,' Koltai said, 'then I adapted it to the Majestic in New York, but then the Majestic went away'.[67] In fact, the venue would soon become the home of

---

[61] Ibid
[62] Nicholas de Jongh, 'Carrie On', *The Guardian*, 20 February 1988, 16.
[63] William A. Henry III, 'Theater: The Biggest All-Time Flop Ever', *Time*, 30 May 1988, available online: http://content.time.com/time/magazine/article/0,9171,967517,00.html.
[64] *Theatre Craft*/Pirani interview tapes.
[65] Ibid.
[66] Smurthwaite, '"Carrie" from Behind the Scenes'.
[67] *Theatre Craft*/Pirani interview tapes.

the record-breaking *The Phantom of the Opera*, which opened in January 1988.[68] The team would continue to struggle to find another theatre with similar stage dimensions to their Stratford base.

Hands and Koltai then accompanied Charles Reynolds, a technical consultant, to a laser factory in Boston ('we decide we can only use lasers if the audience doesn't realise they're lasers. We don't want it looking like a disco . . .'[69]) to explore ideas for the show's destructive finale.

Meanwhile, Reid created a series of concept costume sketches for Hands. 'He [Hands] prepared a kind of chart, and he broke [the show] up into different sections. . . starting off in the gym, and he wrote roughly what he saw . . . We had actually discussed the classical theme,' said Reid, 'I'm not going to say it's a Greek tragedy – and yet there is an element of that in it. I took him hundreds of little drawings of girls in aerobic costumes jumping about, and he puts a tick opposite the ones he likes. I'd done about a hundred and I got about twelve [ticks] out of him!'[70] Reid and the interviewer laugh about Hands' propensity to tick the 'correct' designs like a particularly fussy school teacher.

'The concept of the costumes is to complete the set, that is to say, they should not be thought of as separate from it,' Hands explained. 'Therefore, we needed a classical inspiration, if you like, and we chose Greek.'[71]

Listening to tapes of Reid's interview about his (eventually much-maligned) Grecian costume designs, one detects a slight sense of embarrassment, as if he is well aware that the company line about *Carrie* being a great piece of classical drama comes across as somewhat grandiose, and that he may have been asked to play it down. Describing one scene, he said, 'I'm scared to use the word "Greek" in case it gets out, because I'm not sure the public would accept that, or get it.' Of his interpretation of Margaret's character, he said: 'She's this sort of "Medea" figure – I shouldn't be saying that to you! – but do you know what I mean?'[72]

Dead end

By November 1986, the show hit a stumbling block: apparently unable to raise the necessary investment, the original production team of the Weisslers and Zollo departed the project.

---

[68]As of this book going to print, *Phantom* – Broadway's longest-running show by some distance – had just posted a closing notice for April 2023, after selling nearly 20 million tickets.
[69]Smurthwaite, '"Carrie" from Behind the Senes'.
[70]*Theatre Craft*/Pirani interview tapes.
[71]Ibid.
[72]Ibid.

Gore   The Weisslers had the authors do a series of dog-and-pony shows in New York for their largely garment district investors, only to show up at Sam Cohn's office months later to tell him they'd been unable to raise the necessary financing. Sam said if they couldn't raise the money, he would like them to withdraw from the show as producers, which is what eventually happened, at a cost.

'They were unable to raise the financing, and we've taken back the rights,' said Cohen at the time. 'But we're devoted and committed to it, the same group [of creatives] is interested, and we won't stop until it's on.'[73]

Whether the dark material and unusual design of the show had played a part in scaring away investors is unclear – a *Chicago Tribune* article alludes to 'a falling out'[74] between the creative team and the producers – but it seems unlikely any potential backers, already aware of the unconventional subject matter, would have been overly keen on investing their money in a show that seemed to be straying further and further away from commercial Broadway fare. Koltai recalled a meeting with 'another American millionaire'[75] at which they proudly showed off the set models, but to no avail.

By the end of 1986, Hands recalled, 'I thought it would never happen.'[76]

---

[73]Gussow, 'Chilling "Carrie"'.
[74]Wolf, 'The Horror of "Carrie"'.
[75]Smurthwaite, '"Carrie" from Behind the Scenes'.
[76]Tookey, 'Flop!'.

2 THE ROAD TO REHEARSALS

With production on pause, those who had auditioned in New York City were left without a resolution.

Kelly Littlefield (Ensemble, Stratford and Broadway)   The rumour was that the show had been postponed.

Rosemary Jackson (Ensemble/Understudy 'Carrie White', Stratford and Broadway)   It went completely quiet, but I was thrilled I had at least gotten the opportunity to dance with Debbie Allen.

Hands continued his work at the RSC, where he had been forced to dedicate more of his schedule to finding new ways to balance the company's books.

Money makes the world go round

This was a tempestuous time for the arts in Britain. Under Margaret Thatcher's Conservative government, the golden age of subsidized theatre was under threat as arts organizations were encouraged to move towards 'self-help' through commercial ventures and corporate sponsorship. Peter Hall, the RSC's founder, told *The Stage* in 1985 that he believed that 'the government, so far from keeping the arts at the existing level, are consciously and deliberately reducing them'.[1]

The RSC's grants from the government-run Arts Council were steadily decreasing: in 1984 they had covered 40 per cent of the company's running costs, but by 1988 this was down to 30 per cent. The grant reduction, combined with a poorly received 1986 London season of plays, forced the company to lay off twenty-two of its ninety-seven

---

[1] Ossia Trilling, Peter Hall profile, *The Stage*, 16 May 1985, 10.

full-time actors and reduce the number of productions from thirty-seven to twenty-seven.[2] By the time work on *Carrie* started, the company was in severe debt; the *Guardian*'s Nicholas de Jongh described the deficit as 'stagnant, menacing and more than a million,' warning that 'a volatile public and a poor season at just one of the company's main theatres [could] send it plunging into the red and towards oblivion.'[3]

To help soften the blow of the cuts, the company had secured commercial sponsorship, forming partnerships with a range of British companies like NatWest Bank and Marks & Spencer.[4] A three-year, £1.1 million deal[5] with Royal Insurance saw its logo prominently displayed on marketing collateral for the company's plays. In 1988, former Artistic Director Trevor Nunn warned of the risks of such deals, describing them as 'unpredictably speculative, offering no financial security on which to base forward planning,' and pointing out 'how easy it would be for the sponsorship tail to wag the subsidised dog,' but reasoning that the industry had little other choice 'with a government actively opposed to the entire principle of arts subsidy.'[6]

Another funding model involved the company forming partnerships with commercial producers. When West End producer Cameron Mackintosh approached Nunn about creating an English-language production of Alain Boublil and Claude-Michel Schönberg's musical adaptation of Victor Hugo's novel *Les Misérables*, Nunn agreed on the 'non-negotiable'[7] condition the show started life as an RSC production and that he could bring on his colleague John Caird to co-direct.[8]

Les Misérables would play for a limited eight-week engagement in 1985 at the RSC's London base, the Barbican Theatre. It starred several members of the RSC's acting company including Roger Allam, Susan Jane Tanner and Alun Armstrong, alongside a crop of performers from the West End such as Colm Wilkinson, Frances Ruffelle and Michael Ball. In exchange for offering up its venue and production facilities, the company would retain the takings from the Barbican sales, with a guarantee of royalties from any future production. When the show moved to the West End's Palace Theatre[9] featuring the same principal cast, Mackintosh would take on the cost of running and promoting the show over time, in exchange for the majority of the takings. 'The RSC had made pacts in the past

[2]Harper, 'STAGE: Horrors!'
[3]Nicholas de Jongh, 'Will to Solvency', *The Guardian*, 16 January 1988, 1.
[4]Royal Shakespeare Company, *Annual Report 1987/8* (Stratford-upon-Avon: Royal Shakespeare Company, 1988), 13.
[5]Antony Thorncroft, 'Carried Away by the Cash', *Financial Times*, 6 February, 1988.
[6]Trevor Nunn, 'The Nunn's Tale', *The Stage*, 29 September 1988, 14.
[7]Edward Behr, *The Complete Book of Les Misérables* (New York: Arcade, 1989), 67.
[8]Nunn and Caird had previously teamed up to stage *Nicholas Nickleby*, a similarly epic (but non-musical) production of Dickens' classic novel.
[9]It later moved to the smaller Queen's (now Sondheim) Theatre, where it still plays with some changes to the original staging.

with commercial producers,' Mackintosh said, 'but what it had never done was to actively produce inside one of their theatres with a commercial producer. I was in control, though, working hand in glove with the RSC departments.'[10]

The company's venture into the commercial musical theatre space was a surprise to many, despite the fact that the company had, apparently, 'toyed with the idea of staging an original musical, and had been looking for a suitable vehicle.'[11] The initial reaction to the plan was sour, and press coverage was laced with condescension for the musical genre. Critics suggested that the company was being taken advantage of by the commercial sector, and that the publicly subsidized company was straying too far from its core field of work. In *The Stage*, Nunn asserted that: 'subsidised theatre is not a generic term for licensed intellectual snobbery, nor is what is commercial by definition unsophisticated, or unserious, or lacking in complexity'.[12]

Despite a shaky reception from reviewers – the *Observer* declared it to be 'witless and synthetic entertainment'[13] – *Les Misérables* would go on to generate significant income for the RSC. It brought the company $846,652 in the 1987/8 fiscal year (when *Carrie* was staged), with the *Financial Times* predicting that figure would top £1 million the next.[14] By 2019, when the original London production was re-staged by a new creative team and the company's royalties renegotiated, *The Stage* estimated the RSC's take to be over £25 million.[15] It was also a cash cow for Nunn and Caird, who each earned a 1.5 per cent royalty[16] and were kept busy for years to come, opening replica productions around the world. Of course, the biggest earner was Mackintosh.

As audiences flocked to *Les Misérables*, it was clear that the co-production model had succeeded. Hands developed a new plan: could *Carrie*, currently stagnating without a producer or funding, be developed as an RSC production with the support of a commercial producer? A second successful musical would create an additional income stream for the RSC, as well as for Hands himself.

Matt Wolf (Theatre critic/journalist) The fuse that had been lit by the British megamusical became such a forest fire that every single British director needed or wanted to be part of it, and it was almost as if they didn't exist unless they were. I was very fond of Terry, and I thought he was a wonderful

---

[10]Behr, *Complete Book of Les Misérables*, 67.
[11]Ibid.
[12]Nunn, 'The Nunn's Tale'.
[13]Behr, *Complete Book of Les Misérables*, 140.
[14]Thorncroft, 'Carried Away by the Cash'.
[15]Matthew Hemley, 'RSC Begins Cunch Talks with Cameron Mackintosh over *Les Misérables* Royalties', *The Stage*, 16 January 2019, available online: https://www.thestage.co.uk/news/rsc-begins-crunch-talks-with-cameron-mackintosh-over-les-miserables-royalties (accessed 2 August 2022).
[16]Nunn, 'The Nunn's Tale'.

director at the top of his game, but he wasn't really proven in the musical theatre world. I remember thinking '*Carrie* is his bid to get onto the musical bandwagon.'

The plan seemed to be an ideal way to finally get *Carrie* off the ground. If the writers still had any concern about Hands' suitability for the project, the notion of their show following *Les Misérables* in the RSC's schedule was understandably alluring.

Now, they just needed to find the money.

Carrie's got the Kurz

Lawrence D. Cohen (Book writer)   Friedrich Kurz, who'd produced a successful version of *Cats* in Germany, connected with our assistant to see if Michael and I might have lunch with him. He wanted to discuss possibly becoming involved. This would be his first time producing a new, original musical.[17] It reflected a certain amount of bravado and chutzpah, and we thought maybe that's exactly what we needed.

The replica production in Hamburg had been hailed as one of the first non-state-funded commercial successes in West Germany, and would eventually run for fifteen years. Kurz – known colloquially as Fritz – was also in the early stages of building a bespoke theatre for a production of *Starlight Express* near Düsseldorf, and was keen to break into the American market, describing it as his 'a dream of mine . . . if you can make it on Broadway, you can make it anywhere'.[18]

Cohen   We put him together with Terry to discuss financing. He had no experience whatsoever of producing a *new* show – be it in England or on Broadway – but that said, he assured us that he had the money.

Hands invited Kurz to a meeting at Ralph Koltai's North London studio, where they talked through the show and the concept in detail. They made their way to Poon's, a Chinese restaurant in Covent Garden, to continue the discussion. 'Halfway through the meal,' Koltai recalled, 'Kurz suddenly says, "I like it" – and that is it. He trusts everyone to get it together.'[19]

Hands and Kurz struck a deal: the enthusiastic producer would co-produce the show with the RSC, fronting most of the capital for a commercial transfer after an

---

[17]Kurz, in his memoir, recalls differently, stating that he met Gore at the Broadway premiere of *Les Misérables* (in March 1987), where Gore told him about the show. He says he wasn't interested until he learned of Hands' involvement.
[18]Kurz documentary.
[19]Smurthwaite, '"Carrie" from Behind the Scenes'.

initial run at the company's base, the Royal Shakespeare Theatre in Stratford. 'Producing a new musical with ... Terry Hands struck me as a virtual guarantee of success,' Kurz later wrote in his autobiography. 'Through *Carrie*, I would have to learn the hard way that such guarantees didn't exist in my line of work.'[20]

The agreement was extremely favourable for the RSC, with Kurz essentially guaranteeing the company a profit from the Stratford run and securing it against loss in a future commercial run. The company would collect an upfront '£220,000 no strings sweetener,'[21] while the take from the three-week Stratford Box Office, estimated at £330,000, would be advanced by Kurz to act as the company's investment in the Broadway leg. In return for developing the show using its resources, the RSC would take 10 per cent of any profits after the show broke even: 'if it lasts on Broadway for more than nine months, it will start to spin big cash,'[22] revealed the *New Statesman*. Hands himself would receive a weekly royalty of 3 per cent in New York.[23]

Kurz would receive a substantial royalty should the show succeed in its commercial life, just as Mackintosh had done with *Les Misérables*. He would also gain the prestigious association with the RSC, and the acclaim of producing a world premiere in its famous theatre led by its Artistic Director. In interviews, Kurz seems genuinely enthusiastic about the project. Perhaps he saw a like-minded associate in Hands, who was even half-German on his mother's side and spoke the language fluently. 'I'm a great admirer of Terry's work,' he said. 'He's essentially a European director – very aesthetic, very pure, very elegant, which is what this piece needs.'[24]

Faced with mounting debts and pressure to increase self-sufficiency, but with the prospect of another commercial income stream and the enthusiastic backing of its Artistic Director, the RSC's planning committee gave the nod for work on *Carrie* to forge ahead.

No turning back

Carrie was announced to the press as part of the RSC's 1987–8 season, with the company explicitly positioning the show as a money-maker to curious journalists. *The Stage* described the company's plans for *Carrie* as the company's 'bloody scheme for survival' and an 'innovative new scheme to cushion its downward slide

---

[20]Friedrich Kurz, *Der Musical-Mann* (Munich: GarthMedien, 2010), 10, translated from German.
[21]Thorncroft, 'Carried Away by the Cash'.
[22]Victoria Radin, 'Blood Money', *New Statesman*, 4 March 1988, 31.
[23]Hummler, 'Weisslers', 129,136.
[24]'Blood and Guts in High School', *The Face*, February 1988.

towards a cash crisis', with a company spokesperson describing the show's inclusion in its programme as 'a result of the new self-help policy at the RSC'.[25]

Artistically, Hands claimed that the show 'seemed a suitable conclusion to our season of American works',[26] which also included the plays *They Shoot Horses, Don't They?* (also with a Koltai set), *The Great White Hope* and a Christmas production of *The Wizard of Oz*.[27]

If the notion of the RSC staging *Les Misérables* with a co-producer had been met with contempt – at least until it became clear that the company was: 'sitting on a nice little earner'[28] – then the announcement of *Carrie* escalated the criticism to another level, with the coverage uniformly criticizing the profit-focussed model of the show. The *Sunday Telegraph* questioned 'if it [the RSC] accepts financial profit as a dominant criterion in choosing its repertoire, why stop here? Why not sponsor pop concerts or all-in wrestling? Perhaps the RSC needs to be reminded what its initials stand for.'[29]

The fact that *Carrie* would only be staged in Stratford as a brief 'try-out' was enough for the press to declare that the RSC was being taken for fools. 'It is sad to see the company prostituting its good name in this way,'[30] the *Telegraph* decried, while an editorial in *The Stage* admitted that 'had *Carrie* not carried an RSC label we would not have cared greatly about its fate.'[31] The trade paper acknowledged the irony of the situation, noting that 'having to a certain extent embraced the market economy by trying to put on shows to make a profit, the horror musical *Carrie* being in the pipeline, it is being strongly criticised for doing so . . . Make no mistake there are plenty of people, both in and out of the theatre, who will not be unhappy if *Carrie* turns out to be unsuccessful.'[32]

The *Financial Times* conceded that the company 'can only hope to maintain its current level of activity into the future by becoming dangerously dependent on transfers.'[33]

Underlying the debate was a condemnation of the show's source material – deemed 'a trashy teen-pulp saga of menstruation and paranormal revenge'[34] by Sheridan Morley in *Punch* – and its relevance to the company's core work. The *Financial Times* agreed, demanding: 'Why is the RSC lending its name, its theatre and the talents of its artistic director . . . to a work whose natural home is an airport

---

[25]'RSC Unveils Bloody Scheme for Survival', *The Stage*, 10 September 1987, 2.
[26]Harper, 'STAGE: Horrors!', 58.
[27]Starring a thirty-two-year-old Imelda Staunton as Dorothy and her husband Jim Carter as the cowardly Lion.
[28]'Carrie on Playing', *The Stage*, 1 October, 1987, 12.
[29]Francis King, 'Blood and Bucks', *The Sunday Telegraph*, 21 February 1988.
[30]*Daily Telegraph* critic' quoted in Terry Trucco, '"Carrie" Ghost Haunts Stage of Thatcher Britain', *Wall Street Journal*, 20 May 1988.
[31]'Finer Feelings and Finance in Conflict', *The Stage*, 25 February 1988, 14.
[32]'Carrie on Playing', *The Stage*, 1 October, 1987, 12.
[33]Thorncroft, 'Carried Away by the Cash'.
[34]Sheridan Morley, 'Carrie on Regardless', *Punch*, 4 March 1988.

bookstall?'[35] Indeed, the genre of King's novel and its film adaptation cast a long shadow. Brushed off by many as 'trashy horror' with little consideration given to its emotional underpinnings, the notion of anyone – let alone the RSC – adapting the story as a serious work for the stage seemed as unlikely and bizarre as a serious musicalization of, say, *Halloween* or *The Texas Chainsaw Massacre*.[36]

The writers – in particular Cohen, with his closeness to King's source novel – were flabbergasted by the reaction.

Cohen   The British press firestorm was upsetting, as it happened without them having read a single word of the script or hearing a single note of the score. What's more, they had the nerve to viciously attack King's widely acclaimed and highly regarded work – by now an iconic novel and equally iconic movie – as trash. If they'd been around in Shakespeare's day, would they have deemed *Titus Andronicus* inappropriate for the RSC? Would they have railed against its graphic violence, mutilations and dismemberments, severed heads and hands, cut throats and blood, blood, blood, blood? I think not. Needless to say, this reception did not augur well for what was to follow.

Hands faced the critics. 'I know I am going to get flak. There will be all the stuff about why am I doing it and why should the RSC be involved. The risks involved with *Carrie* are huge but I absolutely believe we're doing the right thing,' he told the *Evening Standard*. 'I believe we are firmly within the RSC charter. I see the company producing one-third Shakespeare, one-third other classics and one-third new work. I see *Carrie* falling within the new work.'[37]

Kurz backed him up in an interview with the *Washington Post*, saying that the company was 'on a shoestring, and they're being criticized for doing commercial ventures! They're vital for the RSC's survival. [The criticisms] make no sense when Thatcher is cutting subsidies.'[38] An 'angry' Debbie Allen told Baz Bamigboye of the *Daily Mail* that:

the RSC can't lose here, because all their costs are being covered by the producers and they will receive [the] profits … What's so bad about that? What's wrong with *Carrie* being done at Stratford? Where else is it going to go? This isn't just a dance show. It is a serious piece of work. It is a musical tragedy that will shock a lot of people in the same way *West Side Story* did all those years ago.[39]

---

[35] Thorncroft, 'Carried Away by the Cash'.
[36] The *Evening Standard* certainly did not find the show 'scary', surmising that 'this account … is about as frightening as a bowl of quivering jelly'.
[37] Owen, '"Carrie on Terry"/"Two in Tune"', 24.
[38] Harper, 'STAGE: Horrors!'
[39] Baz Bamigboye, 'Debbie Causes a Carrie On', *Daily Mail*, 1 March 1988, 20.

Hands continued to defend the show's suitability. 'We have always had a musical tradition, and it comes from our interest in Shakespeare,' he told the Associated Press. 'He uses music endlessly: his musicals, of course, were the late plays . . . The RSC's job is to provide drama, and for people to choose what they want to see. If I can help that service by making us some money here and there, we should do so.'[40] The *Daily Mail* wasn't convinced, calling Hands' justification of the project 'intellectual hocus-pocus which quite defies comment,'[41] sarcastically declaring that the company should abandon its focus on Shakespeare and rebrand as the RFC – the Really Frightful Company. The *New Statesman* suggested that the company's self-help argument was merely used as 'a pretext for a member of a classical drama company to have a shot at Schlock.'[42]

Amidst the slew of eagerly defensive interviews from the team, it is hard to ascertain whether others within the company genuinely shared Hands' belief in the show's validity. In a rather stark confession, presumably believing he was 'off the record', an unedited, taped interview with Ralph Koltai includes the designer's assertion that 'the show hasn't got anything to do with the RSC, but don't say that. That's another story I'm not going to get involved in! No, the only thing the show has to do with the RSC is the fact that the show takes place at Stratford, it opens there, and Terry Hands is the Executive Director of the company, and I happen to be an associate of the RSC. That's where it ends.'[43] Koltai appears to be insinuating that Hands' motivation for directing the show was a more personal one, and that the company's involvement was a means to an end. If Koltai's beliefs reflected the way that the show was perceived by Hands' own staff, we might assume that Hands was facing scepticism about the project from within the organization, as well as from outside of it.

The show was scheduled for a three-week run in February 1988, during the 'dark' period between the annual seasons of Shakespeare plays. These months had traditionally been used to generate rental income from visiting theatre, opera and ballet companies, but with many such organizations struggling to afford the increasing costs of touring, such revenue had begun to dry up.[44]

The RSC's General Manager, David Brierley, said that 'it makes sense to . . . do something completely different, especially something so potentially lucrative.'[45] Brierley also seems to have been given the unenviable task of responding to the aggravated letters about *Carrie* published in the local newspaper, the *Stratford Herald*. In a carefully worded response to one complainant, he pointed out that the

---

[40]'Stephen King's "Carrie" Lands on London Stage', *Associated Press* reproduced in *Standard-Speaker*, 24 February 1988, 8.
[41]Mark Steyn, 'Period Pains', *The Independent*, 20 February 1988.
[42]Radin, 'Blood Money'.
[43]*Theatre Craft*/Pirani interview tapes.
[44]Fetherston, 'Broadway Goes for Blood', 72.
[45]Thorncroft, 'Carried Away by the Cash'.

region should be proud to be hosting the world premiere of a major new musical, that taxpayers' money was not being squandered, and that the company had no choice but to rely on a range of commercial ventures to secure its future.[46]

A classy out-of-town try-out

A West End run of the show was initially considered, presumably opening prior to (or in parallel with) the Broadway production. Audition notices in British trade publication *The Stage* described the show as a 'major West End musical' which would 'open out of town prior to West End opening April' (Image 2.1).[47]

However, by October 1987, articles about the show start to reference a plan to 'transfer *Carrie* straight to Broadway after its opening in Stratford-upon-Avon, skipping the West End,'[48] with a May 1988 opening. The *New York Times* suggested that 'a West End production would then follow [the Broadway run], if the show is a success'.[49] Hands later said that the decision to bypass the West End and move the show directly to Broadway was 'by chance really. We could not get into any London theatre large enough to take it.'[50] Kurz said that 'everything was fully booked for years. *Cats*, *Phantom of the Opera* and *Les Misérables* already had staked out their permanent places. There was no room for *Carrie* . . .'[51] It would be safe to assume that the negative press reaction to the show's announcement had done little to convince any of the big London theatre owners to leap at the opportunity to host a show that was being so openly derided.

The decision provoked a further round of uproar from the press, with critics pointing out that relatively few Brits would get to see the show before it moved State-side. Hands tried to brush aside the notion. 'I regard Stratford as our main engagement, then we are going on tour,' he said, insinuating that a long life was planned for *Carrie*. 'Our first stop happens to be Broadway.'[52] American press reports seem rather more impressed by the show's unique testing ground, with the *New York Times* describing the Stratford run as 'a classy out-of-town tryout'.[53]

After their enforced hiatus, Koltai and Reid returned to work on their set and costume designs.

---

[46]David Brierley, '"Carrie" a Money Spinner', Letters page, *Stratford Herald*, 19 February 1988.
[47]*The Stage*, 3 September 1987, 26.
[48]Jeremy Jehu, 'Equity Backs Hands across the Water Deal', *The Stage*, 15 October 1987, 1.
[49]Jeremy Gerard, 'Drowsy Broadway about to Be Stirred', *New York Times*, 7 December 1987, 69.
[50]Owen, '"Carrie on Terry"/"Two in Tune"', 24.
[51]Kurz, *Der Musical-Mann*, 12.
[52]Michael Goldfarb, 'From the Shakespeareans, a Carrie for Broadway', *Washington Post*, 21 February 1988, 23.
[53]Enid Nemy, 'Good News from the Rumor Mill', in 'On Stage' column, *New York Times*, 20 November 1987, 66.

IMAGE 2.1 Audition ads for singers and dancers in *The Stage*. Courtesy of *The Stage*.

Acknowledging the complexity of the machinery that would be needed to achieve the desired effects, Koltai started consulting with Peter Kemp – the esteemed theatrical engineer responsible for constructing the impressive, dynamic sets of *42nd Street* and *Chess* – and a small army of other scenic contractors.

In a rehearsal interview, Reid recalled his continued struggle to align his costume designs with Hands' abstract ideas, recounting the many rounds of sketches he presented during the long design process. 'It wasn't torture, but it was heavy-going because I wasn't terribly sure of what he wanted,' he said.

This is the strangest [show] I've ever had to do. If you're doing a period costume, say it's from Charles I's time ... you're guided by certain things. The bodice is going to be cut in a certain way, and the skirts are going to have a certain width, and the men have got that cavalier look. But this was very much an unknown, amorphous kind of thing. We'll just have to wait and see now if it's a success. And if it's not a success, it's not for the want of trying![54]

Glimpsing the designs for the costumes and set for the first time, the writers were less than impressed.

Michael Gore (Composer)   Truthfully, they worried us. We expressed our concern about the set being a white box with absolutely no furniture or props, and nothing on the walls to help orient the audience into the story. Worse, the gym clothes for the schoolgirls made them look as if they were wearing Greek togas, a potentially fatal and risible misdirection for an audience.

Dean Pitchford (Lyricist)   That was a real, 'Whoa, wait a minute!' moment. We felt that we had taken a real 'hard left'. We were waving our hands and saying, 'No, no, please don't.'

Gore   Terry told us we were thinking too naturalistically. When that failed to persuade us, he responded by telling us we didn't have the experience to know how to properly look at sketches in spite of our experience doing just that on films and other pieces of theatre. He insisted that once we saw the fully realized costumes, we'd be happy.

Pitchford   There was a slow accretion of wrong decisions. Terry was very adept at soft-selling things, and he had an expression – he'd say, 'Leave it with me!' – which was his way of saying, 'I don't want to talk about this anymore,' or, 'I don't know what I'm going to do,' or, 'I know exactly what I'm going to do, but I'm not going to tell you!' From the moment we saw the set and costume sketches, we did a lot of, 'Wait, hang on, please ...' and he would throw back a lot of assurances. 'It's going to be wonderful. It's going to be marvellous. You'll see. You'll see ...'

Broadway, baby

In New York, Kurz secured a commitment from the Jujamcyn Group to house the show in its Virginia Theater.

---

[54] *Theatre Craft*/Pirani interview tapes.

Jujamcyn had found itself struggling to fill its portfolio of five theatres with consistently long-running shows. Its houses were regarded as less desirable than others, being smaller and further away from the Theatre District's busiest thoroughfares. The Virginia – though only a few minutes' walk from Times Square – felt distant from the cluster of theatres situated there, and had sat empty between May 1984 and March 1986. Owner James Binger had brought in Rocco Landesman to help develop the company, both as a landlord and a producer. Landesman was a former Yale drama professor, whose first major foray into producing – the multi-Tony-winning musical *Big River* – had opened at the group's Eugene O'Neill Theatre in April 1985 to great acclaim.

Landesman agreed not only to host *Carrie* but to plough a $500,000 investment into its budget[55] in exchange for a 5 per cent share of net profits.[56] It was a decision he would come to regret: later, he would tell *Time* magazine that *Carrie* was 'the biggest flop in the world history of the theater, going back to Aristophanes'.[57]

Variety published the details of a private placement memorandum – a document setting out the risks and terms of an investment – which explained the 'labyrinthine route of the show'[58] to the stage and its complex profit model. As well as Jujamcyn's royalty, Cohen and Gore would receive 0.5 per cent each, in addition to their collective 6 per cent author royalty (shared with Pitchford), plus 5 per cent of future net profits, increasing to 7.5 per cent at double recoupment and 10 per cent at triple recoupment. *Variety* described the author royalties as 'unusually heavy'.[59]

In exchange for sourcing the remainder of the required capital, Kurz would receive 40 per cent of net profits, and his investor pool would split 47.5 per cent.[60] Kurz would retain the option to produce the show in 'all other venues in the US, Canada and Great Britain'.[61]

The split from the original production team, Barry and Fran Weissler and Fred Zollo, would prove to be costly. Having formed a joint venture to develop the project, they were reimbursed $113,766 for expenses incurred as part of the sale of the rights to Kurz, with Zollo receiving an additional $45,825 for his out-of-pocket costs, according to *Variety*.[62] In addition, the outgoing producers would retain a stake in the project as part of their agreement to depart: they would be paid 0.5 per cent of the weekly box office and 2.5 per cent of any net profits.

---

[55]Michael Riedel, *Singular Sensation: The Triumph of Broadway* (New York and London: Avid Reader Press), 78.
[56]Hummler, 'Weisslers', 129,136.
[57]Henry III, 'Theater'.
[58]Hummler, 'Weisslers', 129,136.
[59]Ibid.
[60]Ibid.: the article notes that this was less than the 'customary 50%' expected of a general partner in a Broadway show.
[61]Ibid.
[62]Ibid.

With a theatre secured, funding in place and revenue splits confirmed, production could ramp up. However, the global spread of the various stakeholders continued to prove challenging.

Pitchford Terry was in England. Kurz was in Germany. I was in Los Angeles and my two collaborators were in New York. Holding meetings and getting work done was like putting the Rockettes on the road. We had time zones and jet lag and all sorts of things working against us, but we ploughed ahead.

The geographical split, combined with their ongoing commitments to other projects, also forced Hands and Allen to work on their own elements of the production separately. Allen focussed predominantly on the 'school' numbers, applying her high-energy, aerobic-style movement style to the teenagers' songs.

'By the time I came to London to work on *Carrie*, I had already worked on the choreography for about five weeks, establishing my own dance vocabulary in terms of what I felt about the show,' Allen wrote in the Stratford programme. 'Through my discussion with Terry Hands, I had a good idea of the style in which the show would be presented and how the set and costumes would function. By the time we started rehearsals in London, I had established the basic dance style for the show.'[63]

Hands was not used to working with a choreographer, but Allen, at least, seems to have embraced the partnership, declaring in interviews that she was looking forward to working as a team. 'I'm here to steal from you,' she later teased Hands in rehearsal footage. 'I want to know all your tricks, I want to know everything you do!'[64] In her programme note, Allen likens their relationship to that of Professor Higgins and Eliza Doolittle, the diametrically opposed leading couple of *My Fair Lady*. 'I'm learning a lot and I think he is, too.'[65]

An equitable solution

Traditionally, acting roles were fiercely guarded by each nation's actors' union, colloquially known as Equity.[66] Then, as now, performers required permission from the relevant union to gain an overseas working visa. As such, it was rare for foreign performers to play a role on Broadway or in the West End if a local actor had the requisite skills and qualities for the job.

Exceptions were possible; a reciprocal trade agreement meant that one American actor could perform in the UK if a British actor was offered a similar placement in America, and vice versa. Permission was also granted in special

---

[63]RSC programme.
[64]Kurz documentary.
[65]RSC programme.
[66]Known today as Equity UK and Actors' Equity Association in the US.

circumstances for internationally recognized or uniquely talented stars to reprise a role in the transfer of a show.

Indeed, the subject had recently been the topic of much conversation in the industry, with Andrew Lloyd Webber threatening to cancel the Broadway premiere of *The Phantom of Opera* after American Equity demanded that the role of Christine Daaé, played by his wife Sarah Brightman, be recast with an American performer. It was a bold statement from American Equity, essentially declaring that nobody was above the rules, however successful their show had been in other markets. Equity eventually relented, allowing Brightman to perform for six months on the condition that an American be given a similarly high-profile role in London.

Aware that he was very unlikely to be granted permission to transfer an entirely British cast to Broadway, Hands was keen to avoid a costly and time-consuming recasting process. Additionally, Allen would most likely have been keen to include dancers from her American network in the show's Ensemble.

Hands urged the Equity unions to grant permission for a mixed British and American cast, split exactly down the middle, which could perform the show on both sides of the Atlantic. It would be the first time such a split had ever been attempted, and would neatly reflect the international mixture of the creative and production teams. The deal would include an assurance that the same structure would be replicated in any future run of the show, guaranteeing equal opportunities for both American and British performers.[67]

The Stage called the proposal 'revolutionary', suggesting such a deal would 'ease tensions surrounding the transfer of artists between Britain and New York', which an RSC spokesperson claimed would be 'an unprecedented breakthrough'.[68] The praise must have come as some relief after the critical hammering around the show's announcement.

It was a proposal that suited both unions: 'It became clear that the only way *Carrie* could occur was an entirely new venture, and the only way Terry could get it off the ground was under the present scope,' Alan Eisenberg, Executive Secretary of Actors' Equity in New York told *Drama*. '100% of nothing isn't as good as 50% of something.' Peter Plouviez, the General Secretary of British Actors' Equity, agreed. 'It's a healthy, encouraging development. We're in favour of the interchange of the best in each other's theatre, because we think by and large that will keep live theatre going.'[69]

---

[67]Technically, not all the performers were British or American, they simply belonged to one of the national unions – two of the 'British' cast, for example, were from South Africa, and one was from Australia.

[68]Jehu, 'Equity Backs Hands across the Water Deal', 1.

[69]Matt Wolf, 'Carrie on Equity', *Drama*, May 1988.

How do you solve a problem like Margaret?

With the Equity agreement in place and an optimistic atmosphere prevailing, it was finally time to cast the show's leading roles.

The team knew that the role of Carrie's ultra-zealot mother, Margaret – played memorably in the movie by Piper Laurie – offered a great opportunity to cast a big-name Broadway actress with an equally big voice.

Gore   *Evita*'s Eva Peron was our vocal role model for Margaret. Betty Buckley, Patti LuPone and Barbara Cook were all candidates on our shortlist. We soon learned how incredibly difficult the part was, requiring not only ferocious acting chops, but insane vocal demands and huge physical stamina.

Buckley – well known for her leading lady status and slew of acting awards – was close friends with Pitchford, having performed alongside him in *Pippin*, and well known to Cohen having appeared in the *Carrie* movie. She also shared an agent, Sam Cohn, with all three writers and Hands.

Pitchford   The success of Margaret's songs depended on hearing an enormous voice peeling the paint off the walls. My contributions to Carrie were always with Betty's voice in my ear. She was gracious enough to come and audition for our director and producers, and they wanted her. We all wanted her.

Cohen   Her audition was brilliant. It absolutely blew the roof off the rehearsal room.

Betty Buckley ('Margaret White', Broadway)   Terry met with me, and he had all kinds of questions about me as a person. I was kind of taken aback by it, because I had worked with his colleague Trevor Nunn.[70] I suggested he go ask Trevor if he had any questions or doubts about me. It just didn't feel like a copacetic start. He was quite confrontational and challenging at that meeting. I remember Terry asked me if I was afraid of heights, because they had thought of flying me, and I said, 'No, I'm not!' I don't know where that came from. I felt quite uncomfortable. These were my friends, and I wanted to help them, but his approach at that meeting put me off.

Pitchford   Things went south. To be honest, Terry didn't push hard enough. He had never been through that kind of negotiation before. He was so used to the idea of repertory theatre back home: the notion that you have a company in which, you know, Dame Judi Dench plays Cleopatra on Tuesdays and then

---

[70]Buckley originated the role of Grizabella in *Cats* on Broadway.

the maid on Wednesdays, and nobody is above anybody else. There's no ranking, no star of the show. That's not how Broadway works.

Frustrated, and with Buckley out of the picture, the team considered other options.

Pitchford   We had to walk away from Betty, which broke my heart, but there's only so much wringing of hands and shedding of tears you can do before you have to move on. And so, we replaced one Broadway legend with another.

The other legend was Barbara Cook. Twenty years older than Buckley, Cook had come to prominence on Broadway in the 1950s, leading a string of hit shows and collecting her first Tony Award for *The Music Man* in 1958. By the time casting for *Carrie* was underway, she had all but retired, occasionally returning to delight fans with a cabaret or solo show. An appearance as Sally in the well-received 1985 concert version of *Follies* at Lincoln Center had endeared her to a new generation of fans, and a series of concerts at London's Donmar Warehouse and Albery Theatre soon after had increased her profile in the UK.

Cohen   The Weisslers had encouraged us to cast Barbara, feeling that her legendary name and her return to Broadway after so many years would make our show an event.

Georgia Otterson, a close friend of Cook, was her de facto assistant during the later stage of her career.

Georgia Otterson (Assistant to Barbara Cook)   She was invited to meet Terry Hands in New York, and she thought, 'Well, I don't know . . .' So many of her friends were asking '*Carrie*?!' She met with him and she thought he was just brilliant. She liked him a lot. He had this idea of it being a Greek tragedy, and she was infatuated, I think, with his plans.

'Terry is a very smart, seductive man, and he explained certain scenes in such clear detail that I could see myself in them,' Cook explained in her autobiography. 'I knew I could perform the show he described, and it was exciting to think of appearing in a Royal Shakespeare Company production.'[71]

In a September 1986 article, she was musing over the role, admitting, 'next year I'll probably do *Carrie*, which Terry Hands of the Royal Shakespeare Company is going to direct'.[72] She was still hesitant about the offbeat material ('It was all a long way from Marian the Librarian,'[73] her prim and proper role in *The Music Man*) but

---

[71] Barbara Cook, *Then and Now: A Memoir* (New York: HarperCollins, 2016).
[72] Peter Hepple, 'Barbara is the Toast of London', *The Stage*, 25 September 1986, 5.
[73] Cook, *Then and Now*, 205.

she liked the score. By November the following year, the news was confirmed, adding some much-needed credence to the project: 'Sometimes, a rumor turns out to be absolutely accurate and sometimes the absolutely accurate rumor brings joy to both the theater community and theatergoers,'[74] gushed the *New York Times*.

'The family element of a show is one thing I have missed,' she said, after performing solo for so long. 'For me, what makes the show really happen is you care about these people as people. If we were just doing a pyrotechnical show, I wouldn't have been interested. People need to leave the theatre crying and, secondly, saying, "so how about those sets?"'[75]

With one leading lady in place, it was time to find the other.

The auditions

Linzi Hateley ('Carrie White', Stratford and Broadway)   I was 16. I was at a theatre school, Italia Conti, and there was an agency attached to the school. There were some really cute-looking children and they got work all the time. I just wasn't that. I had a really powerful singing voice for my age, but I was a shy, chubby teenager, so I didn't fit in.

Open auditions for British cast members were held at the London Palladium on 7 and 8 September 1987.

Hateley   I didn't really know at that point that I was going for the part of Carrie. The first day was a dance audition. I went along with my leg warmers and probably even a headband for my big 1980s hair, knowing me. I remember very clearly standing on the Palladium stage thinking, 'My God, I've died and gone to heaven before I've done anything!' I really did think, well, even if I don't go any further, this is a dream come true.

One person made Hateley starstruck.

Hateley   I grew up watching *Fame*, so to have Debbie Allen in front of me was a bit surreal. I learnt a routine with all these phenomenal dancers. They were all quite a bit taller and a lot thinner than me, but I just went with it. I thought, 'Well, maybe they're looking for all different shapes and sizes . . .' We learnt a routine to Michael Jackson's 'Bad'. They blasted it through the sound system and it sounded amazing. I can almost remember the routine!

The following day, Hateley returned for a singing audition with Pitchford and Gore. Unaware that she was being considered for the title role, Hateley arrived looking rather different to the downtrodden teen.

---

[74]Nemy, 'Good News', 66.
[75]'Stephen King's "Carrie"', 8.

Hateley   I was sixteen and I had thought, 'I'm never gonna be employed unless I make myself look as old as possible.' So, I'd put my hair up and had lots of make-up on and put my heels on . . . I didn't really know what I was doing. I chose to sing 'On My Own' from *Les Mis*, because I'd just recently heard the cast recording, and I was obsessed with Frances Ruffelle. My Auntie Violet had seen the show and said, 'Ooh Linz, there's a part in *Les Mis* that you'd be perfect for . . . Eponine! Honestly, I could see you doing that one!'[76] I sang it once, and Dean – who was and always remained such a warm and gentle person – came up to me, and said, 'Would you mind putting your hair down, and taking off your make-up, and just looking like you naturally?' So, I took all my make-up off. I remember sitting in this dressing room. There were a lot of other beautiful girls there, and I seem to remember being fascinated by Sally [Ann Triplett] . . .

Sally Ann Triplett ('Sue Snell', Stratford and Broadway)   I was in the Ensemble of *Follies* at the Shaftesbury, and I understudied a part.[77] I didn't have an agent for about fifteen years when I first started out, I used to find all my own work, and I just managed to keep working and not let go. I heard about this show and I thought 'I'm gonna just try my luck.'

Hateley   I just remember thinking 'She's fierce!' She seemed to be so confident – she might not have been – but she came across as so full of fun and really feisty! Anyway, I went back in, sang 'On My Own' again. There was a noticeable excitement from them. I didn't know what that meant.

Cohen   After months and months of casting on both sides of the Atlantic, and just as we'd given up hope that we'd ever find the right girl to play Carrie, up popped this sixteen-year-old schoolgirl. Two lines into her auditioning with 'On My Own', the three authors all looked over at each other and without speaking, realized we needed to look no further. We'd found our girl.

Hateley   They said, 'Right, can we teach you a bit of the title song?'

Cohen   We asked her to go off for a little while and learn it, and then come back to sing it.

Gore played the opening notes of the show's title number.

Hateley (*sings*)   'Doesn't Anybody Ever Get It Right? Carrie!' And as soon as I heard that, I thought ,'This is amazing. This is absolutely amazing.' It just hit me. I instantly connected with it. I can't read music. Still can't. But I think I've got a good ear, so I picked it up very quickly. They said, 'Right now do it again, and really mean it.' So, I just blasted it out of the park as much as I possibly

---

[76]Hateley breaks out into a broad Midlands accent for her impression of the enthusiastic Auntie Violet.
[77]The UK premiere of Stephen Sondheim's show opened at the Shaftesbury Theatre in July 1987 – Triplett would eventually take over the role of Young Phyllis.

could. There was a sense of something . . . something felt good in there. And that was it. I went home and I thought, 'Well, that was an amazing experience!' I went into college the next day, and I didn't hear anything all day. I just thought, 'Oh, well, maybe that's it.' It was my seventeenth birthday. I was called up to the agency, which was on the top floor, late in the afternoon. I thought, 'I hope it's not bad news, because it's my birthday!' I walked in and they gave me this birthday card, I opened it, and it said, 'Happy birthday, Carrie!'

Hateley's casting – making her the RSC's youngest ever leading lady at the time – caught the imagination of the British press, with the *Daily Mirror* describing her achievement as a 'rags-to-riches fairytale'. When asked what she might do with her wages, she informs the reporter that she plans to send her parents on holiday – 'somewhere hot where they'll get a sun tan' – as thanks for paying her drama school fees. 'I know it will be hard work and that I've never done anything like this before, but when I walk on to a stage I feel at home,'[78] she said.

She told *The Times*, 'You dream of this sort of thing happening at the end of your career, not the beginning. It's unbelievable.'[79] To the *Liverpool Echo* she said, 'I put it all down to fate, and I couldn't be happier . . . I saw the film and it really frightened the life out of me, but the musical is not like the book at all. This production is more down to earth.' Her focus on the role at such a young age is clear; when questioned whether she feels she will be missing out on 'the things girls of her age usually do', she responds, 'Oh no, I will look back in years to come and be grateful for all I have already achieved. What young, aspiring performer wouldn't want that? . . . If it's a great success I should be spending my eighteenth birthday in America.'[80]

Despite her surprise and delight at winning the role, there was some nervousness from her parents, familiar with the disturbing nature of the source material.

Hateley   I think they were concerned. To go from being at school to suddenly playing the title role in a Stephen King show which has strange, dark, abusive subject matter. But Terry made a point of taking my parents and I out, and he explained what he thought the process would be. He guaranteed me that I wouldn't have to expose myself or anything like that, because they had seen the film with Sissy Spacek, so they knew it was full on!

Meanwhile, Triplett had a decision to make: continue in her *Follies* understudy role for the remainder of her contract, or find a way to take the principal role of Sue in *Carrie*.

---

[78]Hilary Bonner, 'Carrie on Linzi!', *Daily Mirror*, 2 November 1987, 1.
[79]Lynda Murdin, 'RSC Gives Star Role to Teenager', *The Times*, 30 October 1987, 16.
[80]Peter Grant, 'Carrie n Linzi. She is Going Places', *Liverpool Echo*, 31 December 1987, 8.

Triplett   If you're in a show in the West End, you're there for the year. You're not let go at all. Mike Cochran, the wonderful director of *Follies*, happened to be in the building that night, and I cornered him on the stairs. I remember it so vividly. I told him the story, and he said, 'Well, you have to make this happen for you! We have to release you.' He was the most brilliant man. And so off I went.

Michèle Du Verney (Ensemble, Stratford and Broadway)   I was doing a class at Pineapple Dance Studios, and a friend of mine told me there was an audition at the Palladium. He said, 'Why don't you come?' and I replied, 'I haven't gone through an agent, I didn't know anything about it.' And he said, 'Just come. The worst that could happen is that you get thrown out!' I managed to get through the door, did the audition, got a recall, and then another one. I remember not hearing for a while, so I took a role in a panto somewhere in Nottingham. One day, I was in a bedsit on my own, hating life, and my agent called and said, 'Michèle, you need to get out of there, you're going to Broadway!'

Michelle Nelson (Ensemble, Stratford and Broadway)   I had been offered a part in the touring company of *Starlight Express*, but I heard there had been an audition with Debbie Allen for *Carrie*. I had missed the first casting but decided to turn up at the second one, being in awe of her and *Fame*. It was fast-paced, high energy, and very exciting.

Michelle 'Shelley' Hodgson[81] (Ensemble, Stratford and Broadway)   I sang 'Papa Don't Preach' and I forgot the words (*extensive laughter*). 'Papa don't preach . . . I'm in trouble deep . . .' and that's all I kept singing. I think Debbie had to say something in the end. 'You seem to be in trouble, honey!' God. That's my lasting memory of that audition. Basically, me singing 'I'm in trouble deep,' over and over!

Catherine Coffey (Ensemble, Stratford and Broadway)   I had a temperature that day, and felt awful, but there was no way I was going to miss this. When I finally met Debbie, she was the happiest, sweetest, most wonderful woman. I remember her speaking to me but I couldn't take in a word she said, I was so starstruck.

Kenny Linden (Ensemble, Stratford and Broadway)   I remember the audition with Debbie. She muttered to her assistant something about not wanting anyone who was out of breath. So, I didn't breathe for the full audition! She came over to me at one point, and said, 'What kind of street dancing do you do?' I said, 'I don't dance in the street!' I didn't have a clue

---

[81]Shelley became known as such because there were three Michelles in the cast: Allen suggested two of them chose variants. Hodgson became 'Shelley', Michèle Du Verney became simply 'Du Verney' to her colleagues (and Michèle in the programme), while Michelle Nelson remained 'Michelle'.

what she was talking about. She should have known there and then that we were not a perfect match!

Suzanne 'Squeeze' Thomas (Ensemble, Stratford and Broadway)   I was doing *Chess*, with [*Carrie* ensemble members] Cath Coffey, Maddie Loftin and Michelle Nelson. Michael Bennett had cast it, so a lot of dancers wanted to do that show. Everyone would go to the same auditions, and then a whole load of us got *Carrie*.

Linden   I was shaking, a bit like my driving test. It was horrible. They took me out, stroked me for a while and said, 'Come back, and try again.' I was a shivering wreck. After that, I didn't hear anything for a while, then I got a phone call saying, 'Can you come down and take some *Carrie* auditions for us?'

Linden had impressed the team more than he realized, and was asked to help audition more dancers in London.

Linden   So, I said, 'Are you gonna pay me?' Yes! So, I went down and I think I got £50 and my train fare. I led all these boys auditioning for Tommy. I taught them the same routine that I'd done in the audition. I can still remember it.

Paul Gyngell, a Welsh actor who had recently appeared in *Joseph and the Amazing Technicolor Dreamcoat* in London, was given the role.

Linden   After that, I said, 'Have I actually got a job?' and they said, 'Oh yes, you're in it.' I ended up understudying Paul, which was nice. I played Kenny, because we were all given our own names.

Hodgson   Kenny is absolutely right. I played Shelley. We created the roles, so we were told that people in future would be auditioning for the part of Michèle, Kenny, Shelley and all the others!

Coffey   I didn't think I had a snowball's chance in hell of getting through. It went my way in the end. Thrilled. Delighted. Flabbergasted. No words to describe that feeling of being in the final line-up.

Next, auditions in New York City – curtailed a year previously – finally resumed.

Littlefield   My roommate and I had moved to New York City. We knew Debbie Allen was currently on Broadway in *Sweet Charity* so we went to ask her if *Carrie* was going to happen. We waited outside the Stage Door at the Minskoff Theatre. Debbie saw us standing there and came over to us and said she remembered us from the audition. She said it was going to be happening soon and to leave our contact information. A week later we were called to come in and sing an uptempo pop song.

Mark Santoro (Ensemble, Stratford and Broadway)   I got a phone call asking if I would come in for a callback at the Mark Hellinger Theater. We had to sing first, and I sang really badly. I thought I blew it. Then Debbie said, 'Go put your dance clothes on!' Her choreography was very athletic, and I remember being out of breath.

Littlefield   We danced again, and then sang on stage. I can remember Debbie's voice talking to me from the empty theatre. I got the call a few days later that I got the job.

Joey McKneely had just finished a run in the short-lived musical *Roza*, which closed after twenty previews and twelve performances.

Joey McKneely (Ensemble, Stratford and Broadway)   I was like, 'Oh my God, I need a job!' The *Carrie* audition appeared and I showed up and got the gig. I was just happy to work. It was interesting, a lot of the best Broadway dancers all got *Carrie*. It had such a huge reputation at that moment. '*Carrie* the Musical? We have to be in that!'

Scott Wise (Ensemble, Stratford and Broadway)   I flew in from upstate New York with a tour of *Song and Dance*. I mainly just remember doing a lot of flips. Then I raced back to do my show that night.

Charlotte d'Amboise was an experienced Broadway dancer up for the principal role of Carrie's nemesis, Chris Hargensen.

Charlotte d'Amboise ('Chris Hargensen', Stratford and Broadway)   I think I danced to Debbie's insane choreography first. Kicking and turning . . . you had to have technique to get past anything! I got all the way to the end. Then I sang, and then I read a scene.

Soon, it became clear that d'Amboise was up against one other performer in New York.

D'Amboise   She was stunning, and Terry Hands was mad for her, and was wooing her, and rightly so! She was totally right for the part! Anyway, she got it, and I was devastated. The next day, she called me up and she said, 'You know what? I read the script. I'm a born-again Christian. I can't curse. I can't. I can't say those words!' I was like, 'Yeah,. . . I have no problem with cursing! No problem!' The part was mine! And then I was leaving for London in a week. It was crazy.

Joining d'Amboise as fellow antagonist Billy Nolan was Gene Anthony Ray, a talented dancer who had shot to prominence playing Leroy Johnson in the *Fame* franchise. 'I'm not an expert on style of dance,' he told the *Daily Mail*:

I've been through so many styles that to categorise is difficult. From Harlem I went right into ballet, to *Fame* with all that jazz dancing, then with the RSC it's classical and jazz mixed, and in the clubs it's real street dancing. A mixture of everything. Like *Carrie*'s a real mixture. My character is a street character, so everything I know comes into it. It's sort of tailor-made.[82]

'I love Gene! Gene! First of all, he's hysterical ... and extremely talented, and I think we work really well together,' d'Amboise said. 'My character is a real rich girl, a snob, and [his] is a street kid that I wouldn't even look at, normally, but I'm sort of rebelling from society.'[83]

'All I want from her is sex, and she promises me that, so I'll do anything for her,' Ray said in his interview, wearing a scarf and shades outside the Royal Shakespeare Theatre. 'That's a little close to my real life . . .,' he jokes. 'It's my first time in Stratford ... it's wonderful with the RSC. I thought it was a dream come true. I was, like, 'Me? Working in a classical theatre? Oh, come off it, never!' But I'm here, I'm doing it, and successfully. And having a good time doing it.'[84]

The role of Carrie's sympathetic gym teacher, Miss Gardner, was awarded to Darlene Love, best known as lead singer of the 1960s girl group The Blossoms and vocalist on hits including 'He's a Rebel' and 'He's Sure the Boy I Love'.

Love had appeared as herself (alongside *Carrie* workshop star Annie Golden) in both the off-Broadway and Broadway iterations of *Leader of the Pack*, based on the life of songwriter Ellie Greenwich; Love had been the original recording artist of many of Greenwich's hits.[85]

Cohen   Darlene's audition was a perfect example of how we, as authors, came from a completely different world to Terry. Our approaches were worlds apart. Darlene came in and sang the hell out of her audition song – as best as I can recall, I think it was 'Sometimes When We Touch' – which impressed everyone. We just assumed – as is always done in auditions – that she would then read a scene from the show, but Terry thanked her and started to bid her goodbye. We called him over and asked, 'Don't you want to hear her read?' Terry replied no, saying that he knew everything he needed to know just from hearing her sing. It was a worrisome moment to say the least, showing the authors that we were coming at things in very different ways.

In her memoir, Love recalled the audition from her perspective. 'Theater was a complete other world for me,' she told *TheaterWeek*. 'I really had no aspirations to do Broadway. It just wasn't in my game plan.'[86] Love said that she agreed to audition for *Carrie* after hearing about Allen's involvement:

---

[82]Danae Brook, '"Leroy" is Just Streets Ahead', *Daily Mail*, 21 February 1988.
[83]RSC documentary.
[84]RSC documentary.
[85]In her memoir, Love (2013), 295, she described her unhappy time in *Leader of the Pack* as being 'like a six-month hangnail'.
[86]Terry Helbing, 'Darlene Love is Here to Stay', *TheaterWeek*, 23 May 1988, 16.

I had never met her before and I'm such a big fan of hers that I immediately got nervous … At the end of the audition, they all applauded! She led the cheerleading section and ran up to me and hugged, and said, 'My dear, where have *you* been? … Well, we found Miss Gardner, I don't wanna see no more Miss Gardners!' When the question of Love's dance ability was raised, she said that Allen cried 'Leave it to me, she'll be *twirling* when I get through with her![87]

Describing her role in the show, Love said, 'I'm the good one in the play; I help Carrie to come out of her cocoon, not to be so shy, and to believe in herself. It's like she's my child.'[88]

Despite the lengthy search for top-notch dancers, Allen continued to hold last-minute auditions in the days running up to the start of rehearsals.

Eric Gilliom (Ensemble, Stratford and Broadway)   I was expecting to go to one of the dance studios, but she called me to her home in Los Angeles. She said, 'We need another guy.' I said, 'How soon till it's starting?' She said, 'You're leaving Wednesday.' This was a Saturday. I had four days to get my life together.

Jackson   By this time, I was working as a dancer on a cruise ship. My mother called me from Louisiana and said, 'Debbie Allen just called. They want you to get off the boat and meet them in England.' I got off the boat in Barbados and flew to Britain. I was shocked. She had tracked me down. What's more incredible, in my opinion, is that she could have had any dancer from New York. I mean, there were a billion amazing dancers in the city. The fact that she remembered me was crazy.

The music men

Michael Gore and Dean Pitchford continued to hone their songs, defining Carrie's two worlds with different musical styles. 'It offered the opportunity to have great, energetic numbers for the kids in the high school, and … much more operatic numbers between the mother and daughter,' Gore said.[89]

As the songs took their final shape, two orchestrators – Michael Starobin and Anders Eljas – were brought in to arrange Gore's piano score for specific instruments and vocal types, giving both worlds of the show a signature sound.

---

[87]Ibid.
[88]Ibid.
[89]RSC documentary.

Gore   We hired Michael to do the mother/daughter orchestral material based on his wonderful work for Sondheim on *Sunday in the Park with George*,[90] as well as several William Finn musicals. As for Anders, the pop record sound and arrangements he created for ABBA and Chess made him seem a perfect choice.[91] The score had a tremendous amount of music, so both orchestrators were happy to be splitting the duties.

Michael Starobin (Co-orchestrator, Stratford)   On most musicals, the composer writes the score for piano only. Even if a composer is capable of orchestrating a song, there usually isn't time because orchestrations aren't written until the show is in rehearsal. So, orchestrations have to be written very quickly in the last four to eight weeks. At that time the composer is busy altering the score and sitting in rehearsals observing and discussing changes with the other writers and the director.

Anders Eljas (Co-orchestrator, Stratford)   I remember Michael [Starobin]'s fantastic orchestrations on his numbers. It was very nice to get inspiration, and work hard and learn. He is also one of the nicest guys you can think of to work with.

John Owen Edwards (Musical Director, Stratford)   I was asked to be Musical Director for *Carrie* by Terry Hands. Like many others, I thought it was an odd idea, but so was the biography of the wife of an Argentinian despot or a musical of T. S. Eliot's cat poems and they certainly did well! I had heard or seen copies of most of the score by the time we went into auditions. It seemed an interesting project largely for two reasons: I would be able to work in New York where I had many friends in the theatre business, and secondly it was a big deal that Barbara Cook, an artist I much respected, was going to be playing the mother.

The trio would seem to form a model team.

Edwards   I was delighted to be working again with my friend Anders Eljas with whom I had had a very warm relationship on the preparation of *Chess* in the West End.[92] An added bonus was that Michael Starobin was to be part of the team, and I had admired his work enormously on *Sunday in the Park with George*.

The British invasion

As the Americans made their way to the UK, preliminary rehearsals began at The Dance Attic, a studio complex in Putney, West London.

---

[90]*Sunday* had opened off-Broadway before transferring to the Booth Theatre, winning the Pulitzer Prize and two Tonys in 1985.
[91]Eljas had toured extensively with the pop group in the 1970s, as well as conducting the London Symphony Orchestra on Benny Andersson and Björn Ulvaeus' *Chess* album and concert tour of Europe.
[92]Edwards was Musical Director.

Littlefield   I roomed with two other American cast members, Jamie Beth Chandler and Mary Ann Oedy. Our flat was in South Kensington.

Mary Ann Oedy (Ensemble, Stratford and Broadway)   I loved staying with the girls. Kelly and I, especially, did everything together. We stayed friends for life after *Carrie*. I went to her wedding! There were three of us in this tiny flat.

Littlefield   I remember having to go through and sign an inventory list of what was in the flat. We joked about the plaster bust of the Greek god in the dining room, like we could fit it in our suitcase or carry it in the first place! It was a lot different from the American housing that I was used to. We had no heat in the kitchen, and a tiny fridge. We could leave the milk on the counter and it would stay cold. We took the Tube to rehearsal each day. I remember walking every morning in the cold drizzly rain from the Tube station over the Putney Bridge to the studio.

Gilliom   I was actually completely terrified when I got there because I didn't know what to expect.

Jackson   They had already been in rehearsals for like two weeks when I got there. I would have probably replaced me ten times in two weeks, but Debbie stuck it out until I could get off the boat and get to London.

Gilliom   The biggest difference I noticed was just how much more chill the British cast members were. I will never forget, on that first day, we took a lunch break and all the Brits went to the pub. 'Yeah, we're gonna have a pint.' I think I got drunk after my first rehearsal.

The Americans made the most of their time in the city. Love spent her spare time finishing off a solo album, working until the early hours.[93] Ray and McKneely found time to explore London's busy nightlife: a *Sunday Express* article said that that the pair 'took off for the clubs whenever they could snatch time from rehearsals', even taking the time to demonstrate some of the latest dance moves for the reporter, like 'the Wag, the Mud and the Limelight'.[94]

McKneely   That's all we did, go to the clubs. Wild times. But we were always at rehearsals turning it out. Oh, to be nineteen again.

With the full company finally gathered in one place, a meeting was called to discuss logistics.

Hodgson   I remember this nervous-looking man from Equity came in to talk about the transport – just the coach to Stratford from London. The Americans were coming out with all of these demands. 'We'll have two seats

---

[93]Helbing, 'Darlene Love'.
[94]Brook, '"Leroy"'.

per person . . . the volume of your Walkman has to be at a certain level . . .' All this stuff. We Brits just sat there with our arms folded, saying, 'This should be interesting!' We were blown away with all the rights they had, with what their Union did for them. Equity was acting for *them*, not for the producers. In this country, it felt like the reverse, at the time.

The arrival of the *Carrie* company on British shores had caused quite a stir, and journalists were dispatched to interview the American principals. Mark Shenton, a cub reporter and keen musical theatre fan, was thrilled to meet Barbara Cook.

Mark Shenton (theatre critic)[95]   She was absolutely fascinating. A lot was riding on the show for her. It was a brand new musical going back to Broadway, where she hadn't appeared for many years. It seemed bizarre, but it also had serious artistic legs. Everybody would have assumed, as I did, that there must be something in it if she's put her name to it.

Matt Wolf attended the same junket, representing *Harpers and Queen* magazine. 'It's an insane idea, let's face it,'[96] Cook told him.

Insane? Perhaps. But with everyone assembled and acceptable Walkman volumes duly ratified, it was time to board the coach and head to the unlikely first home of the latest new megamusical: the leafy Midlands town of Stratford-upon-Avon.

---

[95]Shenton had various touchpoints with the show in 1988, interviewing cast members and reviewing the show on both sides of the Atlantic, as well as working for the show's marketing agency, Dewynters.
[96]Matt Wolf, 'Carrie on Singing', *Harpers and Queen*, February 1988.

3 STRATFORD: DOESN'T ANYBODY EVER GET IT RIGHT?

The *Carrie* company's new home was the Ashcroft studio (Plate 3), a sunny, wood-panelled rehearsal space above the RSC's recently opened Swan Theatre in Stratford-upon-Avon. The cobbled streets of the medieval market town were still quiet in the cold, early weeks of 1988: it would be some months before the tourists swarmed to explore the haunts of the town's most famous son, William Shakespeare.

> **Mark Santoro** (Ensemble, Stratford and Broadway)   I knew Stratford was a very prestigious place. I remember seeing actors in Shakespearean costumes in the hallways.

> **Dean Pitchford** (Lyricist)   I stayed in RSC housing, which is not as glamorous as it sounds. It was like something out of *Mrs. Miniver*![1] There was a little row of houses, each with a tiny sitting room and a very narrow staircase up to a single bedroom. On the wall was a little vending machine, into which you could plop coins to get heat. Every night, I had to remember to get enough change to make the heating work, then each morning I would pray I had enough hot water to have a shower. It was a baptism by fire. Or rather, by ice.

> **Scott Wise** (Ensemble, Stratford and Broadway)   Dean and I had homes next to each other, both over 500 years old. I could hear him every night on a keyboard, banging out new tunes for the show.

The first week of January was a busy one for Costume Designer Alexander Reid. 'We had fifty-two fittings on Friday,' he told an interviewer. 'We had four costumiers,

---

[1] The patriotic 1942 movie set in wartime England.

and each girl went in in turn. They are lovely to work with, young and enthusiastic. It's refreshing to get youngsters that are still keen, and they're all crazy [keen] to go on and do it. Barbara Cook was lovely too.'[2]

Rosemary Jackson (Ensemble/Understudy 'Carrie White', Stratford and Broadway)   We didn't understand a whole lot of things, but we were young, and if we were going to wear these Greek-looking costumes, I guess that's what we were doing. I think as a cast, we just trusted the powers that be. We trusted the music and the score, and we trusted the vision, as bizarre as it was.

As pioneering as the half-British, half-American casting process had been, there were still logistical complexities.

Pitchford   We had more than thirty performers, half of whom were living out of suitcases. When we started planning for New York, we realized the *other* fifteen would be living out of suitcases, for who knows how long. There were difficulties with expenses and accommodation, and all of those things.

Michelle 'Shelley' Hodgson (Ensemble, Stratford and Broadway)   I remember there was a disparity in wages, based on the different Equity rules. That caused some tension between us all.

According to *Drama* magazine, the minimum wage for American performers was three times more than for Brits, but, as pointed out by the General Secretary of British Actors' Equity, the figures could be deceptive: 'I'd have to spend hours combing the West End to find one person earning the minimum salary; in New York I'd spend hours on Broadway finding someone who earned above the minimum.'[3]

By the time a meeting was called to discuss the issue, the Brits had learned to stand their ground.

Kenny Linden (Ensemble, Stratford and Broadway)   It came to a head when we were told about our digs in New York. We'd been told we would be put up in apartments, but then we heard that they'd discovered the apartments were too expensive, so they were going to take some of our wages away to pay for them. We just said, 'No,' *en masse*, all of the Brits. We all sat there at a meeting and said, 'We're not going then!' It's the only time in twenty years that I saw a company stand together and say, 'We're not going to Broadway unless you sort this!' Can you imagine? Terry shrugged and said, 'Okay. We'll have to pay then . . .'

---

[2] *Theatre Craft*/Pirani interview tapes.
[3] Wolf, 'Carrie on Equity'.

Party time

Hodgson   We all quickly found a common thread in Stratford. We were all out of our home environments, and we bonded hugely. I remember going out to this dodgy disco below a hotel. We would go in and just throw shapes.[4] People were sitting there with their warm pints, staring at us. We trashed a few hotel rooms, if I remember rightly.

Jackson   It was all just a party. It would be rehearsals and then a party every single day.

Catherine Coffey (Ensemble, Stratford and Broadway)   We turned Stratford upside down!

Jackson   Rehearsals were gruelling. They were long. They were meticulous. They were fun as hell, though. I mean, I don't think I've ever had that much fun on a job in my life. Everybody was just so excited and enthusiastic about the possibilities of this thing that we were creating.

Suzanne 'Squeeze' Thomas (Ensemble, Stratford and Broadway)   One day I started a water fight. The whole cast was running around me. This is at the Royal Shakespeare Company! This sort of thing had never happened before! You know, they were all reading sonnets in the corner, and suddenly there were all these dancers, running out of the shower, half-naked, throwing water at each other.

Pitchford   The cast was full of energy, and they all wanted to go out and have a couple of beers after rehearsal. There was this pub next to the theatre, and it was dead of winter, and so we would take over the place. Everybody had spent the day dancing and singing. The only person who was fresh was Lillias White,[5] who would get up and sing. It was her chance to let rip. It was like a church in there! The people of Stratford didn't know what had hit them.

Coffey   We would all dance on tables, on the streets, in pubs. Singing and dancing like the Kids from *Fame*!

Sally Ann Triplett ('Sue Snell', Stratford and Broadway)   The fact that Gene Anthony Ray was jumping around Stratford, Shakespeare Land, was something in itself.

Coffey   He was exactly like he was in *Fame* . . . maybe naughtier!

For the RSC, Ray and his *Fame* co-star Debbie Allen were rare draws for younger audience members.

---

[4] A uniquely British slang term for dancing exuberantly.
[5] White – an eventual Tony winner (1997) and now a Broadway veteran – was understudying Darlene Love as Miss Gardner.

IMAGE 3.1 Gene Anthony Ray and the male Ensemble in rehearsal. Suzanne Thomas (photographer).

Pitchford   *Fame* was enormous in England and across Europe. It was crazy. Every time they finished a season of the TV show, they'd put them out on tour, rake in the money, and then come back and shoot another season. Not only did we have *Fame*'s choreographer, we had one of its biggest stars.

Charlotte d'Amboise ('Chris Hargensen', Stratford and Broadway)   When we would go out to restaurants, people really recognized him. He wasn't always happy about that. He was uncomfortable being recognized.

In an interview with the London *Evening Standard*, Ray credits a sold-out *Fame* show at the Royal Albert Hall for his decision to try more stage work. 'That audience made the show different, and made you do different things every night,' he explained. 'I knew I wanted to work in front of audiences, not cameras, and that meant a musical.'[6]

Maybe I'll dance

In spite of the impromptu water fights and late-night disco antics, the cast had to be up and ready each morning for Allen's vigorous daily dance rehearsals.

---

[6]Owen, '"Carrie on Terry"/"Two in Tune"'.

Thomas   Every morning we had to do whistle sprints, which are what the army does to keep fit. Then we had to do the ballet barre, and then a jazz course. We would do two and a half hours of dancing before we even started rehearsal. But it didn't do us any harm!

Kelly Littlefield (Ensemble, Stratford and Broadway)   Whistle sprints and sing, whistle sprints and sing, whistle sprints and sing . . .! We would also do push-ups with our feet on chairs, and sit-ups galore.

Coffey   Debbie trained us like we were athletes. I had never worked physically as hard before, nor since! Honestly, I would have done anything for that woman. Blood, sweat, tears!

Mary Ann Oedy (Ensemble, Stratford and Broadway)   She would always keep pushing and pushing me to 'go up another gear.' I'd think, 'Why is she pushing me? I'm doing good!' Later, on opening night, she came running toward me, and I thought, 'Shit! I failed. What did I do wrong?' But she grabbed me and said, 'That's what I was talking about!' I had 'gone up a gear.' When I think back on it, it wasn't that I was holding out on her, it's just that I kind of 'pop' once I get on stage. I go into that other gear in front of an audience. But what I learned from Miss Allen is . . . don't wait for the show to go up into that gear. Go into that gear right from rehearsals!

Michelle Nelson (Ensemble, Stratford and Broadway)   We would do each dance number repeatedly, and as we ended she would scream, 'Now sing!' We would have to go straight into a song, all feeling very short of breath. She was intent on building stamina.

Santoro   It was a lot like the *Fame* TV show!

Nelson   She took no nonsense and was super-professional. There was always fun and laughter though.

'I work this cast hard,' Allen told the *Daily Mail*. 'I am a perfectionist and can be difficult, sometimes, but after the hard work, we have fun, and that's the way I work.'[7]

Linden   I trained as a ballet dancer and sort of fell into musicals. I certainly never really trained in jazz and all that stuff, so I was learning on the job, and I was always very slow to pick things up. Debbie couldn't cope with that, so she didn't warm to me. I needed a lot of rehearsal, I needed to know it really well before I could actually perform it. I think I struggled, and that was tough. She wasn't always terribly lovely to me.

---

[7] Bamigboye, 'Debbie Causes a Carrie On'.

Allen's dynamic is apparent in footage captured by two film crews shadowing the rehearsal process.[8] During a rehearsal for the song 'Don't Waste the Moon', Allen – praising each pair of dancers in turn – says to a bemused Linden 'Alright Kenny, a little sloppy, but it's coming!'

Santoro Debbie had her favourites, and you always had to prove yourself. You had to give 100 per cent every time.

Linden The Americans, from day one, were so amazing. We'd say, 'Oh, God, they're going to be phenomenal!'

Hodgson Debbie would pit us against each other and say, 'English girls do this, English boys do this, American boys do this, American girls do this.' We [the Brits] would stand there, giving evil eyes – resting bitch face, as we call it now! – as if to say, 'We're not circus monkeys!' We thought it was a very strange setup considering they wanted us to feel like one cast. Separating us, making us compete against each other, didn't feel like the best way to do it.

Triplett All the Americans would stand at the front and get it right away, and all the English dancers would stand at the back by the ballet barre, looking at each other saying, 'No, I won't go! They're going to think we're rubbish!' We'd really doubt ourselves.

Thomas I used to just laugh because they'd be whooping and hollering, and there we were, hesitating at the back.

Triplett Then, slowly but surely, as time went on, we became more and more confident.

Eric Gilliom (Ensemble, Stratford and Broadway) I always kind of felt like there was this weird expectation from Debbie that we [the Americans] had to constantly deliver.

Hodgson I think the English quickly got a little bit more American and the Americans got a little bit more English! We did rub off on each other, but the beginning was frosty, to say the least.

Jackson The divide disappeared almost immediately because we had so much in common, we were all young, we were all hungry, just these amazing dancers who really wanted to do this thing really, really well.

Coffey Everyone was pretty equal in terms of talent and zest for life!

Oedy One day the boys surprised us with a performance of our entire routine from 'In'. It was hilarious!

---

[8]One crew seems to have been commissioned to the RSC – likely capturing footage and interviews for video tapes dispatched to potential group bookers – and another was filming a 'behind-the-scenes' documentary about the work of producer Friedrich Kurz (it is not clear if it ever aired).

Linzi Hateley described her perspective to *TheaterWeek*. 'At first I found the Americans very forward, sort of pushy,' she said:

> If you stood British and American actors in front of a glass wall, the British would punch forward and come to the glass and stop, but the Americans would lash out and have themselves completely through it. But what has happened is that their energy and aggressiveness has rubbed off on the others. The whole company has great energy.[9]

Pitchford I would visit rehearsals and look around the room and think how grateful I was that these kids were upending their lives to do our show. It was an enormous gift from them to us.

Two worlds

Jeremy Sturt was only twenty-two when he was offered the role of Deputy Stage Manager, overseeing rehearsals and eventually 'calling the show' during performances.[10] He had been working on a similar role at *Chess* in the West End and was recommended to Hands by that show's director, Trevor Nunn.

Jeremy Sturt (Deputy Stage Manager, Stratford and Broadway) He told me that Terry Hands was desperate for it to be the next *Les Mis*, so he needs a musical Stage Manager to be there to call the show, and we've obviously got nobody [suitable] here at Stratford.

In rehearsals, the cast and crew quickly realized that Hands and Allen would work almost entirely independently. While Allen repeatedly thrashed out the dance sequences, Hands would work alone with Cook and Hateley on their mother and daughter scenes.

Pitchford Basically, Terry cut the show in half. He sent Debbie off to rehearse the school scenes. It freed him up to deal with the high drama and the operatic immensity of Margaret and Carrie and their scenes.

Linden Debbie did everything with us. Terry didn't really tell us what to do or where to go. He was just a nice man who'd wear a lot of black and occasionally say 'good' and then walk out again. It felt like Debbie had been told to go and choreograph a great number to this song and we'd sing and dance to it, and then at the end of it he'd throw in a bit of acting, if you were lucky.

Thomas I only remember one time Terry directed me. He said, 'Okay, we've got a little tableau here. You stand there, and you just crouch down next to her.'

---

[9]Ledford, Larry S (May 23, 1988) 'Linzi Hateley's Date with Broadway', *TheaterWeek*, 10
[10]Normally the DSM would do this from the wings at the side of the stage. Due to the show's boxed-in set, Sturt would 'call the show' from the back of the audience.

And I was, like, 'Why would I crouch down?' I remember saying to him, 'Why am I sitting on the floor?' As an actress, I couldn't understand why I was doing what I was doing. But later I realized it tied into the whole Greek thing – he was making these little 'tableau' freeze-frames.

Linden   When we eventually came together with Linzi and Barbara, it was like seeing a different show.

In one particular section of footage of a full-cast number, Hands and Allen can be seen literally taking turns to direct the company in one scene as it segues from dance to dialogue.[11]

Linzi Hateley ('Carrie White', Stratford and Broadway)   I remember clearly when I first started rehearsing with everyone else, it was just terrifying. I think that they actually made a choice to keep us separate, to build this massive contrast between the two worlds. Because, until we really started putting the show together, I had no connection with any of the Ensemble. I was so impressed by these phenomenal dancers that could not only sing, dance and act, but looked incredible. I felt massively intimidated by that.

Joey McKneely (Ensemble, Stratford and Broadway)   Debbie is a very strong-willed woman, and she was very creative. She had a certain outlook of

IMAGE 3.2 Linzi Hateley rehearses with director Terry Hands. Mary Ann Hermansen (photographer).

[11]There is, by coincidence, a line of tape on the floor of the studio, literally dividing them.

how the show should look, which was a very American, sort of, adolescent energy and feel. And then you had Terry, and he had a completely different vision of it.

Pitchford   It quickly became obvious that we were getting a show that was created by two different people in two different spaces and then brought together and welded down the middle. Everybody was working at cross purposes.

Hodgson   I remember thinking, 'how will they actually marry these two worlds?'

Linden   I think the director's job, with a choreographer, is to discuss the way each musical number should be so that it gels with the next scene, and figure out how to transition between the two.

Pitchford   What Terry was doing with those Margaret and Carrie scenes, yes, it was wonderful. And at the same time, Debbie was creating these extravagant dance numbers. But it would have been lovely if someone had stopped at some point, and found a way to massage the two segments of the show together.

Some cast members found themselves facing the challenge of navigating the two rehearsal regimes. Charlotte d'Amboise was faced with a tall order. In the principal role of queen bee Chris Hargensen, she had to deliver a convincingly villainous performance – but as a featured dancer, she also had some of the show's most complex routines to nail.

D'Amboise   Terry was very softly spoken, and very smart. He pretty much let me do what I wanted to do. He didn't have much input into my performance. When I first started doing it, Chris was just this basic villain. I remember Debbie saying to me 'You need to find the light there, have fun with it more. I want to see you have fun with it.' It just totally switched the whole character. I was able to find her. She was totally right.

Ensemble member Rosemary Jackson also found her time split between the rehearsals of Allen and Hands.

Jackson   One day, Terry called me over and asked me to sing the title song. He said, 'Okay, you're going to be Carrie's understudy.' I was, like, 'Cool! Of course, Linzi is never going to get sick, but this is awesome!' And so my time was divided a lot. I was doing my Ensemble work, for the most part, and then I would go and catch up on the Carrie part. Or sometimes Linzi had an interview or a fitting or whatever, and I would jump in and do blocking so that we could keep the ball moving forward. It was a lot of juggling.[12]

---

[12]Jackson never had the opportunity to perform as Carrie.

Creative tensions

As the cast rehearsed, work continued on honing the show's score in preparation for orchestration.

Michael Starobin (Co-orchestrator, Stratford)   I dropped by cast rehearsals to observe – and one did that a lot more often back in the day before it was so easy to make a video on a phone and send it to the orchestrator. Watching the rehearsals, I just had a sense that it wasn't coming together.

John Owen Edwards (Musical Director, Stratford)   In the early days a lot of my time was taken up teaching the company the music. The cast was great and I got on well with them all, and with Debbie Allen. Unfortunately, the same could not be said for Michael Gore, the Composer.

Michael Gore (Composer)   In London, Larry [Cohen] and I had seen John conduct *Chess* in the West End. He did a very good job conducting that show, and as a result, we hired him. But when it actually came to working with the singing talent in rehearsals early on, I felt that we weren't on the same page. There was really no animosity on my part: he was a very nice guy. I just came to feel, after watching him rehearse the cast for a few weeks, that he wasn't a good fit with our particular material.

Edwards   From my standpoint, the musical director of a show is responsible to several people: the producer who employs you, the director – nominally the artistic head of a production – but the ultimate boss is the composer, whose work rests largely in your hands. In London, Terry was very sympathetic and told me to hold on: when we went to Stratford, he would be on home ground and things would be easier. Perhaps against my better judgement, I agreed. Things, however, did not improve and shortly after we arrived in Stratford, things became very difficult with Michael and reached the stage where Terry summoned me to his office and fired me. Again, he was very sympathetic, and I suspected he was having his own difficulties.

A *Telegraph* retrospective described 'a personality conflict'[13] between Edwards and Gore; indeed, the press soon announced that Edwards would be departing the project.

'There were some difficulties between John and the people who wrote the music,' Kurz told the *Daily Mail*. 'It was mutually agreed he would leave.' Edwards commented only to say that 'it's a dance show with very, very skilled dancers'.[14]

---

[13] Tookey, 'Flop!'
[14] 'A Carrie on Over Music at the RSC', *Daily Mail*, 30 January 1988.

Edwards   The news leaked out pretty quickly and by the end of the day, an old friend rang me and asked me if I would be interested in coming in as a guest conductor on another production. So, after a good meal out with plenty of wine, I said my goodbyes and headed back to London ready to start work on another show the following week.[15]

Gore   My collaborators and I felt we would do better with an American at the helm. As a result, we parted ways with John and hired Paul Schwartz who came over to England and conducted both the Stratford and Broadway runs.

Paul Schwartz (Musical Director, Stratford and Broadway)   I gathered that Michael Gore was not feeling musically supported in Stratford. I think he felt that he needed someone younger, and an American, and for some reason he thought I had a pop music background, which I totally did not! I think they thought that I would come in and kind of get all the pop numbers. Michael's background was as a record producer, I mean, apart from, you know, scoring *Fame* and all of that, his main thing was that he was a record producer. He came from a 'Pop with a capital P' background, and he wanted more of that Pop feel in the pop half of the score. So, he kind of initiated this thing of flying me over, which I think Terry was totally against. So, my initial arrival there was a little bit fraught.

Schwartz arrived in Stratford in late January.

Schwartz   I remember arriving for my first moment of rehearsal, literally fresh off the plane. I was sitting there talking to some of the dancers and Terry walked in, and I walked up to him with my hand out saying, 'Hi, Terry, I'm Paul,' and he just didn't react to me at all. I took a few vocal rehearsals. I made very quick, fast friends with the two orchestrators, we really got along very, very well.

The rehearsal period in London and Stratford lasted an exhausting twelve weeks, twice as long as most new musicals.

Linden   A twelve-week rehearsal period is just insane, because it allows for too much messing around. People aren't focussed enough. You need someone to say, 'This is what we've got to achieve and we've only got six weeks to do it.' There were some weeks where we ended up only rehearsing for half a day here, half a day there.

As the show moved from the rehearsal studio to the stage of the Royal Shakespeare Theatre, the writers recall feeling increasingly cut out of the process. Tensions rose and frustrations grew.

Gore   Terry chose to create a very tight rehearsal relationship, and he made it clear he didn't want our input, any input, during that process. This turned out

---

[15]Edwards says he regrets never seeing the show performed but he 'felt that appearing like a spectre at the feast would not be a good idea'.

to be a harmful decision on his part because there were many things we could have changed and made better if we were to have been included. Put bluntly, we were living writers working with a director who was, with few exceptions, mostly used to working with dead authors.

Pitchford   We were not happy about being cut out. We agreed to a daily meeting, but often he would cancel it, or send an assistant.

Cohen   At one point he actually even went so far as to seriously suggest that the three authors might like to go off and vacation in Europe on holiday – then return to Stratford in time for the opening!

Gore   As head of the RSC, he was accustomed to getting his way without being questioned. Whenever we gave him notes, he replied in his very brisk British way, 'Leave them with me,' which we came to learn meant that they would be promptly ignored and forgotten.

Cohen   One of the RSC production team staff, sizing up the increasingly tense situation, confided in us that with Terry, we were dealing with a master chess player. If we wanted to win, we would have to be the same. The truth, however, was that Terry was a master at the game working on his own turf. We were, frankly, outmatched.

Simon Opie (Production Manager, Stratford and Broadway)   The key issue with the process was that the show was coming together from disparate cultures, and that made communication and collaboration difficult. The poles of UK versus USA culture, classical RSC theatre versus Broadway musical, huge differences in experiences and points of reference all contributed to make it hard to find a consensus on how to shape and improve the show.

Gilliom   I found myself on many a day of rehearsals, thinking, 'What the fuck is going on here? Something is terribly wrong!' Terry and Debbie would be sitting in the front of the theatre, you know, having these little conferences. I sensed from the get-go that it wasn't gelling the way I think that everybody had hoped that it would.

McKneely   I remember once there was a very heated discussion about a basketball. Debbie's husband was a basketball player, Norm Nixon. [Hands] wanted the boys to come across with this white ball, and she shouted, 'Get a basketball! They've got to be bouncing a basketball! That doesn't make sense! It's America. We've gotta have a basketball!'

Promoting *Carrie*

Meanwhile, promotion for the show began in earnest. Early marketing materials featured the show's name in a jagged, red 'horror movie' typeface with black and white headshots of the cast, with promises that 'a best-selling book and acclaimed film becomes a spectacular new stage musical'. The cast was pictured in the local press, cheering in front of a specially branded *Carrie* bus (Plate 4), and the local branch of bookseller Waterstones celebrated the arrival of the musical with a dedicated *Carrie* window display, featuring attractively arranged stacks of King's novel.

Perhaps in an attempt to shift public perceptions (and expectations) away from 'horror' towards Hands' more dramatic interpretation of the story, the scrawled title treatment was quickly replaced with a simpler white font on a black background as opening night approached. Marketing materials soon bore a new logo, developed by the graphic designer Russ Eglin of London marketing agency Dewynters. Eglin had led the creation of iconic emblems for other musicals including the memorable reflective *Cats* eyes and the *Phantom*'s white mask, reproduced on countless print ads, posters, TV commercials and T-shirts across the world.

The *Carrie* logo was simple and stark; a selection of thin, curved, red and white lines forming the abstract shape of a girl's face, with a single red tear rolling from her eye (Plate 7).

The lines resemble 'Zener' symbols[16] found on cards used to conduct experiments around telekinesis and extra-sensory perception, though it's not clear if the good people of Stratford would have clocked the reference. At a 2013 memorial party for Eglin, Cameron Mackintosh praised the designer's genius as well as the 'improvisatory aspect' of some of his work, including the 'accidental, random spattering of red paint blobs'[17] that made up his *Carrie* logo.

Whether the show's branding was too obtuse or not hardly seemed to matter: with only a three-week run and plenty of unique selling points, tickets sold quickly.

Pitchford   The locals came, people from London came. It was their only chance – it was like they all agreed to schlep out to the countryside. It was a very hot ticket.

To promote the show, Allen made a memorable appearance on the BBC's *Wogan* talk show, teaching host Terry Wogan some seductive moves from the show, much to the delight of the studio audience.

Journalists were invited to Stratford to watch rehearsals and meet some of the young cast members. When asked who the show would appeal to, an exuberant Ray said – in a line presumably not endorsed by the RSC's marketing department[18] – 'eight to 80, blind, crippled and crazy, blue-haired women and little children!'[19]

---

[16]Named for psychologist Karl Zener, who created the deck of cards in the 1930s.
[17]Michael Coveney, 'West End Poster Boy Russ Remembered in a Muse of Fire', *WhatsOnStage*, 28 October 2013, available online: https://www.whatsonstage.com/london-theatre/news/michael-coveney-west-end-poster-boy-russ-remembere_32445.html (accessed 19 September 2022).
[18]An RSC handbill was firm in its assertion that the show was 'not suitable for young children'.
[19]Kurz documentary.

Many reports focused on Hateley's debut as the company's youngest ever leading lady, with the *Guardian's* Tim Madge describing it as 'the biggest thrill of her young life', and confidently predicting the show was 'going to be a smash hit'. According to Madge, Hateley received 'a spontaneous burst of applause from both cast and onlookers'[20] as she sang her title song in rehearsal for the first time. Michael Owen of the London *Evening Standard* met with Hateley and Ray who, he said, 'get on like a house on fire'.[21]

Cook's upset

Away from the cameras, a crisis was brewing.

Barbara Cook, preparing for the role of Margaret, was growing increasingly frustrated. She was irritated by what she considered slow progress, substandard material, and a creative team without the requisite experience. 'Soon after we started rehearsals, I realized that not one person involved had ever put together a new musical from scratch,' she recalled in her memoir. 'The most basic, essential building blocks eluded the creators ... I knew from day one that I was not doing my best work because I was never comfortable with the material.'[22]

Others believed she was struggling with the physicality of the role and demands of the score.

Pitchford   The demands of her role were extremely taxing. She was older, and marshalled her resources. Her rehearsal schedule was planned to make optimum use of the energy that she would have. She would be released early, because she needed her sleep. She knew what she needed to do, and she was an athlete in that respect. She was always the hardest worker in the room, but there wasn't a lot of, you know, 'Let's go grab a burger after rehearsal.'

Cohen   Barbara had been initially very nervous about returning to Broadway after so many years. She had vacillated about accepting the role, and grew increasingly more anxious every day of rehearsal. Her beautiful voice was extremely well-suited to certain numbers – really gorgeous – but the more dramatic and ferocious duets with Carrie demanded killer, all-stops-out vocals, and determined to protect her voice, she refused to push it into that all-out blasting register.

McKneely   I don't think she knew what she had gotten into. Barbara was old-school Broadway. She was a very classy woman, never raised her voice, never demanding. She just really walked in, did her thing, and sang beautifully.

---

[20]Tim Madge, 'What a Carrie-On Up at the Good Old RSC', *The Guardian*, 17 February 1988, 38.
[21]Owen, '"Carrie on Terry"/"Two in Tune"'.
[22]Cook, *Then and Now*, 206.

Hateley   She was wonderful, not only a wonderful artist and a stunning vocalist, but she was a warm, gorgeous person. But it quickly became apparent that she wasn't happy. She had a reputation to maintain. She'd had a wonderful career. *Carrie* was going to be her first thing back on Broadway after a long time away and it needed to be right for her. I think that from very early on, the writing was on the wall. The fit wasn't right.

Cook grew more and more frustrated that Hands seemingly couldn't comprehend that the show had problems. She encouraged him to seek advice on how to make improvements, 'but no one was willing to acknowledge the need for help in nearly every department'.[23]

Georgia Otterson (Assistant to Barbara Cook)   I remember her saying [to Hands and the writers] . . . 'On Broadway, we're used to having these theatre "doctors". They come in, they look at a show and they say, you know, "This might be a beautiful number, but you gotta cut it out." ' I'm not sure that folks listened to her. And so, she asked Tommy Tune and Wally Harper to come over and offer some advice.

Tune, the prodigious Broadway director, actor and dancer, had staged a number of Cook's cabaret shows, and Harper had loyally served as her accompanist and musical director on her concerts and albums for over thirty years.

Gore   Wally Harper was primarily brought over to make her feel more comfortable. She was extremely anxious about making her return to Broadway after a long absence between shows, and it was hoped that his presence would help give her more confidence. He stayed for a short period of time and then returned home.

'The Composer, Michael Gore, was furious when Wally arrived,' Cook recounted in her memoir. 'I think he was afraid Wally might want to change some of his music.'[24]

Cook rarely minced her words when making her feelings known. Lillias White, standby for Miss Gardner, remembered arriving in Stratford and being led into the dark theatre during a rehearsal. 'I hear Barbara Cook say, "I haven't been on Broadway in eighteen years and I am going back in this piece of shit?" she said in an interview. "Barbara Cook is a tough cookie, honey. Barbara Cook is a no-shit-taking cookie with the voice of an angel." '[25]

---

[23]Ibid., 207.
[24]Ibid.
[25]Eddie Shapiro, *Nothing Like a Dame: Conversations with the Great Women of Musical Theater* (Oxford: Oxford University Press, 2014), 208.

Schwartz   I remember after we got the 'And Eve was Weak' orchestration. I invited Barbara to come in, and she stood on the edge of the pit in the theatre and we played it . . . smash! Bang! Bang! You know, it's like 'Ride of the Valkyries' and everything kind of rolls into one. When we finished, I turned around to look at her and she said, 'Well, I can sing smart, but I'm not sure I can sing that smart.' Because it was just so huge.

Starobin   Barbara was standing on the stage one day, and they were about to do her scene – which came after the 'kill the pig' number – and they said, 'Barbara, you need to move back. We're going to close up the pit where the pig comes out.' And she said, 'Well, you better shovel all the shit into it first.' At that point, she had had it with everything. It had reached that point where we all kind of knew . . .

One of Cook's concerns was the lack of character development for Margaret. After repeated requests, Hands agreed to speak to Gore and Pitchford about writing a new song which would be better suited to Cook's lyric soprano style, and which would explore Margaret's motivations in more depth. The writers replaced 'Once I Loved a Boy', Magaret's aria from the workshop, with a new song, 'When There's No One'. Despite the change, Cook remained unconvinced.

Sturt recalls chatting with Cook after a rehearsal when Hands approached.

Sturt   Barbara just went silent. Terry said, 'Right . . .' A pregnant pause. He said, 'Well, Jeremy obviously knows this, but I just want to tell you that I think I've sorted it all. We're going to do this. We're going to do X or Y as opposed to . . .,' and he listed all of this stuff he wanted to do. She put her hand on his arm and said, 'All you're doing is rearranging the deck chairs on the Titanic.'

Otterson   At one point she told me, 'Go down to the hardware store and get a . . . what do they call those big things? You know, a hammer?' I said, 'Oh, like a sledgehammer?' So, I found an ironmonger and I bought this huge sledgehammer . . .

The next day . . .

Otterson   I think we had practically everybody there, standing around Terry. I took the sledgehammer down, and Barbara presented it to him. I have a picture of her writing something on it. The concept was 'Do something!' Barbara was never totally subtle. She was always very, very direct, but it came from a good heart and a lot of wisdom.

Triplett   I remember her coming up to me and saying, 'Hey, Sally, I don't think I can come to Broadway with this one.' I replied with something like, 'Well, you should follow your heart, and if you don't feel like it's you, then you shouldn't do it.' She was iconic. The most beautiful, incredible singer. But she just wasn't suited to it.

Hateley   She was always kind to me, and very mothering, actually. But at the same time, I was working with someone who wasn't happy and wanted out. And that was a very strange thing for me to deal with. I just thought rehearsals were going really well at this point. I didn't understand her concerns and I remember feeling confused by that.

Sturt   One night, I said, 'You're not coming, are you?' And she said, 'No, I'm not coming to Broadway, I'll see this [Stratford] out. I'll do that. But I'm not doing Broadway, because it would be my homecoming. I'm not going to do that.'

With Cook now formulating her exit strategy, the creative team began to consider potential new Margarets. Suspecting that a replacement may be needed at short notice, they decided to cast a 'standby' for the role sooner rather than later.

Audrey Lavine (standby 'Margaret White', Stratford and Broadway)[26]   I was doing a show in a regional theatre, and I got a call to go into the city. I went back to New York and did this audition, and then I didn't think anything else about it. But a week later, they called and said, 'You're going to Stratford.' It was crazy. It happened in like a week. When I got there, Barbara was clearly not happy. She reached out to me right away and let me know that she might be leaving. We became good friends.

Lavine learned that the producers were in discussions with a potential full-time replacement: their original choice for the role, Betty Buckley.

Lavine   They were courting Betty, negotiating. They hadn't come to an agreement yet. But they thought I could bridge the gap between Barbara – who I was probably more like vocally – and Betty, who I was probably more like as an actress.

Betty Buckley ('Margaret White', Broadway)   They called my agent and asked if I would fly to London to take over the role. I asked to see some video, and I saw some pieces of it. I felt like I had an interpretation of the role I could offer. Barbara Cook was a wonderful performer and human being, but I recall her performance being rather 'stationary', if you will. I was a more athletic performer, I guess one could say.

All hands on deck: tech

At the end of January, Ralph Koltai arrived in Stratford to oversee the remaining set build. 'There is a slight hiccup over one area of scene painting, so I've decided

---

[26]Levine was also a cast member in 1986 *Rags* which was, until *Carrie*, reported to be Broadway's most expensive flop.

to do it myself,' he wrote in *The Listener*. He described another issue, saying that there was 'no point blaming anyone, but somewhere along the line we acquired a 16-inch gap between the upstage wall and the ceiling, which doesn't look very nice'.[27] Perhaps unaware of the unfolding dramas, he said of rehearsals, 'it all seems calm at the moment, 'though I dare say all hell will break loose when it's about to open'.[28]

Tech rehearsals – the process of marrying together every element of the show on stage for the first time – began. Problems and strife are not uncommon during 'tech'; in fact, it would be hard to find a director who could claim they had experienced an entirely problem-free one. In *British Theatre Design: The Modern Age*, Peter Hall describes the process as 'the last lunatic days . . . when the lighting, the music, the costumes and the set are all put together in a seemingly impossible jumble of problems.'[29] But when time is short and tempers fraught, the tech process can become a crucible in which rifts and tensions come to a head.

> **Opie**   The time available to install the show, [tech] rehearse and open it in Stratford was ludicrously short. We worked round the clock, but in reality the time available was not sufficient for a musical of such technical complexity.

> **Mark Bailey** (Assistant to Set Designer Ralph Koltai)   The tech period in Stratford was very chaotic and I think the writing was on the wall, but one has to keep faith to be able to continue to work on a piece. There were quite a few 'issues' – it was a huge and very challenging show technically, so it isn't surprising.

Koltai's 33-foot wide set, though slick and simple at first glance, was deceptively complex.

> **Sturt**   It was the biggest tech show out there at the time.

> **Opie**   Finding ways to mechanically organize each of the overlays within the same space was complex, and to keep running costs down, the transformations were completely mechanised. Motors and control systems work well, but take time to commission and are costly. Within the basic box, there were two large stage lifts that introduced large elements – such as the shower scene – from under the stage, and which were also lowered at times to provide troughs for action, such as the infamous pig-slaughtering scene. Another important element was the house 'truck' which represented Carrie's home. This arrived from behind the back of the set. It had its own back wall, which pirouetted to allow the truck base to pass underneath it as both elements arrived on the stage. A complicated and challenging feature.

---

[27]Smurthwaite, '"Carrie" from Behind the Scenes'.
[28]Ibid.
[29]John Goodwin (ed.), *British Theatre Design: The Modern Age*, rev. edn (London: Orion, 1998), 13.

Sturt Walls wouldn't turn, trucks misaligned . . . you have to remember, in 1988 we were right at the cutting edge of technology, electronics and hydraulics. Looking back, it was a hugely dangerous but also momentous shift forward in stage machinery. Shows like *Carrie*, *Miss Saigon*, *Starlight Express* were massive, and very dangerous. There were no courses that covered it, we were all learning new stuff every day.

Opie In addition, the stage at Stratford was raked – sloped to the front – and this made geometries and mechanics additionally challenging.

Martin Levan (Sound Designer, Stratford and Broadway) A challenge for me was the broad scope of the music. The score contained a lot of pop/ rock-style music together with some incredibly emotional and intimate writing for the scenes between mother and daughter. Historically, sound systems tended to be good at one or the other – either loud, rock music or intimate, sensitive music – and we had to present both equally well. We developed a method of integrating two completely different sound systems set up side by side, with some technology to morph one into the other during scene changes.

Sturt The liaison between the designers, scenic constructors, stage carpenters and stage management was critical.

Peter McKintosh,[30] then a twenty-year-old Theatre student at nearby Warwick University, had contacted Hands about observing his processes as part of his studies.

Peter McKintosh (student designer) He said, 'Well, we're not doing any Shakespeare at the moment, we're doing this musical.' He said, 'But I will be busy. So really, all I'm saying is you can come and sit at the back of the Stalls for a week.' So I did. I don't think I spoke to anybody, I really didn't meet anyone. I just watched this thing unfold.

McKintosh quickly noticed that things were not going as well as hoped, and pressure was high.

McKintosh Within the week, I saw many, many surprising things happen. To be fair, as I've learned since, things go wrong in techs all the time, that's what they are about. They are ways of solving problems. But the combination of all of them in the week seems to have been quite a lot to contend with.

McKintosh recalls one example involving the polycarbonate 'shower screens' used during an early Act One number, 'Dream On'.

---

[30]McKintosh is now an Olivier Award-winning scenic and costume designer.

IMAGE 3.3 Work on Koltai's complex set during tech rehearsal. Mark Bailey (photographer).

McKintosh   In the show, a very long wall of plastic doors – about as wide as the stage – comes out of the floor from a slot that can't have been more than 10 centimetres deep. Each door would revolve as the girls came through them in the song. So, this thing came out of the floor, the stage filled with smoke. All the girls came out in their underwear, strangely, and sang the song. Now, the brilliant thing about Ralph Koltai's brain is that he managed to distil images into the perfect solution, and this was a really economic solution. Brilliant. I was sitting there thinking, 'Wow, so clever, and a really clever thing is that they're going to have to get all of those doors back in line before somebody presses the button for it to go back through the floor into the sub-stage. I just can't wait to see how that happens.' Even before the thought had really finished formulating in my mind, somebody had pressed that button, and all you could hear was smashing plastic and fibreglass, and the whole thing buckled. And that was the end of the tech for that day.

Bailey   For several days after, they were held together by a lot of black gaffer tape until replacements could be made.

McKintosh   It seemed, possibly, symptomatic of things to come.

Video footage of the tech rehearsal for 'And Eve was Weak' shows the 'house set' failing to move into place, preventing Hateley from accessing the sub-stage trapdoor. Stagehands sprint on to the stage, dodging around Cook to manually close the trap. At the end of the number, Cook shrugs resignedly as the company cheers her on. In her memoir, she recalls deciding to keep a journal about her exasperation with the tech process, in case nobody outside the show believed her.[31]

Pitchford   Terry was an award-winning Lighting Designer, and he had decided that he would do the lights for *Carrie* as well as directing it. By the time tech started, you could forget any work on the book or the music or the lyrics or performances. He put down his script and picked up his lighting chart, and wandered around a microphone around his head, talking to the crew, calling out lighting cues. He became unavailable to us.

Cook also found Hands' distraction frustrating, recalling in her memoir an afternoon where 'the entire company and orchestra sat doing absolutely nothing while Terry Hands lit the show. Tens of thousands of dollars were flying out the window.'[32]

IMAGE 3.4 Barbara Cook awaits her next cue in the elongated Stratford tech rehearsal. Mark Bailey (photographer).

---

[31]Oh, to get hold of that journal . . .
[32]Cook, *Then and Now*, 207.

Performances begin

Due to its short run in Stratford, the show already had a 'suicidally short'[33] preview period before its scheduled opening night on Thursday, 18 February. Due to the tech rehearsal process over-running, the first preview on Saturday, 13 February 1988 was cancelled at short notice, meaning that 'the cast had less than a week to suit up for opening night,' and that early audiences would see 'a startling ... still rough-edged ignition of the play'.[34]

> **Cohen**   As our first preview approached, it was clear to the authors that the show was clearly not ready to open and that we needed to postpone for at least a few days. Terry was adamant that the RSC only considered the first performance to be a preview, and that the show would 'open' the following night as scheduled; in spite of all of our concerns, that was going to happen here, too. Yet on the day of the preview, it became abundantly clear to everyone that we weren't ready and he cancelled the performance.

The Stage got wind of the delays, revealing that the cancellation had been 'prompted by difficulties in getting some of the show's complex special effects to work during rehearsals,' and that the show has 'apparently been prey to a few gremlins', but reassuring readers that the teething problems were 'apparently more technical than supernatural in origin'.[35] Ticket-holders, many of whom did not discover the cancellation until they arrived at the theatre, were apparently offered seats to Tim Piggott-Smith's (rather different) theatrical anthology *Passages to India* playing at the Swan next door.

The cancellation was an irritating distraction for the RSC – still attempting to ramp up goodwill for the show – and led to disgruntled locals expressing their dismay in the regional press. An irate letter from a P. A. Bisson of Redditch in the Birmingham *Evening Mail* complained about the 'lack of any consideration shown'[36] by the company regarding the issue, after being given less than a day's notice. With the run sold out and no chance to re-book, an extra performance should be added, urged the disappointed Mr Bisson; alas, the RSC's packed schedule prevented any extension.

As previews started, technical issues continued to plague the set, with technical crew often seen sprinting on to 'move recalcitrant scenery'.[37]

> **Santoro**   The hydraulics of the set always broke down, and Stage Management had to pause the show so the stage crew could fix it.

---

[33]Tookey, 'Flop!'
[34]Francis X. Clines, '"Carrie" Churns towards U.S.', *The New York Times*, 2 March 1988, 67.
[35]'Cast Ignore Glitch and Carrie on Regardless', *The Stage*, 18 February 1988, 1.
[36]P. A. Bisson, 'Show Should Go On – for Us', Letters, *Birmingham Evening Mail*, 22 February 1988.
[37]Tookey, 'Flop!'

Carrie finally reached its long-awaited official opening night – when members of the press are invited to review the show – on Thursday, 18 February.

Steve Rich (audience member, Stratford)   I was there. Stephen King was huge amongst us sixth-formers back then. I was also musical theatre crazy. *Les Mis* was still red hot, so the RSC was the place to be if you wanted to boast about seeing an early performance of the latest big show. On arrival the audience was buzzing, but the mood became increasingly tense as curtain time was delayed around thirty minutes. I remember being told that some effects didn't work and were being axed as we waited.

Paul Clayton (audience member, Stratford and RSC actor)   I had to be there. I remember that it all smelt of the RSC doing something for purely commercial reasons, particularly as it had been stuck into the winter hole of February and March between major RSC seasons. There was something not right, but a big musical based on a Stephen King horror film directed by the wunderkind at the RSC was something not to be missed.

Philip Argent (audience member, Stratford)   I had never been to the RSC in Stratford before, but Barbara Cook was my favourite musical diva, so I knew I couldn't miss this. Everybody was talking about it.

Michael Berg (audience member, Stratford)[38]   We went up to Stratford. We were gobsmacked. Probably the best opening night I've ever attended, for many reasons. I actually fell in love with the show and have always remained a fan.

Mark Shenton (theatre critic)   What I remember is a kind of incredulity as the main response. People were sort of watching with their mouths agape, a bit like 'Springtime for Hitler' in *The Producers*.

Gilliom   I think by and large, the British audience was going, 'What the fuck am I watching?'

Jackson   It was very, very quiet, and when there was applause, it was a little delayed. We had to take a beat, to kind of let them know 'you can applaud now!'

Argent   There were many moments where I couldn't quite believe what I'd just seen or heard, and I couldn't help laughing.

The performance would not go smoothly, with an infamous set malfunction leading to a very visible on-stage incident, reinforcing Cook's decision to depart.

Bailey   The back wall of the stage had a 'goal post' frame set into it, and this could move downstage towards the audience. As it did so, the section filling in

---

[38]Berg was, at the time, manager of Dress Circle, a theatre memorabilia shop in London, which many musical fans look back on fondly as *the* place to hear about brand new musicals.

the goal pivoted up and over as the wooden floor below it slid forward. The infill would complete its pivot and land in place upstage, now showing the reverse, which was a planked back wall to the White's living room at home.

On the moving-floor platform was Cook, seated. However, it took longer to move into place than intended, while the rear wall panel continued to rotate.

Sturt   What did not click in, in this case, were the safety limiters, which would have automatically held the pivoting wall until the truck was safely through. One of the Stage Management team called it to me and I stopped it to allow the truck through. It was a manual stop, and because the wall juddered, it probably looked way worse than it actually was.

To the audience, it appeared that the rotating rear wall of the set was spinning slowly but directly towards Cook's head.

Triplett   She was mid-stage with this huge piece of set hovering just above her head. It was a nightmare!

Sturt   We then couldn't move the wall, because we had stopped it half way through its movement, therefore Barbara and Linzi did the whole scene with the 'garage door' in an open position. It looked terrible. After the scene ended, we had to manually close it and move it off.

The unnerving incident didn't go unnoticed from the Stalls. In its review, the *Guardian* informed readers that 'the complex machinery even imposes a drama of its own by looking set to decapitate Miss Barbara Cook',[39] whilst Matt Wolf's *Chicago Tribune* review pointed out that: 'the opening night was marred by technical mishaps, including at one point a wall-panel that looked as if it might rest on top of Cook'.[40]

Matt Wolf (theatre critic)   I remember that very vividly. Obviously, we could see what she couldn't see: that the set was kind of coming up and pivoting behind her. I seem to recall people in the audience shouting 'Duck!' at the stage, but maybe I have just dreamed that! She ducked down, and that bit of stage machinery passed above her. So, she was physically unscathed, but it must have been, emotionally, pretty harrowing.

Hateley   She was like, 'You know what? This is not for me.'

Kurz recalls Cook's rather more irate reaction in his autobiography. 'After the initial shock, she stormed furiously into her dressing room and nobody could comfort her,' he said. 'Finally, I set out to win back the stunned actress. There lay

---

[39]De Jongh, 'Carrie On'.
[40]Wolf, 'The Horror of "Carrie"'.

Barbara on her dressing-room bed, offering an exceedingly unflattering sight – a plump dowager with a pouting mouth. "Where is that lousy director? Isn't he worried about me at all?" she bellowed at me. She kept screaming, becoming even hoarser, something a singer naturally can't afford. And suddenly she stopped – and shook with laughter. She grabbed me, thirty years younger, by the hands and said almost affectionately, "Kid, save your Deutschmarks and put an end to this shit."[41]

Unaware of the backstage drama, the critics filed out of the building. Cast members and their guests headed to a drinks reception, which had been set up in the rehearsal studio. An enormous cake featuring the faces of the two leading ladies had been duly provided by a local baker.[42]

The nervous chatter about the impending reviews was interrupted by loud bangs in the quiet night sky over Stratford. Kurz ushered everyone over to the floor-to-ceiling windows of the room, overlooking the town's public sports fields and the river Avon.

Sturt   I was standing next to the Production Manager when all of a sudden he said, 'Oh, my God, he's lit up the whole of the playing fields.' Suddenly, these fireworks went off, enormous explosions which went on for a good ten or fifteen minutes. It was pretty stunning

Rich   'Carrie' was spelled out in pink firework letters on a huge frame at the climax of the ten-minute display.

D'Amboise   I was like, 'Wow, they have some money!'

'Even as I send this report,' Michael Coveney wrote in his *Financial Times* review, 'a deafening firework display on the Avon is blotting out sensible reflections.'[43]

Sturt   As they died away, coming towards the playing fields you could see blue lights flashing. Somebody had obviously woken up the police, because they must have thought it was World War II again, or something. The next day, you could see the damage that the fireworks had done to the playing fields, which, of course, Fritz had to pay for.

The onslaught

The morning after opening night, and with Kurz and the RSC management presumably attempting to repair relations with the local authorities, the reviews landed.

---

[41]Kurz, *Der Musical-Mann*, 11.

[42]The cake weighed 42 pounds, about 19 kilograms – unfortunately, the fondant faces of Hateley and Cook were not edible, a local news article soberly informs us.

[43]Michael Coveney, '"Carrie"/Royal Shakespeare Theatre, Stratford', *Financial Times*, 22 February 1988, 19.

Berg   My lasting memory, apart from the show itself, was the following morning in our hotel. We went down for breakfast and sat at a table right next to Debbie Allen and her friends. They had a pile of newspapers. Watching their faces as they read those reviews, which was obviously what they were doing – as we were doing it as well – was priceless.

Gore   The reviews expressed all of the authors' worst fears in print – everything that we'd told Terry repeatedly but were powerless to get him to do anything about.

If the sold-out audience response to the show had fluctuated, the reaction from the critics was more clear-cut. It was unsurprising that the earlier arguments about the validity of the project were rehashed in the reviews, but nobody was prepared for the scathing reaction to the show itself. Indeed, such a savaging had not been witnessed for some time in the Arts pages.

The *Guardian*'s Nicholas de Jongh had been dispatched northwards to investigate the 'horrible goings on' in Stratford, declaring the show 'a resounding mistake' and opening his review with an extended fairy-tale metaphor about Hands being lured in by mysterious folk from 'a faraway place called America' offering money and a Broadway transfer, declaring that this state of affairs is the natural conclusion of the government's focus on self-sufficiency in the arts. The production 'vibrates with energy and speed', de Jongh concluded, offering his only hint of praise, 'signifying little'.[44]

'The fable has been thoroughly sanitized and undergone a latex injection of romance,' *The Times*' Irving Wardle said, comparing the show to the novel. 'The special effects are fine, but like the rest of the production they remain detached episodes.'[45] The *Sunday Times* declared, double pun intended, that the RSC should have 'washed its Hands of it. Period.'[46]

Trade paper *The Stage*, which had given over notable column inches to the state funding debate, called it 'the biggest load of codswallop since *Time*' in a review darkly titled 'Post Menstrual Tension'. Despite the Anglo-American cast, it accused the show of being 'considerably more American than Anglo.' Hands should 'get back to the Bard as soon as possible,'[47] it advised.

Jane Edwardes of *Time Out* predicted that: 'this is the kind of show that will drive people out of the theatre and into the cinema for years to come … [it] cops out on the horror and presents a line-up of precocious chorus girls calculated to appeal to the tired businessman rather than an honest portrait of the agonies of pre-pubescence'. Koltai's staircase finale and set pieces were 'spectacular' but Hands'

---

[44]De Jongh, 'Carrie On'.

[45]Irving Wardle, 'What a Carrie On . . ', *The Times*, 20 February 1988.

[46]Kenneth Hurren, 'A Rocky Horror Show', *The Sunday Times*, (21 February 1988).

[47]Peter Hepple, 'Post-Menstrual Tension – Bad Blood at the RSC', *The Stage*, 25 February 1988, 15.

production is so 'inept' that 'he can think of nothing to do with them'. 'Shame on the RSC for housing such a tawdry event,'[48] she concluded.

In the *Financial Times*, Michael Coveney had mixed feelings, comparing the music to 'a discotheque spin-off of *Fame* and *Flashdance* with second act concessions to ballad requirements' and suggesting that the subject matter had sent Hands 'spinning into an utter cultural vacuum of dance studio robotics with a hint of cultural and classical pretensions,' conceding that 'much of this, I hasten to add, is enjoyable in a masochistic way'.[49]

In *Punch*, Sheridan Morley swung a blow at the clearly wounded director: 'We are left wondering why a director with the taste and intelligence and courage of Terry Hands should have devoted so much time and rehearsal effort to the kind of airport-bookstall shocker that teenagers throw away with their hamburger cartons and their empty drink cans'.[50]

The Telegraph's Charles Spencer decreed that 'one quickly tires of the ubiquitous pelvic thrusts and simulated copulation . . . Carrie's special powers are suggested by a couple of conjuring tricks which would seem dull at an end-of-the-pier variety show . . . A tragedy of wasted effort and directorial hubris . . . It is sad to see the company prostituting its good name in this way'.[51]

Mark Steyn's *Independent* review – headlined 'Period pains' and set around a cartoon of a disgruntled-looking Shakespeare clutching a copy of *Hamlet* stamped with the word 'Rejected' and muttering, 'Not enough songs, I suppose' – declared that: 'there are faults in most every department of *Carrie* but the most ludicrous are those committed by the British participants rather than their more artless American collaborators'. The design of the show was 'fundamentally flawed' and 'there is an awful lot of frenzied movement which appears to have no material connection with its motive cause'. The songs were 'undramatic, non-specific and incapable of propelling the plot'.[52]

The *Sunday Telegraph*'s Francis King called the production 'totally misconceived' with the final scene in particular 'particularly unsatisfactory' when Carrie has a bucket placed over her head, 'a fate which, by then, I'd have gladly imposed on Terry Hands'. King does call out Gore's 'brilliant' music, and the performances of Cook, Hateley and Ray, who danced 'with thrilling panache'.[53]

Milton Shulman of London's *Evening Standard* was disappointed by the special effects, commenting that Gore's music occasionally rises 'to an impressive melodic crescendo' but questioned 'whether the idea and the production were really necessary', assuring anyone considering taking a 'nervous elderly aunt'[54] to the

---

[48]Jane Edwardes, '"Carrie" Review', *Time Out*, 24 February 1988, 23.
[49]Coveney, '"Carrie"/Royal Shakespeare Theatre, Stratford'.
[50]Morley, 'Carrie on Regardless'.
[51]Charles Spencer, 'A Tragedy for the RSC', *Daily Telegraph*, 20 February 1988.
[52]Steyn, 'Period Pains'.
[53]King, 'Blood and Bucks'.
[54]Milton Shulman, 'Carrie with Rock is a No Horror Show', *Evening Standard*, 19 February 1988, 10.

show need not worry, whilst the ever-prudish *Daily Mail* gravely warned readers 'that this misguided aria is graphically signalled by a schoolgirl shower scene' and an 'unsavoury story . . . it looks and sounds like a mess'. The show was 'sanitised and yet vaguely unpleasant', 'aggressively vulgar' yet 'entirely sexless' with music 'ranging from soupy, soppy ballad to disco . . . [it] leaves behind a confused and exhausted impression of someone having applied a food mixer to musical notes'.[55]

'Kicking a leg, thrusting a buttock here and a groin there . . . [*Carrie* is] a bedizened whore from Thatcher's Britain', declared Victoria Radin in the *New Statesman*, who focused on the 'spiritual famine' facing the RSC thanks to the funding cuts. The tunes are 'totally unmemorable' and Carrie's revenge 'leaks out spectacularly'.[56]

Maureen Paton of the *Daily Express* did not hold back, announcing that the show was 'a dreadful hammy piece of nonsense . . . clumsily directed . . . a cliché-ridden farce . . . a laughably trivial show'. Her assessment of Gore's score was 'appalling', and of Allen's choreography, she declared that she had seen 'better movement at a jumble sale'. Presciently, she warns that there could be a 'bloodbath'[57] when the Broadway reviewers get their hands on it.

A handful of reviews were mixed, with some edging towards positive. Felix Barker of the *Sunday Express* declared that the show was an impressive demonstration of 'what a group of clever people can do if they have six million dollars to burn', calling the production 'dazzling' and that the 'glitter girls and leather lads outdo *Chorus Line*'.[58] The *Observer*'s Michael Ratcliffe acknowledged that it needed improving before its move to Broadway but that 'there are many good things about *Carrie*', the opening number was 'breathtaking' and that the RSC had 'confounded doubts they should be involved in the enterprise at all'. Hands' lighting was 'gorgeous' but the songs were 'served sequentially like club sandwiches – some sharp and tasty, others processed and dull'.[59]

The critics did agree on one thing: Hateley's performance as Carrie was the highlight of the evening. 'A star is born,'[60] declared the local *Birmingham Express and Star*, making comparisons with Judy Garland. Wolf praised the show's young lead as a 'powerhouse presence . . . already one Tony nomination appears guaranteed . . . When the show locks its two leading women in an eternal mother–daughter conflict, it frequently ignites'.[61] *The Stage* called Hateley a 'genuine find, and in Barbara Cook, [it] reintroduces a shining older one'.[62] Wardle called the voices of

---

[55]Jack Tinker, 'Oh Dear, Girls, What a Dreadful Carrie On', *Daily Mail*,19 February 1988.

[56]Radin, 'Blood Money', 31.

[57]Maureen Paton, 'What a Carrie On', *Daily Express*, 19 February 1988.

[58]Felix Barker, 'A Horror Glory', *Sunday Express*, 21 February 1988.

[59]Michael Ratcliffe, 'Strutting Their Stuff', *The Observer*, 21 February 1988, 24.

[60]Peter Rhodes, 'Terrific Linzi Carries Off an Epic Triumph', *Birmingham Express and Star*, 19 February 1988.

[61]Wolf, 'The Horror of "Carrie"'.

[62]Hepple, 'Post-Menstrual Tension'.

Hateley and Cook 'the most thrilling sounds of the evening'.[63] The *Guardian*, though describing Cook as 'miscast', praises her 'exultant, soaring' voice. 'Their scenes together have a resonance that suggests *The Glass Menagerie* as rewritten along the lines of Greek myth,'[64] praise that must have delighted Hands. The *Mail*'s Jack Tinker, otherwise dismissing the show as a tawdry mess, declared that: 'I hope sincerely that Broadway takes Miss Hateley to its heart. It can take the rest wherever it pleases.'[65]

The show must go on

The team tried to work out how to tackle the critical assault. According to *The Telegraph*, 'Hands' creative authority over the production started to come into question, in a series of niggling arguments with the writers'.[66] Meanwhile, the *Independent* called the Broadway transfer 'a doubtful prospect'.[67] Perhaps seizing upon the more positive reaction to the Carrie and Margaret scenes he'd placed so much focus on, Hands doubled down on his focus of elevating the scenes and trimming the book, adjusting or cutting lines that had received an inadvertent laugh from the audience or a sarcastic aside from a critic, or which he felt held back the pace of the show. He later claimed that he had always expected poor reviews, saying that he knew the show would be 'deservedly drubbed'.[68]

Even after press night, at which point most shows are no longer changed, *Carrie* continued to be altered daily.

> **Bailey** There were endless script changes and some changes of musical numbers. The show was being rehearsed pretty well daily from the first performance in Stratford until the press night in New York.

In a preview piece for Broadway readers, Hands told Frances X. Clines of the *New York Times* that three new scenes, additional special effects and fresh lyrics had been added to the performance they watched together. Clines observed that alterations were being 'rushed daily into the production as the musical is frantically basted and audience-tested eight times a week', with 'new chunks of dialogue and lyrics, plot and ersatz pig's blood' added to each show. '"It's terrifying every night," d'Amboise told him.'[69]

---

[63]Wardle, 'What a Carrie on . . .'.
[64]De Jongh, 'Carrie On'.
[65]Tinker, 'Oh Dear, Girls'.
[66]Tookey, 'Flop!'
[67]Steyn, 'Period Pains'.
[68]Tookey, 'Flop!'
[69]Clines, '"Carrie" Churns towards U.S.'.

Pitchford, Gore and Cohen were dismayed by the show playing out in front of them. It was far from the *Carrie* they had envisioned. Their early fears – that Hands' vision was too complex and abstract – had been reinforced by the critical reaction, but the generally enthusiastic response from the audience did not help their case. Acknowledging that their own lyrical, musical and book contributions had not been immune to criticism, they were keen to do what they could to fix the issues that had been raised by the press; indeed, Clines' article noted that 'the writers already were darting up the aisles with their notes for another night of hectic revisions'[70] by the time the bows started.

> **Pitchford**   We would go to Terry and Debbie with our notes. Could you please take a look at this moment? Could we please get in there and rewrite this section? And they would say, 'No. You hear the audiences, they're loving it. Are you kidding? Don't fix what's not broken.' It was painful for us, because once the show started playing – and playing as well as it did – we lost any leverage for getting our changes into it.

The writers strongly suspected that seasoned Broadway audiences would be far less forgiving, and that the New York critics would be even harsher than their British counterparts: the snarky previews and opinion pieces already running in the American arts pages suggested that the reviewers were ready to pounce. They implored Hands to think twice about the transfer without some substantial structural and design changes, but found their requests brushed aside.

Perhaps the director's mind was elsewhere. Throughout everything, Hands had been keeping the news of Cook's imminent departure to himself, but the news soon got out.

> **Pitchford**   We did not know that she had spoken to a columnist in London, Baz Bamigboye. He had interviewed her over the years, whenever she was in London, so she trusted him, and she let slip in a phone conversation that she was leaving.

'I will not continue with this show,' she had told Bamigboye. 'I will not go to Broadway with it. It is too chaotic.' Cook said she would honour her commitment to finish the Stratford run, but would also be more than happy for a replacement to step in. 'We haven't been told officially that Miss Cook won't continue,' a rather forlorn-sounding RSC spokesperson chipped in. 'In any event, we're still going to New York. The reviews have not deterred us.'[71]

The 26 February, *On Stage* column of the *New York Times* broke the news to disappointed Broadway theatregoers, with Cook's manager, Jerry Kravat, more

---

[70]Ibid.
[71]Baz Bamigboye, 'I Just Can't Carrie on Like This, Says Star', *Daily Mail*, 23 February 1988.

delicately confirming that 'the decision was made by her and the producers and that Miss Cook would continue with the production in Stratford-upon-Avon'.[72]

In her autobiography, Cook strongly asserts that 'the one smart thing I did was sign only for England. There was no mention in my contract of my appearing in the transfer to Broadway',[73] suggesting that whenever the topic was brought up during rehearsals, the producers would dismiss any concerns from the Company Manager about Cook's post-Stratford plans. In a letter to a fan who had seen the show, she said that, 'Even before the reviews came out, I told the powers that be that I would not continue after Stratford – only eleven performances to go . . .'[74]

Hands later told the *Los Angeles Times* that they had parted on good terms. 'It was clear that the part wasn't going to exhibit her soprano-legato voice, and her ability to break one's heart,' he said. Kurz was less impressed. 'I read about her decision in the press, about ten days before the end of the run,' he said in the same article. 'She could have potentially jeopardized the show.' Hands goes on to explain that he hadn't informed Kurz of Cook's imminent departure as he didn't want to 'unduly add more pressure on Fritz's end than there already was'.[75]

Cook stuck to her word and saw out the remainder of the Stratford run, though perhaps her heart was not in it: despite praising her singing voice, the *Guardian* described her performance as being like a 'stiff, unmotivated martinet, for whom fanaticism seems an utter embarrassment'.[76]

McKneely   And so, all of a sudden, we finished in Stratford, and all of a sudden Barbara was not with the show any more.

Wise   Barbara Cook was a dream and a class act. Always rising above the inadequacies.

Jackson   I think she was trying this thing on for size. She gave it a try, it just wasn't the right fit. I mean, I think a lot of us were relieved . . . no, relieved is the wrong word, but it was hard. We had an unhappy cast member, you know?

Otterson   I remember she was invited to go to the [Broadway] opening, I think, and to walk the carpet. But she had a conflict. I think she was gonna go later . . .

'I did go to see it during its very brief run on Broadway . . .' Cook recalled in her memoir. 'It was still a disaster, and they hadn't solved any of the basic problems, let alone details like why the gym teacher was leading class in high-heeled pumps . . . I was incredibly relieved not to be a part of the show.'[77]

---

[72]'Barbara Cook', in 'On Stage' column, *The New York Times*, 16 February 1988, 58.
[73]Cook, *Then and Now*, 206.
[74]Letter from Barbara Cook to Philip Argent, 26 February 1988.
[75]Harper, Timothy (Mar 27, 1988) 'STAGE: Horrors!'
[76]De Jongh, 'Carrie On'.
[77]Cook, *Then and Now*, 208.

Edwards   Many years later I was doing some recording in New York at the same time as my old friend Elaine Paige was appearing as Mrs Lovett in *Sweeney Todd* at the New York City Opera. The night I went to see it, Barbara was also in the audience and we both found ourselves in Elaine's dressing room after the performance. Barbara, not surprisingly, did not recognize me, but on being reminded that we had worked together on *Carrie*, she laughed loudly, flung her arms around me and said, 'Honey, were we right!'

Brave faces

In New York, barely a week passed without one news outlet or another nodding to the show's various dramas, many liberally playing with 'What a *Carrie* on'-style puns in their headlines and gleefully quoting extracts from the scathing British reviews.

Hands, Allen and Kurz put on a brave face. Hands emphasized the exalted performance of Hateley, hinting that she would almost certainly win a Tony Award. Kurz told the New York *Daily News* that 'enormous improvements have already been made', claiming that early press reports were harsh because they had seen an early 'unfinished' preview without his consent, and that 'the performances have got better and better, we've improved the special effects, changed some costumes, added scenes that make the plot clearer, and have improved the orchestrations and the sound so you can understand the lyrics'. Kurz was adamant that the Stratford reviews shouldn't count against the show and that critics should wait until the Broadway opening before casting judgement. 'We still have a lot of work to do . . . I feel that's when all the changes will have been made and that's when we'll be ready – and that's when *Carrie* should be reviewed.'[78] Allen told the *Los Angeles Times* that she considered the Stratford run a 'work in progress', and that 'things need to be clarified and redefined for Broadway. The basic structure is there, but the characters need a little more developing.'[79]

On home turf, the London *Evening Standard* – seemingly without evidence – reported that 'morale at the Royal Shakespeare Company is at an all-time low, and a vociferous faction . . . is now calling for the resignation of the artistic director . . . the culprit, as everyone knows, is an American adolescent with a severe personality disorder. Her name is Carrie . . .' According to the report, the repeated reassurances from Hands, Kurz and other spokespeople that the show was a runaway hit were wearing thin, with suggestions that members of the RSC's resident acting company were preparing to decamp to the National Theatre *en masse* in embarrassment, and that an in-joke nickname for the company had been circulating: 'No Cash and

---

[78]Marilyn Beck, '"Carrie" On', in 'Extra Entertainment' column, *Daily News*, 4 March 1988, 60.
[79]Harper, 'STAGE: Horrors!'

Carrie.[80] According to the *Guardian*, who labelled the *Standard* article 'bizarre', every RSC director subsequently signed a letter denying any such plot existed and suggesting that the rumours were maliciously circulated by the company's rivals. 'Hanging over Hands,' the article says, 'is the awful recent experience of having had almost every critic in the land slate the production.'[81]

Despite its chaotic time in Stratford, *Carrie* – as a revenue generator – had done its job for the RSC. The British leg of the show had sold extremely well, and had not cost the company anything to stage.

David Brierly, the long-term General Manager at the RSC, said:

It was a Midlands, non-Shakespearean audience, and we had full houses every night. It was terrific to have offered something which made the connection between them and us. And we probably had a bigger and more favourable postbag about *Carrie* than about anything we've done for donkey's years. It is the most extraordinary example of something on which the critics and the public were simply poles apart.[82]

The company's ambition to use the show to attract a younger and more mainstream audience appeared to have been successful: 'Youthful locals who wouldn't dream of sitting through *Hamlet* streamed in, screaming and storming the actors' dressing rooms, which certainly hasn't happened at recent performances here of *Much Ado About Nothing*,'[83] a reporter from the *Wall Street Journal* noted. Hands' former colleague Trevor Nunn later told *The Stage* that, 'Hands saw it [*Carrie*] as a work of dramatic force and raw theatricality which would interest thousands of Midlands youngsters and bring them to Stratford. He was right … the production sold out and played to nightly standing and cheering demonstrations rarely experienced at Stratford. We know from the many young people who have written to us that The Royal Shakespeare Theatre is no longer for them an exclusive and daunting temple of culture, and that they have returned to see the company's Shakespeare work with a feeling of belonging.'[84]

Many new musicals beset by scathing reviews, major technical problems, artistic differences, fall-outs, sackings and resignations might admit defeat, close quietly and fade into relative obscurity. Evidently, Hands, Kurz and Allen still believed that *Carrie* was Broadway-worthy. Or, perhaps they felt there was no option but to press ahead: a theatre was booked, investors had signed on the line and an opening night was in the diary. Hands would surely have been aware that

---

[80]'Hands Carries the Can for Rocky Drama', *Evening Standard*, 11 March 1988.
[81]John Vidal, 'The Selection of the Fittest', *The Guardian*, 7 April 1988, 33.
[82]Tookey, 'Flop!'
[83]Trucco, '"Carrie" Ghost'.
[84]Nunn, 'The Nunn's Tale'.

his personal fee, and the RSC's long-term royalty, depended on the success of the show in New York. The critics must be proven wrong.

D'Amboise   I remember thinking 'Oh, we've got to go to New York. Is that going to happen?' And then suddenly it was like 'Absolutely, we're going to New York!'

Bailey   We all went to Broadway hoping for a hit.

In the passionate New York theatre community, rumours were swirling about this brand new musical, plagued with problems and savaged by the press. For those fascinated by theatrical flops, it would be the season's hottest ticket.

4 BROADWAY: THEY'LL MAKE FUN OF YOU, THEY WILL BREAK YOUR HEART

Stephen Dolginoff (audience member, Broadway)[1] Obviously, there was gossip from Stratford. You would buy this magazine called *TheaterWeek*, open it to the gossip column and there might be a little paragraph about the show you're interested in, so I'd heard that Barbara Cook had left the show.

Scott Briefer (audience member, Broadway) One rumour going around was that Tommy Tune had gone down on his knees and pleaded with them to not bring it to New York because it was so terrible. So, you can imagine how interested we all were!

The buzz about *Carrie* had gradually permeated the New York theatre scene for some time. What started as early excitement in the press about a promising new show featuring Barbara Cook's long-awaited return to the stage was soon overtaken by chatter about its delays and general state of readiness. Its hectic reputation was soon reinforced with cynical summaries of the scathing British reviews and the surprise news of Cook's departure. Headlines like *TheaterWeek*'s cover splash *Will Carrie Make It to the Prom?*[2] fuelled the hearsay, and several US-based newspapers hurriedly dispatched critics to sleepy Stratford to get the scoop on the musical which was 'likely to arrive in New York as a show whose production history is more intriguing than the onstage event'.[3] The *New York Times* soberly informed its readers that: '*Carrie* Churns toward U.S.',[4] as if a particularly turbulent storm was headed across the Atlantic.

---

[1] Dolginoff would later create the musical *Thrill Me: The Leopold and Loeb Story*.
[2] Ironically, the magazine didn't hit newsstands until the show had closed.
[3] Wolf, 'The Horror of "Carrie"'.
[4] Clines, '"Carrie" Churns towards U.S.'.

Before long, *Carrie*'s late April arrival on Broadway was firmly marked in the calendar of anyone with an interest in theatrical curios or car-crash entertainment. Mandelbaum reflected that 'for those who care about collecting flops', attending the first preview would be '*de rigueur*'.[5]

Despite the anticipation amongst the flop-curious crowd, advance sales for *Carrie*'s open-ended Broadway run were not particularly strong, lurking at $2.7 million,[6] considerably less than other recent big British imports like 1982's *Cats* ($6.2 million),[7] 1987's *Les Misérables* ($16 million)[8] and 1988's *The Phantom of the Opera* (an 'unprecedented' $18 million).[9]

Carrie had not been cheap to produce, with a highly publicized budget in the region of $7–8 million (*Cats* had cost $4.5 million).[10] The complex physical production and the competitive advertising landscape meant that its diminished 'war chest' of funds would not keep the show open for long unless it caught the imagination of the wider ticket-buying public. A lot was riding on strong word of

IMAGE 4.1 The omnipresent *Cats* logo in New York City, pictured in May 1988 just as *Carrie* opened. Suzanne Thomas (photographer).

[5]Ken Mandelbaum, *Not Since Carrie: 40 Years of Broadway Musical Flops* (New York: St Martin's Press, 1991), 4.
[6]Rothstein, 'After Seven Years'.
[7]Jessica Sternfeld, *The Megamusical* (Bloomington, IN: Indiana University Press, 2006), 124.
[8]Ibid., 233.
[9]Michael Kantor and Laurence Maslon, *Broadway: The American Musical* (New York: Bulfinch Press, 2004), 391.
[10]Michael Riedel, *Razzle Dazzle: The Battle for Broadway* (New York: Simon & Schuster, 2016), 293.

mouth from preview ticket-holders to help stimulate sales; the beleaguered public relations team had to work fast to position it as the season's must-see hit, and keep their fingers crossed for kindness from the critics.

Finding an audience

Promotion for the show began in earnest. Friedrich Kurz – renowned for utilizing modern marketing and sales techniques for his German productions – set about targeting the previously untapped youth market, putting together ticket deals for young people who 'would not normally go to a Broadway show' and actively promoting the show as a 'pop rock opera'.[11]

> **Dolginoff**   There were huge posters all the way down the street. They had rented out the windows of an entire vacant building and covered them in posters. I loved the artwork.
>
> **James Noone** (audience member, Broadway)   I was in Times Square a lot, and I remember there were telephone booths covered in the *Carrie* logo and the slogan, 'She's just around the corner' or 'Call her!' with the box office number. That was kind of intriguing.
>
> **Mark Silver** (audience member, Broadway)   I was walking down some street and I looked over and saw the handbill pasted on the wall. It said, '*Carrie*: There's Never Been a Musical Like Her'. A musical about *Carrie*! Stephen King! I just couldn't believe it. I got very excited.[12]
>
> **Mary Ann Oedy** (Ensemble, Stratford and Broadway)   Someone had a *Carrie* stencil and spray-painted the logo around the streets of Midtown Manhattan.

Time claimed that the $500,000 advertising blitz was 'teasingly mysterious rather than hard sell'.[13] The logo lacked the instant clarity of the *Cats* eyes or the beret-wearing waif of *Les Misérables* – two ubiquitous icons plastered over every available New York surface. Wags joked that the strapline, 'There's Never Been a Musical Like Her', might well turn out to be true . . . but not necessarily in the way the ad-men hoped.

The 1980s on Broadway

As *Carrie* arrived on Broadway in Spring 1988, there was strong competition for the average theatregoers' buck. Just a few years earlier – around the time the show was being developed and workshopped – it was a different story.

---

[11]'Hands Carries the Can'.
[12]Silver was so taken with the logo that, many years later, he had it tattooed on his leg.
[13]Henry III, 'Theater'.

With the notable exception of the high-profile transfer of *Cats* from London in 1982, Broadway in the late years of the 1970s and the early 1980s had been dominated by a spate of innocuous revivals and plays rather than new work. Broadway still felt 'conservative, nostalgic, and rigid'[14] in terms of the development of new home-grown shows, its approach to theatrical innovation and its willingness to welcome different audiences. A visit to the Theatre District – the busy heart of Midtown Manhattan around Times Square – was an unsavoury prospect for many; despite a series of attempts to clean up and modernize the neighbourhood in recent decades, it was poorly lit and still scattered with sleazy shops, run-down bars and stretches of buildings on the verge of collapse.

Attendance dwindled, with only thirty-one shows opening in the 1984–5 season, down from fifty a couple of years earlier.[15] So bad was the state of affairs that the 1985 Tony Awards eliminated the Best Actor in a Musical, Best Actress in a Musical and Best Choreography prizes for lack of eligible candidates.

Many lifelong, hands-on producing impresarios retired. The AIDS epidemic tragically laid waste to a generation of theatre-makers; *A Chorus Line* creator Michael Bennett, who withdrew from the community in 1986 due to his illness and died the following year, was one high-profile example. As Broadway's 'old school' vanished, production models changed, and it soon became more commercially savvy for theatre owners and producers to import tried-and-tested musicals rather than risk creating them from scratch, either from subsidized or subscription-funded regional theatres (with the resources to test and nurture new work) or from the West End (where production costs were lower). As Jessica Sternfeld writes in *The Megamusical*, 'for the first time in modern American musical theater, a dominant style emerged that was not American'.[16] The critic Frank Rich agreed, stating that 'in the eighties, 'Broadway lost whatever claim it still had as a source for American theater; it became instead a showplace for theater that had originated elsewhere.'[17]

The so-called 'British Invasion' of the late 1980s had seen a trio of these imported 'megamusicals' – *Les Misérables* (1987), *Starlight Express* (1987) and *The Phantom of the Opera* (1988) – take advantage of the lull in American-made musicals, and move into prime Broadway houses for lengthy, high-profile runs. Defined by their impressive and complex scenery, epic plots and enormous budgets, the megamusicals raised audience expectations in terms of scale, and their popularity (and running costs) led to a steep hike in ticket prices. Backed by the deep pockets of Cameron Mackintosh or Andrew Lloyd Webber and hot on the heels of sold-out seasons in London, they arrived in a whirlwind of publicity, omnipresent

---

[14]Sternfeld, *The Megamusical*, 173.
[15]Riedel, *Razzle Dazzle*, 336.
[16]Sternfeld, *The Megamusical*, 2.
[17]Rich, *Hot Seat*, xii.

advertising and familiar tunes. The shows sold out for months on end, with tickets often changing hands for astronomical prices on the scalpers' market. Along with the perennially sold-out *Cats*, these new shows offered ample opportunity for potential *Carrie* ticket buyers to spend their hard-earned cash elsewhere.

Aside from its controversial subject matter, the team were well aware that *Carrie*'s teenaged characters and pop- and rock-infused score might struggle to attract the traditional, often older Broadway crowd with enough disposable income to give the show momentum.

Sternfield's definition of a megamusical includes another point: they are 'generally not loved by critics' but that their opinion 'largely ceased to matter'.[18] Indeed, mixed reviews for the London productions of *Cats* and *Les Misérables* had not deterred the ticket-buying public, and word-of-mouth had helped to make them two of the biggest selling musicals of all time. It is safe to assume that the *Carrie* team, after dealing with the humiliation of the British press reviews, hoped it would follow a similar path.

Tony trouble

The Tony Awards, held annually in June, have always provided a vital platform for promoting new Broadway shows: nominations, wins or even a performance at the televised ceremony can provide invaluable publicity and lead to a spike in ticket sales. Hopes were high that Linzi Hateley would scoop an award; others suggested Hands' futuristic lighting or Ralph Koltai's high-tech set might be worthy of gongs.

Shows must be open by a particular cut-off date – usually in early May – to be eligible for nomination, and Broadway seasons are delicately shaped to ensure shows benefit from the attention that the annual celebration brings.

> **Dean Pitchford** (Lyricist)   When you live and work in the New York theatre world, you know that every date in the calendar has significance. The opening date of a show is important. The Tony cut-off date is sacrosanct. Good producers know that.

Carrie's scheduled opening date changed numerous times. Early press listings suggested the show would open to the press on 1 May 1988, just in time for the Tony eligibility cut-off three days later.

> **Joey McKneely** (Ensemble, Stratford and Broadway)   The moment I realized that we were destined to fail is when they pushed our opening night date back.

Newspapers soon reported that a 'technical glitch' meant that the show's set had not been shipped from the UK in time, forcing a two-week delay to the show's opening night, missing the 4 May Tony cut-off.

---

[18]Sternfeld, *The Megamusical*, 4.

Jeremy Sturt (Deputy Stage Manager, Stratford and Broadway)   [The producers] hadn't filled in the carnets properly. So, the set got impounded in the Port of New York.

McKneely   To not even get a shot at a Tony nomination? That was a kiss of death. You're not even part of the discussion.

Reluctantly, the opening date was pushed back to 12 May (meaning that the show would only be eligible for awards the following year) and the Virginia stage would sit empty until the set arrived.

Pitchford   Our hearts sank. Missing that date and having to run eleven months before we could possibly get another Tony nomination? It was disastrous.

Kurz does not mention the incident in his memoir, but does say that the set transportation operation was such a major undertaking that 'we even had to enlist the Royal Air Force to transport some bulky sets to New York'.[19]

Sturt   We were four weeks behind on the build. We went to three-day-week rehearsals. So, we rehearsed for longer in New York than we should have done.

The delays 'cost a fortune and used up our reserve funds',[20] Hands later admitted to the *New York Times*.

The young cast, now assembled in New York City, made the most of the spare time.

Audrey Lavine (standby 'Margaret White', Stratford and Broadway)   When the kids from England came to New York, they were all agog. They were having such a wonderful time. They were gorgeous, beautiful young dancers. They were shocked at the size of the portions in New York restaurants, and they were all afraid to get fat before the show opened!

Suzanne 'Squeeze' Thomas (Ensemble, Stratford and Broadway)   We could get into all the clubs for free. 'We're in *Carrie*!' we'd say, with our best British accents, and they'd let us in!

Charlotte d'Amboise ('Chris Hargensen', Stratford and Broadway)   I remember that they put up Sally Ann Triplett in a gorgeous apartment on Madison Avenue, and she was, like, 'This is boring as hell. I cannot be on the East Side!' So she ended up renting a boat!

Some found time to reunite with former castmate Barbara Cook. Stage Manager Joe Lorden organized an afternoon tea at his apartment, during which the company

---

[19]Kurz, *Der Musical-Man*, 12.
[20]Rothstein, 'After Seven Years'.

spent an apparently raucous few hours going over the ups and downs of their time together in England.

Music changes

In the weeks between the Stratford and Broadway productions, a decision was made to overhaul the arrangement of the show's musical score. A new orchestrator, Harold Wheeler, was engaged to rework the orchestrations devised in Stratford by Michael Starobin and Anders Eljas.

Paul Schwartz (Musical Director, Broadway)   Terry was looking for something to pin the blame on, and he said at the company meeting – the day after we opened in Stratford to the worst reviews in the history of the British theatre – 'Don't anyone worry about this, as soon as we get the orchestration sorted out it will be fine.'

Michael Starobin (Co-Orchestrator, Stratford)   So, they hired Harold Wheeler, who rewrote some of our orchestrations. But a lot of them remained.

Pitchford   We sat through the sitzprobe[21] in Stratford, and it was a massive sound. It was thrilling, but it would have felt better placed in the Metropolitan Opera House. We felt worried that our singers and the plot and story was being overwhelmed by this gorgeous, massive orchestration, especially in moments of underscoring where dialogue was being spoken on top of it. And so, we decided, let's just get the whole show re-orchestrated. Let's not double back and rethink ourselves or second guess ourselves now. Let's thin the tracks just so that we can bring the drama forward.

Michael Gore (Composer)   Harold was brought in when we were moving to Broadway in order to streamline the orchestrations and create more consistency, and link between the operatic Margaret/Carrie songs and the high school numbers.

Pitchford   The idea was 'Can you help us without losing the character of this? Can you help us thin this out so that it does not roll like a tidal wave over the cast, but instead we can place the cast inside these orchestrations?' And that was Harold's great contribution to the show.

Wheeler – who had recently arranged the score for the Broadway production of *Dreamgirls* – gave the show a rockier edge. In a 2010 interview, he reminisced:

It was a wonderful score, the only thing wrong with it ... well, there were a lot of things wrong with the show that made the critics hate it, but musically when

---

[21]The first time the cast and orchestra perform the score of the show together.

Carrie was at school, it was *Grease*, and when she was at home with her mother, it was Stephen Sondheim. The two never met. They never even came near meeting. So, it was as if you were in two different shows and there was no mesh between the two.[22]

Anders Eljas (Co-orchestrator, Stratford)   Michael [Starobin] told me that Harold called him and said, 'I don't see anything wrong with these scores! I will call you if I change something.' He never called. I think he thought it wasn't a big deal about the changes he made. I'm sure my stuff was improved by him, and I thank him for that!

Starobin   Harold said they were also asking him what to do about the show in general, to which he responded, 'I can help you with the music, but I don't know, I'm no book writer.'

Schwartz   I am in no way knocking Harold's work because his work was all really beautiful, but the original orchestrations [by Starobin and Anders] were absolutely extraordinary. They were really, really good from both fellas. I mean, *really* good. Anders' stuff was just quirky and weird and exciting, and Michael just ran whole hog into the whole Wagnerian thing!

Margaret White 2.0

After Cook's departure, negotiations with Buckley had recommenced. But with time short, other performers were asked to audition in case the discussions collapsed again.

Kim Criswell (actress)   I was in rehearsal for *Jesus Christ Superstar* at Paper Mill Playhouse in New Jersey, bringing the whitest Mary Magdalene in the history of the world. I'd been paying attention to all the gossip that was coming across the Atlantic. All of a sudden, they're looking for a new Margaret White. Everybody assumed, including me, that they would get Betty Buckley. She'd been in the film, it'd be a great coup. I got a call from my agent, and I was surprised to hear that I had an audition for it. I was like twenty-nine or thirty!

Cook had played the role in her early sixties.

Criswell   I went to the audition, and we talked about the show, and I put some songs on tape for them to send back to England. I said, 'Guys, you do know I'm too young for this? I mean, I can't have a teenage daughter! I'm not

---

[22]Elizabeth Vincentelli, 'A Chat with Orchestrator Harold Wheeler', *New York Post*, 19 April 2010, available online: https://nypost.com/2010/04/19/a-chat-with-orchestrator-harold-wheeler/ (accessed 15 October 2022).

old enough!' And they said, 'Well, we don't care. You can sing it. They said Barbara Cook was too old!'

Criswell maintained she wasn't quite right for the part.

Criswell I said, 'I heard you guys were getting Betty Buckley.' And they were like, 'Well ...' and they basically said that negotiations weren't going well. They were getting some other options.

Pitchford We saw an American woman who Fritz [Kurz] flew in from Germany, who was a musical star there. It turns out – only after the fact did we discover – that he was dating her! Soon after that we drew a line.

Lawrence D. Cohen (Book writer) My collaborators and I gave Terry and Fritz an ultimatum that we wouldn't agree to the Broadway transfer – something that we, as authors, had the power to stop – unless Terry cast Betty as Margaret. After her original audition, there had been difficulties with the producers over her contract 'asks', and they reached a stalemate. Concerned, we asked Terry to sit down with her to try and sort it out, only for him to return from the meeting and declare that he would never, ever work with her. We told him that casting her was the only way we'd agree to go forward.

Pitchford We made the case – and we made it very persuasively – that the only way we could recover from such bad press was to come in with star power. You can't have open auditions and put somebody else in the role, and move an entire company and sets and everything else to New York on the basis of an unknown. So, we told them to go in there and make Betty's deal. And they did.

Betty Buckley ('Margaret White', Broadway) A few days before they started rehearsals for Broadway, my agent called and said, 'Look, here's the thing, we have a guarantee of a certain number of weeks, all these people will end up out of work if you don't do the role, Betty.' And these were my friends. So, I agreed, and I went into the show.

As well as her recent Tony-winning performance in *Cats*,[23] Buckley was a familiar Broadway name thanks to roles in *1776*, *Pippin*, *Song and Dance* and *The Mystery of Edwin Drood*, and was well-known to television viewers having appeared in three seasons of the ABC sitcom *Eight is Enough* from 1977–80. A neat selling point was her memorable appearance in the 1976 *Carrie* movie as the gym teacher. As well as the marquee value she would add to the production, the writers hoped she would bring more dynamism to the role of Margaret.

---

[23] A 1994 *New York Times* article about musical flops entitled 'Kitty Litter' poked fun at the similarities between *Carrie* and the somewhat more successful *Cats*: both 'featured barn-size pieces of scenery flying around in an ostensibly audience-rousing manner, both told stories no one could possibly follow, both climaxed with Betty Buckley dying amid aphasia-inducing lighting effects'.

Buckley – who had also spent many years as an acting coach – accepted the role on the condition that she was guaranteed time to work closely with Hateley, delving into the psychology of the complex mother-daughter relationship to heighten the impact of their shared scenes.

The two leading ladies formed a strong bond from the start. In a May 1988 interview, Hateley commented, 'We've only worked together for a couple of weeks and I've learned so much from her already.'[24]

Linzi Hateley ('Carrie White', Stratford and Broadway)   When we started rehearsing in New York, Betty said to me, 'What time is your car picking you up in the morning to take you down to rehearsals?' And I was like, 'Car? What do you mean?' I was seventeen in a big city, still supposedly having to be chaperoned. I was walking the streets of New York trying to find my way to the rehearsal room. She said, 'Right, I am going to start picking you up. My car will pick you up on the way.' She took on that responsibility of making sure I was safe. I mean, what a wonderful gesture from her. She was a big star, she was in a totally different league to me, but there was care and nurturing for a naive seventeen-year old.

Buckley encouraged Hateley to throw everything she had into their duets, showcasing the physical violence between the warring mother and daughter in a way that the much frailer Cook had been unable to.

Hateley   Terry had done the groundwork in Stratford – he had spent a lot of time with me and Barbara. And I think that he got out the structure of what he was hoping to achieve between mother and daughter. When Betty arrived, I think he basically wanted to give her whatever she needed to facilitate the best environment. I think he did that by sitting back or listening and occasionally suggesting something, which in a way you had to commend. There's no question the scenes were the way they were because of what Betty brought to them, and brought out of me.

Buckley   I told her to trust me and look me in the eye. We did a lot of improvisation to keep things spontaneous between us. She was fantastic to share a stage with, and she trusted me implicitly.

Hateley   The working environment with Betty was very different to how it had been in Stratford with Barbara. It was intense, very moving, extremely honest, and at times even scary! Betty would want to talk about and analyse the scenes, and she was very passionate about her choices. I was so new to that way of working, but I completely trusted her and I know she respected me for that. I believe that's why we still remain so close, as we went through a very

---

[24]Larry S. Ledford, 'Linzi Hateley's Date with Broadway', *TheaterWeek*, 23 May 1988, 10.

personal experience together. Betty always says that our working together has been a highlight of her career which is a massive compliment! I wanted to please her, because I could see how brilliant she was, and she was making the scenes so much more powerful. I embraced everything that she offered. I think that's what made the relationship so intense and raw. It was a very brave and special experience together.

Buckley   In the rehearsal room with Terry we created, I think, a very authentic psychological portrait of a gifted, young girl and her abusive mother. We created some very violent sequences.

Hateley told an interviewer, '[Betty] doesn't always stick to the script. There is a lot of improvising . . . It's a much more realistic way of doing things, but I'm more used to being directed into it.'[25] The interview ends with Hateley chirpily saying, 'time for another Betty Buckley beating!' as she returns to rehearsal.

Hateley   Every single performance, you never quite knew what was going to happen. We felt scared of each other at times. In the car after each rehearsal, we'd just sit there in a state of shock and exhaustion.

Lavine   I sat in on all of Betty's rehearsals. Now, I am a lifelong compulsive knitter. So, I was sitting there in rehearsal, knitting, but I'm watching and pitching in, and at one point, the Stage Manager came over to me and said, 'Betty says if you're not gonna pay attention then you shouldn't be in the rehearsal,' and asked me to leave. I have to preface that by saying she was always lovely to me. Even years later, we're Facebook friends and all that. It wasn't an ugly thing, just that her process is so intense!

The cast were blown away by the shift in energy and intensity in the company once Buckley took over the role.

Rosemary Jackson (Ensemble/Understudy 'Carrie White', Stratford and Broadway)   It was an amazing shift. We really got to feel what the show could be. Watching her was like a complete college course.

Simon Opie (Production Manager, Stratford and Broadway)   Her performance was terrifically powerful. One hundred per cent committed, the ultimate professional and truly spellbinding in the best bits.

McKneely   Betty is a tempest. You know, she comes in full force, very demanding. She has high, high expectations of herself and everybody around her. So that created another sort of drama. But her singing was just off the charts.

Sally Ann Triplett ('Sue Snell', Stratford and Broadway)   The show went from 'here' to sky-high. Just the intensity of it. The darkness, the singing. She's

---

[25]Ledford, 'Linzi Hateley's Date'.

actually very warm-hearted, and incredibly passionate about what she does. One day, she said, 'Sally, would you like to go to the best singing teacher in New York?'

Triplett was thrilled by the opportunity.

Triplett She said, 'Okay, tomorrow, one o'clock. Wonderful. Amazing! I'm going to take you in my car!' Wow. She put me in the car, and she bought me a sandwich at Carnegie Deli – their sandwiches were amazing, like 6 inches high! And we went into this apartment by Central Park. I sat on the sofa with my giant sandwich, and for the next hour and a half, I listened to Betty Buckley's singing lesson. It was an invitation to listen to her! Lying on the floor, doing the breathing and everything! Only Betty could invite you to see the best singing teacher in town and not tell you that it was going to be *her* singing! Hats off to her, you know, what a gal!

D'Amboise I remember her calling me in the middle of the night, late. 'Hi, it's Betty!' in her sweet little voice. And I'd be like, 'Hi, . . .?' She would just want to talk about the characters. She would ask me about my character, which, mind you, I hadn't thought about very much. She would *make* me think about it, really make me dig deep. And she was also trying to figure it all out. She wanted to feel the part, and what our relationship was. She's that kind of an actress, which is why she's so brilliant. Only retrospectively did I realize that she was actually trying to help me, maybe, find out what the hell I was doing!

No changes

Unable to start the tech on stage until the set arrived, the cast rehearsed at the 890 Broadway studio complex, the location of the 1984 workshop presentation. The Ensemble – having rehearsed, performed and re-rehearsed the show for several months – found themselves spending the majority of their time drilling the vigorous choreography, while Buckley and Hateley worked with Hands on their material separately.

Buckley We did develop a lot of our work away from everybody else, and when the run-throughs began, we came in and brought that style of performance to the show.

Cohen Terry chose to work in private on the Carrie and Margaret scenes which definitely heightened their impact, but he ignored the other 'high school' half altogether and never addressed the ongoing problems that could have made the show much better.

D'Amboise   Where they messed up was the time between Stratford and New York, where real changes should have happened. We could all see what was working and what was not working.

Indeed, the British press had made pains to list the issues that 'require urgent attention before the April opening in New York',[26] primarily the mismatched tone ('is this a universal tragedy or an excuse for high-volume aerobics, a primal family drama or so much kinetic kitsch?').[27]

Cohen   We just assumed extensive work would be done on the teen half of the show to address our and the critics' criticisms. Terry chose not to do anything except to work in private with Linzi and Betty, and poor Debbie Allen just ended up drilling her dancers again and again, marking time. Nothing changed in the text except for Terry cutting back more and more dialogue, which resulted in making the story seem even weaker and harder to follow.

Thomas   To the dancers, it felt like it was Debbie's show. She was doing everything. We hardly ever saw Terry once we got to New York. He left Debbie to it.

Opie   The set was a huge fixed element and made it hard to make significant changes, so most of the changes were around particular scenes – the telekinesis scene ['I'm Not Alone'] for example, which took more attention than was really warranted. It was impossible, I would say, to make radical change, and that eventually became frustrating for everyone involved.

Pitchford   We were not getting any of our requests in, so it became pointless to go to rehearsals. We were just not listened to.

Triplett   One night, Debbie went to the opening night of *Into the Woods* because her sister[28] was playing the lead. She, you know, maybe had a couple of drinks, whatever, and she went home late. Next day, she got to work a few minutes late. She had on these big dark glasses – she was always so showbiz – you know, she always just wanted to make it fun. She came into the room and she just, like, tipped her glasses down and didn't say anything. She just stared, because Terry Hands was re-choreographing the opening number. He was literally down in a lunge with us girls trying to . . . [laughs]. God bless your soul, Mr Hands. Debbie was just like, 'Mmmm-mm, no!' She was fabulous.

A comparison of the Stratford and Broadway recordings shows that some scenes were trimmed substantially, making the show pacier but likely rendering

---

[26]Ratcliffe, 'Strutting Their Stuff'.
[27]Wolf, 'The Horror of "Carrie"'.
[28]Phylicia Rashad, who played the Witch in Stephen Sondheim's new musical, which had recently had a cast change a few blocks away at the Martin Beck Theatre.

the telekinesis plot more difficult to follow than before for the casual viewer. The *New Yorker* would later describe the Broadway book as 'minimal'.[29] Whereas the Stratford programme listed the show's run-time as two hours plus an interval, a reviewer from *The Stage* noted that the Broadway running time was down to two hours in total, and subsequently 'the plot skipped from one melodramatic episode to another, without much linking material, so it became almost unintelligible'.[30]

In an interview following the show's closure, Hands alluded to a change in his directorial approach for Broadway, commenting that 'what we went for in New York was a Jacobean tragedy ... shock sensation, song, dance, dumbshows, all telling a story but all extremely improbable'. He mentions that he recently watched and was inspired by a production of Middleton's *The Revenger's Tragedy* which featured 'five murders and incest, two rapes, poisoned skulls, all by the interval'.[31]

Hands may have adjusted the historical era of his tragic influences from Greek to Jacobean, but in real terms, the gap in tone between the school and home scenes was widening. The incongruous costumes remained, Carrie's power was still vague, and, according to the critics, the supposedly 'epic' finale still felt flat. Aware of the company's agitation, Hands gathered everyone for a pep talk.

D'Amboise   I think he had his idea, and he was holding on to it.

Lavine   He said he knew what was wrong with it, and he knew how to fix it, and that we should be confident in that. The mood was not great.

D'Amboise   I remember Terry coming up to me and telling me how the show was going to surprise everybody, and that *Phantom* had nothing on this show. I remember thinking, 'Am I hearing that right?' I felt there was a little bit of delusion in that sense. I think that they were hoping that Betty would come in and change it all, but it wasn't just about the performances. It needed a different kind of structure.

Eventually, the well-travelled set arrived, and the crew worked long hours so that the tech rehearsal process could finally begin. As the build commenced, one of Kurz's major investors, CBS Records, withdrew their funding. This, combined with the lower-than-anticipated ticket income, led to a cash flow crisis.[32]

Opie   We suspended technical work at the Virginia several times during the build period due to financial uncertainty. I believe that the financial pressures were probably extreme.

---

[29]Mimi Kramer, 'Bloody Awful', *The New Yorker*, 15 May 1988, 85.
[30]Oleg Kerensky, '"Carrie"', Broadway review, *The Stage*, 2 June 1988, 11.
[31]Mark Lawson, 'Hands on His Knees', *The Independent*, 27 May 1988.
[32]Tookey, 'Flop!'

In scenes eerily reminiscent of the Stratford tech, time was running out to ensure the Virginia could accommodate one of Broadway's most technically complex shows to date.

Opie   The challenges lay in the re-installation of machinery and control systems that had been commissioned in the UK and the fact that certain features of the Stratford stage – such as the stage lifts – had to be recreated in the Virginia. These demands were technically complicated but also expensive in the context of Broadway working practice. Money became a very tight constraint and we had to control the work to fit the cash-flow, which was obviously stressful.

Mark Bailey (assistant to Set Designer Ralph Koltai)   Everyone was very concerned about having a hit and so pressure mounted, costs were soaring and people started to lose nerve.

'We've got to make great big holes in the stage, like that lift with the shower doors,' Koltai said when describing some of the difficulties in retrofitting the set. 'Theatres always have trunking and cleaning systems running underneath the stage at precisely the point where you want to cut into the stage floor! This is no exception, it's all got to be taken out and re-routed or whatever. A fair bit of money has to be spent . . .'[33] In addition, the 'rake' or slope of the Stratford stage had to be recreated at the Virginia to accommodate the set, taking up further time, budget and resources.

A gas pipe the length of the stage was installed to enable flames to leap high into the air, and the auditorium walls were painted pitch black to create an eerie atmosphere and provide a striking contrast with the bright white set. Hands was particularly taken with the functional style of the Virginia's interior: 'the stage dominates the auditorium; you have no decorations, no chandeliers . . . with the stage feeling as though it's taking up 50 per cent of the space for audience and performance. That gives the show an increased impact. If you're going to a show which is as unusual as this, then one does need an unusual space.'[34]

Ready, set . . . previews

Pitchford   The early audiences in New York were very mixed. Keen theatre fans, those who were genuinely interested, many people who wanted to see Betty Buckley do this role. Some had heard gossip about the show and wanted to make up their own mind. And then there were people who just wanted to dance on our graves.

---

[33]*Theatre Craft*/Pirani interview tapes.
[34]Ibid.

Dolginoff   I just knew that I had to go to the first preview. I went to see if I could get a ticket, and I remember the woman said, 'Yeah, I think we can get you in. The special effects are gonna knock your socks off.' I was really excited. My ticket was probably $40, maybe $45, the fourth row centre.

Peter Michael Marino (audience member, Broadway)[35]   I was there for the first preview in the third row. I saw the show at least five times. Oh yeah. I 'second acted' it.[36] And of course, that's the best act. Linzi was brand new to Broadway, so it felt like we were discovering this new talent, and of course we were also getting to live our *Fame* dreams by seeing Gene Anthony Ray.

Silver   I went to the TKTS ticket booth in Times Square, and I bought my ticket. It was $50 – that was the most expensive ticket at that time – and my ticket was for Row A, Seat 1.[37]

Noone   A friend of mine who worked in the theatre had tickets to the first preview so he asked me if I wanted to go. We were in the third row, I think, dead centre.

Gil Benbrook (audience member, Broadway)   I got us the half-price tickets to see a preview on Tuesday, 3 May. I remember walking up to the Virginia to check out the marquee and see if there were any understudies posted. There was a work truck parked in front. A woman appeared and started talking to one of the workers, and I overheard her asking something about building a small step to help her to get on or off part of the set. As she turned to walk away, I realized it was Betty Buckley, but she was gone as quickly as she'd appeared.

Stafford Arima (audience member, Broadway)[38]   You know, I was very lucky. I think it will probably be on my tombstone, it'll say that I was one of the only Canadians who got a chance to see the original *Carrie* on Broadway. My mother took me to a matinee performance.

Dolginoff   So, first preview, it's like 7.45 pm and they haven't let us in, and that felt kind of weird. It gets to 7.50 pm and they haven't let us in, and that's *really* weird. People are now murmuring 'Are they going to send us home?'

Concerns were raised that, as in Stratford some weeks before, the first preview might be cancelled. Ed Blank, Broadway critic for the *Pittsburgh Press*, noted the

---

[35]Marino would later create the musical *Desperately Seeking Susan* (a self-declared flop).

[36]The now seemingly extinct practice of sneaking into a show during the intermission, finding a vacant seat just before curtain up and enjoying the second act for free.

[37]A photo of a Box Office 'Scale of Prices' sign reveals that tickets for the show were priced between $32.50 and $50, and that performances took place at 8 pm, Tuesday to Saturday, with matinees at 2 pm on Saturday and 3 pm on Sunday.

[38]Arima would go on to direct the 2012 off-Broadway 'revisal' of *Carrie*.

delay was down to 'last-minute rehearsal problems', and that there was also an unexpectedly long 'thirty-minute intermission, another sign of backstage grief'.[39]

Forty-five minutes after the advertised start time, eager ticket holders were rushed into the auditorium and a Playbill thrust into their hands.

Briefer   The Virginia is one of the ugliest theatres on Broadway. It's not a Broadway gem, that particular space, but I thought when I walked in, 'wow'. They had painted all the walls black, and all of the house lights were red.

Dolginoff   It was very black and there was a big black scrim, and that was it. I remember thinking, 'Well, I've got a really good seat.' I remember looking around and it wasn't full, but it wasn't empty.

Pitchford   I have one very specific memory of the first preview's intermission. There was a hallway leading to the restrooms and there was a row of payphones on the wall. I remember going to the mens' room, and every single one of the phones being used. People were plugging in their coins and going, 'Oh my God, you won't believe what we're seeing!' They didn't even wait until the show was over before they started dissing it.

Arima   I was a kid from Toronto, I had no idea what made a good musical or a bad musical! But I sat in that theatre and was mesmerized by everything about it. There was a rock concert energy. I had never experienced that kind of visceral reaction to theatre.

Benbrook   Even with its flaws, we loved Betty and Linzi and most of the music, and even the cheesy costumes and choreography. Even though it wasn't a perfect musical, we couldn't stop talking about it.

Most audience members were unaware that the show was very much still in flux.

McKneely   We were cutting and shaping and re-choreographing every day through previews. We'd put things together again, and it wouldn't make sense. So, they'd have to scramble to try and make it make sense. We'd be in twelve-hour rehearsals and in tech constantly.

Michelle 'Shelley' Hodgson (Ensemble, Stratford and Broadway)   We never did the same show twice. It felt like we'd lost the plot. There were so many cuts and so many changes and tweaks. Joe [Lorden], our Stage Manager, while making his backstage pre-show announcement, got to the point of saying, 'Now, guys, remember, Scene Three is now Scene Four. This is cut. Don't wear your wigs. Boys, the pig's blood is cut in that bit. This is cut, that's cut, we're sticking that back in. We're trying this tonight . . .' and he'd go through this

---

[39]Ed Blank, 'Reviewing Broadway', *Pittsburgh Press*, 8 May 1988, 99.

entire enormous list of constant changes, daily. There was one performance where he said, 'Oh, I don't know what's going on, just go out there and do whatever you can! Guys, if you can remember what the hell is going on . . . good luck!'

Lavine   Watching the previews every night was how I learnt what changes went in. As a standby, that was my rehearsal. But it did give me the opportunity to see what worked from the audience. I would say, 'Tonight it's going to be a hit!' The next night, 'Oh, this is the worst thing ever!' The next night, 'Oh, it's just fabulous!' It was a rollercoaster.

'As the audience files out, some appear thrilled, others appalled, the word most frequently banded about is "unbelievable". For show freaks, this has been a night unlike any other, the kind for which they have waited a lifetime,' Ken Mandelbaum described in *Not Since Carrie*. 'These fans will tell their friends to get to the Virginia Theatre immediately, and many of them will return to *Carrie* two or three times during the two weeks of previews that remain . . .'[40]

Triplett   It was becoming like a cult.

Noone   I saw it six times. I spent every penny. I was just a poor designer back then, and I just kept running to the bank to get some more money to buy cheap tickets. I would tell all my friends that they had to go see this thing. I'd seen really bad musicals before, but this was somehow bad *and* incredible. I knew this thing was going to close, and I just needed to see it as many times as I could.

Some people may have returned to the show on multiple occasions, but others left the theatre infuriated by what they saw. One letter from an irate audience member was so extreme that it was proudly displayed on the company's backstage noticeboard (and later saved by a cast member). Dated 28 April 1988, it read:

```
Dear cast of Carrie,

Last night was the first preview of your show, and
simultaneously, a first for me.

I have been a theater-goer for many years; open minded,
liberal, interested. No matter how much I dislike a
show, or disagree with a performance, or piece of
writing, I have never been disrespectful. As a teacher
of drama and theater at the high school level, I have
taught that good manners are essential for the respect
of the actors as well as the audience members.
```

---

[40]Mandelbaum, *Not Since Carrie*, 9.

Yet, despite all I have taught, last night I booed. And I booed angrily and vociferously. I was appalled by this tasteless, vulgar, degradingly abusive "entertainment".

I booed hugely talented people who worked so hard for so little reward. I booed my favourites; like Betty Buckley, for embarrassing the two of us by appearing in this worthless trash, I booed the producer, the director, the gyrations of Debbie Allen's offensive choreography. Most of all, I booed the state of theater, the state of mind that could actually produce this.

I have never been more offended by any production I have ever seen, and I apologise for being rude. But you owe me an apology as well.[41]

Aware of the brewing negativity and baffled by the seemingly inconsequential daily changes, the writers braced themselves for the impending critical response.

Pitchford   I stopped going to see the show. I stayed in my apartment and I ate a lot of ice cream. You know, I never gained any weight when I performed in New York, and not since. But during that preview period, I gained fifteen pounds. I only left the house to buy new pants.

To encourage sales, Buckley was drafted into promotional appearances on local television, where she quickly encountered some of the cynicism facing the production. 'The show's definitely gonna open!' she told one probing interviewer. 'We're getting standing ovations every night since we started previewing . . . the audience loves it.'[42]

A television commercial was filmed; in it, the camera zooms in on a teenage girl cowering in a mysterious corridor as voices whisper 'Carrie' above a cacophony of flashing lasers and red lights. A voiceover at the end tells the viewer that 'There's never been a musical like her.' It never aired.[43]

Opening night

The show officially opened – finally – to the press on Thursday, 12 May 1988. Gathered on stage before the doors were flung open, the company cheered dancer

---

[41]A tasteful fold on the Xeroxed copy of the letter disguises the sender's signature.

[42]CarrieTheMusicalcom, *Carrie: The Musical: Betty Buckley TV Interview*, YouTube, 1988, available online: https://www.youtube.com/watch?v=SXxyosPA5-E&t=16s (accessed 5 May 2022).

[43]At the 2003 Tony Awards ceremony, while the real commercial breaks were playing on TV, old TV ads from infamous Broadway shows were projected onto the stage curtain. When *Carrie*'s ad appeared on the big screen, Debbie Allen is said to have stood up and shouted, 'That's my show!'

IMAGE 4.2 Ensemble member Scott Wise receives his 'Gypsy Robe' on stage before opening night. Suzanne Thomas (photographer).

Scott Wise as he was awarded the 'Gypsy Robe', a traditional ceremony in which a robe decorated by the casts of other Broadway shows is awarded to the Ensemble member with the most credits in a new show (Image 4.2).

Audience members, critics and celebrity guests including Stephen King, Kevin Bacon, Joan Jett and Allen's husband Norm Nixon crowded into the theatre past the flashbulbs of the press.[44] Each attendee was given a Playbill and a copy of King's novel, freshly reprinted with the musical's logo.

Company members exchanged gifts. Kurz handed out Tiffany pendants engraved with the show's logo. McKneely gave his fellow cast-mates T-shirts emblazoned with a memorable quote from the show, 'CARRIE WHITE EATS SHIT!'

It was the night the writers had been dreading, and tensions were high. The run in Stratford had been a fixed length and well sold; the British reviews may have been harsh, but they had little impact on potential sales for its limited run. In New York, the critics could make or break a show; indeed, it was not uncommon for badly received productions to post closing notices in a matter of days. The reviews were the one element over which producers, investors and theatre owners had to relinquish control.

---

[44]Footage in the 'Kurz documentary' shows the producer asking his assistant if Donald Trump is coming. She confirms he is not.

The performance went off without a hitch – nobody came close to decapitation, at least – and the cast received a standing ovation. One journalist commented that he hadn't 'seen a Broadway crowd react like this in a long, long time'.[45]

After a brief meet and greet with Stephen King backstage,[46] the company headed to a post-show party at a nearby nightclub, Stringfellows, where Kurz's documentary crew waited to solicit thoughts and feedback from the invited guests. In the footage, Hands responds confidently in German, saying that he thinks 'Fritz is a great man, a friend, he loves theatre and he wanted to do an American musical on Broadway. He had to do that, and he did it, by himself, and for me, because he's a friend. I'm happy and it's an adventure.'[47]

The voiceover introduces a reluctant-looking Andrew Lloyd Webber who, when pressed for his thoughts, says, 'I'd rather not say ... you shouldn't ask me.'[48] Kurz himself recalled more enthusiasm from the young composer, writing in his autobiography that, 'Andrew Lloyd Webber sat next to me until the wee hours. We discussed the show, praised the highlights, and appreciated the musical ideas. [He] seemed impressed and I listened to the words of the Master that night with great pleasure.'[49]

D'Amboise When you go to an opening night party, you can feel in the room within an hour whether it's bad reviews or it's good. You always know. I hate that so much.

Mark Santoro (Ensemble, Stratford and Broadway) We kinda knew the show wasn't good, but you keep your hopes up. I was young and naive and wanted so bad to be in a Broadway show ...

Triplett I remember the papers coming in. It felt like being in an old MGM film. Somebody literally came in with a pile of *New York Times* and they were given out, and we all flipped through and then, you know, the penny dropped because of the opening sentence ...

Wreckage

'Those who have the time and money to waste on one Anglo-American musical wreck on Broadway this year might well choose *Carrie*,' declared Frank Rich, the so-called 'butcher of Broadway', alluding to his less than complimentary recent

---

[45]Jacques le Sourd, '"Carrie" Fires Up Audience with Gothic Fun', *The Daily Times*, Mamaroneck, New York, 13 May 1988, 65.
[46]In footage, Buckley can be heard reminding King that they have met before at an audition, likely for the *Carrie* movie (Kurz documentary).
[47]Kurz documentary (translated).
[48]Ibid.
[49]Kurz, *Der Musical-Mann*, 13.

review of *Chess*. 'Most of *Carrie* is just a typical musical theater botch'. The cast wear 'grotesque, sub-Atlantic City costumes', and Allen 'shouldn't wait another moment to return to her performing career'. 'The only surge in Michael Gore's otherwise faceless bubblegum music is in those songs in which Carrie and her mother do battle', while Pitchford's lyrics are full of 'whopping clichés' and Cohen's book scenes are nothing more than a 'plodding series of song-and-scenery cues'.[50]

Kurz was well aware of the damage that a scathing *Times* review could cause. 'That venerable newspaper wielded a virtual monopoly in those years … A rave review was like a big check – a pan sent the entire team into a deep depression. On that night, Frank Rich struck a blow', he recalled in his autobiography. 'When a butcher sharpens his knife and writes in a fit of bloodlust, you don't stand a chance. That's what we experienced on that memorable night … We were victims of one of the nastiest theatre critics ever to be published.'[51]

Buckley   I remember going to the party and hearing about the reviews. I was driven home, and I asked the driver to stop at a news stand, so I could pick up the *New York Times* and read it for myself. Frank Rich loathed the show. But he did like Linzi and me. His kind comments were buried in all of the negativity. I remember sitting in the back seat, laughing, because it was worded so carefully that it was clear he wanted the show to die, and he wouldn't even give a quote about us that we could use.

Rich's review was not the only stinker: the onslaught had only just started.

In the 'ludicrously campy high school scenes', *Time*'s William A. Henry III cruelly declared that the girls 'look and dress like twenty-eight-year old hookers',[52] whilst *Newsday*'s Linda Winer – whose review was arguably harsher than Rich's – agreed that the high school scenes were 'populated with twenty-eight-year-old Playmates'.[53] In comments that would raise more eyebrows nowadays, the no-doubt picturesque Howard Kissel from the *Daily Post* declared that 'the girls don't look like teenagers at all. Their bodies don't have the bloom of youth. They're either too angular or too fleshy. Their faces are hard and haggard, like they've just come off a rough bus-and-truck tour playing the hookers in *Sweet Charity*'.[54]

Thomas   All these comments about middle-aged women! Bearing in mind that not one of us was over the age of twenty-three. I was like, 'I'm twenty, twenty! She's twenty-one!'

After getting his observations on the female cast members' bodies out of the way, Kissel accurately predicted that *Carrie* was 'likely to become the new reference point

---

[50]Frank Rich, 'The Telekinetic "Carrie," with Music', *The New York Times*, 13 May 1988, 63.
[51]Kurz, *Der Musical-Mann*, 14.
[52]Henry III, 'Theater'.
[53]Linda Winer, '"Carrie": Staging a Horror on Broadway', *Newsday*, 13 May 1988, 221.
[54]Howard Kissel, 'Don't "Carrie" Me Back to Ol' Virginny', *Daily News*, 13 May 1988, 59.

for Broadway atrocities'. In another flashback to the previous month's frosty reaction to *Chess*, he recalled that 'halfway through *Carrie*, I suddenly wished I could take back some of the nasty things I said a few weeks ago about *Chess*, because *Carrie* is so disgusting it makes *Chess* look adorable … Everything about the show is tacky', he declared. 'Allen's choreography, apart from one number that reminds you of the Bob Fosse steps she did in *Sweet Charity*, is disco stuff, energetic but meaningless …' Gore's music is 'either monotonously hard-driving or tiresomely sweet', and the lyrics contained 'enough gratuitous vulgarity that I wouldn't send a child'.[55]

Winer pulled no punches in her critique of the show beyond the girls' appearances, declaring within two paragraphs that the 'music is numbingly senseless', the choreography 'like an aerobics workout for a Vegas take-off of *I Dream of Jeannie*', and that the show, overall, was 'stupendously, fabulously terrible – ineptly conceived, sleazy, irrational from moment to moment, the rare kind of production that stretches way beyond bad to mythic lousiness'.[56] Ouch.

The *New Yorker*'s Mimi Kramer joined the onslaught off the bat with the headline 'Bloody Awful'. She compared *Carrie* to other teen-dance stories like *Saturday Night Fever, Flashdance, Dirty Dancing* and *Footloose* in which characters use their dance ability to escape their dreary backgrounds, but that '*Footloose* and *Dirty Dancing* actually have some good numbers; *Carrie* doesn't.' 'It's hard to say which is more vulgar, Miss Allen's choreography or Mr Ray's performance,' she continues, 'but the three performers who, with Ray, form the quartet of principal high-schoolers are almost as unpleasant to watch as he is … it's sad to see a Broadway stage filled with so many manifestly untalented performers'.[57]

The *Los Angeles Times* took a swipe at Hands and the British tryout: 'Maybe American musicals should have American directors and try out in Boston.'[58] John Simon in *New York* suggested the pioneering Equity split would 'have been better used elsewhere', praising Hands' lighting but not much else, declaring the show a 'gutless shocker' and a 'flavourless fricassee … an unstable mixture that crumbles on exposure to the stage'.[59]

The *Washington Post*'s David Richards declared that 'if Caesar's Palace were to go in for contemporary opera, the results might look like this', with special effects that were 'eye-catching', but a score that was not 'particularly distinctive' with 'insipid' lyrics. 'By abstracting the tale … the creators have robbed *Carrie* of everything that is troubling, funny, scary … the musical is vague and vaguely ludicrous'.[60]

[55]Ibid.
[56]Winer, '"Carrie": Staging a Horror'.
[57]Kramer, 'Bloody Awful'.
[58]Harper, 'STAGE: Horrors!'
[59]John Simon, 'Blood and No Guts', *New York*, 23 May 1988.
[60]David Richards, 'N.Y.'s Hairy "Carrie"', *The Washington Post*, 13 May 1988, available online: https://www.washingtonpost.com/archive/lifestyle/1988/05/13/nys-hairy-carrie/cb4fe984-9a9e-4be4-8322-a194fa373489/ (accessed 5 May 2022).

The evening TV news shows – not a fixture that the team had had to worry about in Stratford, but very much part and parcel of the New York theatre landscape – leapt on the opportunity to regurgitate the scathing critiques to their late-night viewers, accompanying readings of the notices with suitably horrified facial expressions and much gleeful gasping. Pat Collins of the *News at Ten* claimed that she wished Stephen King's rabid dog character Cujo would show up and put an end to it all. 'In all my years of reviewing, this is right up there in the Top 10 of the worst musicals I have ever seen,' she concluded. Over on Fox's *The Ten O'Clock News*, Stewart Klein declared from the off that '*Carrie* is a catastrophe'.

'This is one of the shows where everything is bad – even the costumes are ugly,' declared Joel Siegel on ABC News. 'This book and score would fail a college course in musical theatre, the direction and staging is even worse . . . *Carrie* is horrible.' he concluded. 'At least the weather's nice,' his co-host chipped in.

Although their praise was somewhat drowned out by the overarching negativity, the leading ladies were treated more kindly, with raves for Buckley's 'powerful, restrained'[61] turn and Hateley's 'lovely performance'.[62] *Time* declared that their shared scenes 'crackled with longing'.[63] Pia Lindstrom's WNBC News review was somewhat more sanguine than the other television critics, calling Buckley 'vividly intense' and Hateley 'talented' but that overall the show 'wears thin' and was 'garish'.

Other reviewers were more appreciative of the endeavour as a whole. British-born Clive Barnes' *New York Post* review was one of the few metropolitan titles to give the show a strong notice, admitting that, despite all of the incidents that 'haunted' its road to Broadway, it 'has unexpectedly emerged as a strong, effective and remarkably coherent piece of terrific total theater', with a finale of 'biblical proportions', 'spartan, epic directness' from Hands and 'wonderfully dense and energized' choreography from Allen. Even the 'unusually special' effects get a positive nod, with performances labelled 'glitteringly venomous' (d'Amboise), 'superbly dramatic' (Buckley, with a 'vinegar and molasses voice') and 'childlike innocence like a fallen angel' (Hateley). The only aspect Barnes cast doubt upon was the 'unmemorable' music.[64]

Jacques le Sourd, a critic for the Gannett chain of newspapers whose reviews were syndicated nationally, said that 'the show has a no-holds-barred boldness and a high-pitched energy that electrifies the audience'. Le Sourd assumed the show's ostentatiousness was deliberate and praised the creators for approaching the material with wit: 'they've done it big, it works, and it's great gothic fun'. The scenic design provides 'bold, stylized settings' and Hands' lighting work is 'relentlessly spectacular', the staircase finale 'a classic of late-20th century showmanship' with

[61]Kerensky, '"Carrie"'.
[62]Winer, '"Carrie": Staging a Horror'.
[63]Henry III, 'Theater'.
[64]Clive Barnes, 'Musical "Carrie" Soars on Blood, Guts and Gore', *New York Post*, 13 May 1988, 19.

Gore's 'throbbing rock score' and Pitchford's 'witty lyrics' rounding out the evening … 'a bloody good show'.[65] Industry paper *Back Stage* dismissed the choreography and most of the songs but praised the leading ladies and the work of Hands, declaring the show 'brilliantly played, superbly directed and dazzlingly lit'.[66]

The *Bangor Daily News* – dedicating substantial column inches to the show as the paper of Stephen King's hometown – took the unusual step of reproducing dual reviews from other titles, one positive, one not so. Michael Kuchwara's negative *Associated Press* notice described the show as 'not quite bad enough to be good … [it] vacillates between serious and schlock', whereas William B. Collins' report from the *Philadelphia Inquirer* praised the show, calling it a 'pop spectacle' with the scenery, lighting and dancing making a 'sensational impact'. He praised d'Amboise's dancing 'of dynamic force … the definitive personification of the gratuitous bully'.[67] A photo of King posing with Buckley and Allen backstage accompanied the piece.

King himself said that enjoyed the show. 'I liked it a lot,' he said. 'In fact, I liked it for most of the reasons that Frank Rich did not. He and I saw the same show. We just drew different conclusions from different perspectives.'[68] An online scan of a Playbill, autographed by King in 1994, is jovially inscribed: 'It was great while it lasted, eh?'

Back on the RSC's home turf, the British tabloids reported on the unprecedented battering, gleefully quoting the most horrible reviews as if to endorse their own recent opinions. 'The Broadway knives are out,'[69] *Daily Mail* readers were informed.

The writers were devastated, despite their long-founded suspicions that the American critics would cast even harsher judgement than their British counterparts.

Cohen   Truthfully, we hoped that the casting of Betty and her dynamic relationship with Linzi would make a huge difference. And it did – their teaming was thrilling and everything we'd hoped, and the preview audiences went crazy at their numbers together. But almost everything else in the show, from the tone to the design to the costumes, made us crazy. Bottom line, if we as authors had loved this production, it would have been easier to accept the negative reviews, but it was painful to read in print the very things we thought were wrong with the show which we had tried to get Terry to address for months, to no avail. That said, for every Frank Rich pan in the *Times*, there was Clive Barnes' rave in the *Post*.

---

[65]Le Sourd, '"Carrie" Fires Up Audience'.

[66]Martin Schaeffer, 'Theatre Reviews', *Back Stage*, 20 May 1988, 30A.

[67]Michael Kuchwara and William B. Collins, 'Broadway Musical "Carrie" isn't Bad Enough to Be Good', *The Bangor Daily News*, 17 May 1988, 16.

[68]Quoted in George Beahm, *Stephen King from A to Z* (Kansas City, KS: Andrews McMeel Publishing, 1998), 31.

[69]'Broadway Knives are Out for Carrie', *Daily Mail*, 14 May 1988.

Pitchford   Some of the reviews had been positive, and even the worst ones had some positive lines buried deep within them, but there was no effort made to amplify those. We could have pulled a page full of wonderful quotes and splashed them across full-page ads in the *New York Times*. But our producer had never produced on Broadway before. He thought that the show was going to sell itself. There was no Plan B.

On Saturday, 14 May, the day after the reviews landed, the company gathered at the Virginia for a two-show day.

Cohen   Before the matinee, Michael and I met with Fritz along with the company manager outside the theatre, and he told us that he'd decided – in spite of the reviews – to make a go of it, and asked that I return home and write ad copy for a radio commercial. His idea was to have Linzi say, 'Hi, this is Carrie. Some people love me, some hate me. Come see me and decide for yourself. If you don't like the show, we'll give you your money back.'

Pitchford   He said, 'We are going to outrun these reviews. Don't be discouraged. We're going to give this a shot. We have the audience behind us. You hear them out there every night . . .'

Thomas   'The audiences seem to love it. We get standing ovations. So, we're going to keep it going and see if word of mouth can keep the show up.' That was what we were told.

Pitchford   Hugs and kisses. Lots and lots of love flowed between him and the cast. They went on to do the show.

Cohen   I went home after the matinee to work on the radio spots. Michael and I came back for the evening show four hours later, only to find that Kurz had posted the closing notice, closed all the bank accounts, and reportedly had gotten on a private plane to return to Germany without as much as a goodbye to the authors, Terry or the cast, leaving no money to pay salaries. We all felt utterly sandbagged.

Pitchford   The theatre owners in New York, who were his co-producers, did not find this out until Monday morning.

Thomas   Someone came on stage and told us all, 'Sorry, change of plan. We're closing.'

Hateley   I recall someone telling me in my dressing room – at least they had the decency to do that – that the show was closing tomorrow. So, literally just before I was about to go on stage, I had to pull myself together and do the Saturday night show knowing we were coming off the next day.

Michelle Nelson (Ensemble, Stratford and Broadway)   I remember arriving at the theatre to a lot of tears. It was the most devastating shock for us all.

Hateley told a newspaper, 'All around me there were tears, but I had to choke mine back. I was going to give a performance in a few minutes' time. It was a tearful one. But it was the best I've ever given.'[70]

Kurz refutes this sequence of events, describing them in his memoir as 'complete nonsense',[71] but declined to be interviewed for this project. In the book, he recalled how – after a turbulent few nights agonizing over how to save the show – he visited the Box Office to see how sales were going, to learn that only $200 had been taken. 'At that moment I had no more doubts: the show was already dead,' he said –

Mentally I put on my businessman's hat. How could the show continue? $7 million was already sunk into *Carrie* . . . Careers, livelihoods, the future of entire families depended on whether it continued. But my passion, my own artistic commitment and even my responsibility to the team, did not blind me to the disaster that we were facing. It couldn't have been worse.[72]

Kurz said he consulted friends in Hollywood who advised him to take immediate action, despite an offer of an additional $2 million from his investors. 'Years earlier on the stock exchange I had learned a wise saying that comforted me now in this difficult hour: "Don't throw good money after bad" . . . [I said], "Nobody's investing another dollar. Over my dead body. We just lost $7 million – not one more cent!"'[73]

Kurz recalled informing Buckley privately in her dressing room: 'She put her slender arm around me and said very tenderly, "Fritz, you're closing the show, right?" I was flustered, took a deep breath, tried to answer, then she added: "A decision like that builds character",' he wrote:

With tears in my eyes I looked at her, I had to cry and laugh at the same time . . . Not for a moment did she think about how much money she would lose and what the quick closing of the show would mean for her career. She saw my frustrated face and, instead of heaping on the reproach, she responded with kindness. I'll never forget that moment.[74]

Buckley The closing notice was a surprise because we had been reassured that more funding was coming, that we were going to keep going.

Hateley Money was pulled very quickly before people had time to say, 'Well, hang on a minute . . .' There were a lot of different elements that created the

---

[70]Anthea Gerrie, 'Linzi Flies Home: The Only Good Thing to Come Out of *Carrie*', *Daily Mail*, 21 May 1988.
[71]Kurz, *Der Musical-Mann*, 19.
[72]Kurz, *Der Musical-Mann*, 16.
[73]Ibid., 17.
[74]Ibid., 18.

drama and the speed of which the show came off. It was a moment of panic and disbelief!

The quick decision to close was a move that would save Kurz and his investors 'an estimated $150,000–$175,000 [on top of the loss], the difference between another week's operating costs and the projected box-office income',[75] William A. Henry III wrote in *Time* the following month. According to Henry's estimates, a reserve fund of around $2 million would have been needed to pay for advertising costs and cover losses for a couple of months, until there was even a hope that word-of-mouth would drown out the notices. 'The technical staff, the press agent, even the creators thought they had been assured of at least one more week.'[76] he wrote. Kurz told Henry, 'I made an economic decision to cut my losses. Broadway is Russian roulette, and I am not a gambler.' Christopher Tookey in *Telegraph* magazine estimated a personal $3 million loss for Kurz alone, not including his team of investors.[77]

> **Hateley**   All I wanted to do was get home. I just wanted to be out of this crazy city and this whole situation. Now, it would be different, I would handle it better. But at the time, all I wanted to do was just leave this place where I felt so unwanted.

Hands had already departed for the UK to start rehearsals for a London production of *Julius Caesar*. At home, he listened to an answer-phone message from Cohen and Gore informing him that the show would close less than twenty-four hours later.

Pitchford, who had returned to Los Angeles the day after opening night to work on a film project, had been expecting to return to New York later in the week to assist with the show's cast recording, only to learn it had been cancelled by the record company.

> **Pitchford**   It was very abrupt. Heartbreaking. All of us were thrown backwards, as if from an enormous blast. Funnily enough, it was Terry who called to tell me. The phone call was a *mea culpa*. It was a lot of 'I wanted to do this, and I don't think that people understood what it was that I was trying to accomplish.' By that time, the trust between us was destroyed. He had sold us a bill of goods that he had never delivered on, and then shut us out of the process and then was trying to do a 'Monday morning quarterback' on, you know, a Saturday.

---

[75]Henry III, William A. (May 30, 1988), 'Theater: The Biggest All-Time Flop Ever', *Time* (http://content.time.com/time/magazine/article/0,9171,967517,00.html
[76]Ibid.
[77]Tookey, 'Flop!'

Cohen   Michael and I made a quick foray to Jujamcyn to see if they would supply an infusion of money to give the show a chance to catch on, but it was too little, too late. We were toast.

Bailey   I think Ralph [Koltai] was pretty devastated. He had been working on the show for nearly three years by this time, and had been repeatedly assured by Terry that they were heading for a hit – there was even talk of a range of *Carrie* clothes based on the costumes for the show![78] Instead it was all over in five days.

Hateley   This wasn't them just saying, 'Very sorry, we're going to give you four weeks' notice.' You know, the treatment we received was catastrophic, and appalling.

D'Amboise   The way they handled it was so poor. It was just sort of like, 'Goodbye!' Sally Ann Triplett, who had a year's lease or whatever on her boat, suddenly had to leave it. The English people were just sitting there . . . They didn't get to spend time in New York. It was devastating for them.

Opie   I think everyone realized in their own way that the show had major flaws, but after such effort and commitment it's hard to accept that it was a complete failure. Should it have lasted longer – yes. Could it have lasted longer – no.

Kenny Linden (Ensemble, Stratford and Broadway)   I used my camera to record everybody backstage on the last day, saying goodbye. Betty makes a speech on stage to the camera.

In Linden's grainy footage, an adamant Buckley says, 'I want you all to know in this audience, watching this video tape on this special occasion, that we here at *Carrie* are proud of our work, we know that we had a great show, we get standing ovations every night, and this is just what can happen in big business, show business. *C'est la vie*!' In the next shot, Ensemble member Scott Wise laments that the show should have done more previews, building up cash reserves before the critics were allowed in. Another says, 'It's the last show, and we don't want to leave, we were very good and we should have stayed.'

Thomas   The last performance, the whole audience stood and cheered, and they wouldn't leave. They put the lights up. We all just stood on stage. They kept clapping. It was like no-one wanted to let it go. They couldn't get people out of the theatre.

One journalist who purchased tickets to what was – unbeknownst to him – the final performance described the closing moments, with Hateley 'standing stage

---

[78]It is fun to imagine which garments might have featured in this range . . .

center bawling her eyes out, streaking the red glop', and Buckley with 'blotches of red on her, too, weeping openly, kissing and caressing her co-star, turning to kiss and hug other red-stained cast members. This was no ordinary curtain call. It all became clear. This had to be the very last performance of *Carrie*.' Earlier he had spotted Allen 'videotaping the twenty-or more chorus members at work' for 'fine-tuning, I surmised, not recordkeeping'.[79]

And that was it. *Carrie* had closed on Broadway after just sixteen previews and five regular performances. Immediate press reports suggested a loss of $7 million, later articles round the figure up to $8 million. It had swiftly overtaken 1986's *Rags* – which had lost $5.25 million – as the biggest flop in Broadway history. Suffice to say, the investment gathered by Kurtz, including the $500,000 from Jujamcyn Theatres, was swallowed up by the closure.

> **Hateley** Betty made a point of telling me 'This is not your fault, and what we achieved was something exceptional.' She said it at the time, and she continues to say that the work we did on *Carrie* was ahead of its time, and something to be very proud of.

> **Pitchford** The cast left after the Sunday matinee. The British cast members had to be told 'Get out of your apartment. Pack your bags. Go.' It was devastating.

At the stage door, cast members were spotted leaving the theatre carrying boxes of their belongings including rolled-up posters and the plastic strips from the lobby cast board bearing their names. Family and friends waited 'sad-faced, as though at a wake'.[80] After an hour, Buckley emerged to sign autographs before returning to her dressing room. Last of all, seventeen-year-old Hateley emerged, 'a RSC pin on her blue dress, her skin still mottled red. "You'd better believe it doesn't come off!"'[81] she joked with the final fans.

The Broadway community was surprised at the speed in which the show ended. It was a disastrous week on the Great White Way: as well as *Carrie*, two other musicals closed quickly after short runs, *The Gospel at Colonus*, starring Morgan Freeman at the Lunt-Fontanne, capitalized at $1.4 million, and *Mail* at the Music Box, which had cost $2.5 million.[82]

> **Hateley** I was in New York for the next three days after it closed and people kept coming up to me saying, 'I can't believe it's come off, we wanted to see it!' It was a very confusing time. I left as quickly as I could, because I just wanted to get back to London, but I wanted to travel home with my parents so we killed a few days so we could all be together.

---

[79]Peter Citron, '"Carrie" Faces Final Broadway Curtain', *Omaha World-Herald*, 17 May 1988.
[80]Ibid.
[81]Ibid.
[82]Ian Ball, 'RSC Musical £3.7m Flop on Broadway', *Daily Telegraph*, 18 May 1988.

'I think they took it worse than I did,' she told a reporter. 'They were so hurt for me about all the things that were said about the show, when, in fact, nothing but good has come out of it for me. Good reviews, great exposure and terrific practice for the future.'[83]

Just before departing for the UK, Hateley received a call from Joe Lorden, the Stage Manager.

Hateley   He said, 'Come down to the theatre,' and I was like, 'Oh, no, I'm not sure.' And he said, 'No, come down!' I went there and he had saved all of the Front of House panels that I was pictured on. He said, 'Take these.' So I have, in my loft, the Broadway Front of House pictures from *Carrie*.

Triplett   I had a really cool boyfriend and we went off to Thailand after that. Then I went straight back into *Follies*. I was really lucky. I've always tried to be, like, 'whatever is meant to be is meant to be'. I was just grateful for the time we'd had and what we'd done.

Thomas   One of the crew had been chasing me about joining his sailing yacht crew on this trip he was planning, and I'd been saying, 'Well, I can't, I'm doing this!' Then, suddenly I was free, so that's what I did next.

Nelson   Debbie invited myself and Michèle Du Verney to go to LA and appear in her television special. So we went, and even stayed at her home.

Mary Ann Oedy (Ensemble, Stratford and Broadway)   It really hurt. I took it personally. A lot of the other dancers just moved on like it was nothing. Lots of them went to audition for *Jerome Robbins' Broadway*.[84] I had the opportunity to audition too, but I wanted to go home to Los Angeles and lick my wounds.

Scott Wise (Ensemble, Stratford and Broadway)   It was sad. You work so hard on something that you know is sinking. You've been living on rehearsal salary for months, so you've put nothing away. I had a wife and daughter to take care of.

Hateley   We were all left without any money. We had nothing . . . I went to London and went back on the dole![85]

Back on British soil, Hands once again faced a press onslaught, the critics now smug in the knowledge that their predictions of a Broadway bloodbath had come

---

[83]Gerrie, 'Linzi Flies Home'.

[84]The anthology show, featuring numbers from shows either directed or choreographed by Jerome Robbins, opened in February 1989. From the *Carrie* alumni in the cast, Charlotte d'Amboise was nominated for a Tony Award for Best Actress in a Musical and Scott Wise was nominated for a Drama Desk Award for Outstanding Actor in a Musical. The show also featured Ensemble members Joey Mckneely and Mary Ann Lamb.

[85]Slang for the UK's unemployment state benefit payment.

true. The *Daily Express* described the RSC as 'shell-shocked,' quoting the repentant director: 'Broadway is an exciting place, but it's like warfare. Don't go without a helmet on. I didn't know what I was getting into. All of us were incredibly inexperienced. It was like wrestling with a boa constrictor.'[86]

In the *Daily Mail*, he placed the blame for the show's fate on Frank Rich's *New York Times* review but appeared to absolve Kurz, noting that: '*Carrie* played to standing ovations but the only way to surmount a [negative] review from Rich is to have a huge advance booking or a huge reserve. It had neither and therefore Kurz ... took the decision to close the show.'[87]

Hands doggedly reminded journalists that the company itself had not lost out financially, despite a slew of headlines focussing on the show's severe overall losses. Facing the rumours that the RSC's Board of Governors was set to sack him or ask him to leave, the beleaguered Artistic Director – suffering from severe hay fever and flu, on top of everything – told the *Independent* that, 'there is absolutely no question of my being asked to go ... nor has there ever been in the history of the RSC that question, and we have had ups and downs, good years and bad. I don't know where this rumour grew up from. Secondly: that I myself would choose to go? It is not something I have contemplated.'[88] Asked a couple of weeks later by the *Independent* how it felt to be at the epicentre of the *Carrie* disaster, he told the reporter, in a convoluted response that took 'fifteen minutes, including pauses,' 'It's difficult to answer and I am not being evasive ... I am in the middle of it so I am still agonising ... You sift out the processes of failure.'[89]

The naysayers in the British press had been proven right about one thing: the RSC had taken a severe reputational risk, and it had not paid off. 'If the New York *Carrie* is dead ... her ghost will haunt the Royal Shakespeare Company for quite some time,'[90] predicted the *Wall Street Journal*.

When *Telegraph* magazine interviewed Hands later in the year, he said, 'Should it have been taken off? My answer has to be: No. I do not believe you should take off a show that has 75 to 100 per cent standing ovations. All my RSC training was saying: you don't do it.'[91] In a retrospective upon his RSC retirement in 1991, he defended the show by focussing on the fiscal rewards from its Stratford season. 'Why should there be such *schadenfreude* about what was, after all, a musical mounted in our Stratford winter season and one which earned us enough money, a quarter of a million, to programme trilogies of Bond and Barker plays?'[92] Though

[86]Philip Finn, 'Musical Carrie is $4.5m U.S. Flop', *Daily Express*, 18 May 1988.
[87]George Gordon, 'RSC Horror as Broadway Curtain Falls on Carrie', *Daily Mail*, 18 May 1988.
[88]Lawson, 'Hands on His Knees'
[89]Ibid.
[90]Trucco, '"Carrie" Ghost'.
[91]Tookey, 'Flop!'
[92]Michael Billington, 'Cash and Carrie', *The Guardian*, 4 July 1991, 24.

Hands appeared to have no regrets about the way he staged the show, he did appear to admit his naivety and lack of experience with the musical genre, telling the *Daily Mail* that 'it has been an extraordinary adventure trying to do something I feel that, to be absolutely honest, I am not sure I am good enough for'.[93]

Journalists caught up with Hateley upon her return to her hometown of Tamworth. She told her local paper that 'it was heart-breaking … the audiences absolutely adored it. They really raved about it – we were getting standing ovations and we were the talk of the town'. An RSC spokesperson said, 'I have no doubt she will go on to succeed elsewhere. She has done incredibly well.'[94] According to the *Daily Mail*, there were three things on Hateley's mind as she landed in London: surprising her boyfriend, having a long, hot bath, and 'the small matter of what to do with the rest of her life'. Proclaiming her to be 'the only good thing to have come out of *Carrie*', the reporter calls Hateley's stint on Broadway 'a personal triumph, an unforgettable experience and a career showcase bar none'.[95]

Those who had not found time to see *Carrie* in its brief Broadway engagement would quickly regret missing one of the most talked-about shows of a generation.

Lavine   If everybody who says they saw it at the Virginia Theatre actually saw it, we would still be running.

According to the Broadway League's published grosses, *Carrie* was seen by 17,752 people in New York. The figures do not distinguish between paid-for tickets and 'comps' for opening night guests, investors and associates of the show, but sales grossed $341,396 during its run. The average ticket price in its first week of performances was $17.75, dipping slightly to $17.42 in its second and increasing to $22.56 in its closing week.[96]

The grosses indicate that attendance was decent, but that the show was certainly not a complete sell-out; during its brief run it achieved a capacity of 72 per cent (week one, five performances), 74 per cent (week two, eight performances) and 62 per cent (week three, eight performances). Statistics for individual performances are not available, but the final week's capacity suggests that either the closing performances were not as well sold as suggested, or the performances at the start of the final week – in the immediate wake of the reviews – were extremely quiet, with attendance spiking once the closure was announced.

In addition, the show's gross potential – the percentage of the greatest possible income figure achieved – was low, at 30 per cent in week one, 28 per cent in week two, and 30 per cent in the final week, suggesting that audiences were buying cheaper tickets or that many of the tickets were complimentary. Giving away

---

[93]Gordon, 'RSC Horror'.
[94]Sue Fisher, 'Star Survivor of a Stage Disaster', *Tamworth Herald*, 20 May 1988.
[95]Gerrie, 'Linzi Flies Home'.
[96]Accessible online: broadwayleague.com.

tickets is not an uncommon practice during the previews of a new musical, but is surprising considering the recollections of tickets being hard to come by. In comparison, *Les Misérables* achieved 95 per cent gross potential and 100 per cent capacity in the same period, and even *Chess* – poorly received by critics – achieved between 79 and 81 per cent gross potential and between 81 and 88 per cent capacity in the same three-week period of May 1988, according to the Broadway League figures.

In far less time than it took to install it, the Virginia Theatre was stripped of the show's iconic set. The stark black and red logo was removed from its marquee. Within days, the only trace of the ill-fated production was the deep black paint on the auditorium walls, which would remain for some years to come.[97]

Philip Argent (audience member, Stratford)   I happened to be in New York just as it closed and I remember seeing the sets being thrown into skips outside the Virginia Theatre. I wish I'd been carrying a camera.

Carrie's short life on Broadway was over. But she had certainly made her mark, and would not be quickly forgotten.

---

[97]The ominous black walls remained until the theatre was renovated in 1994 (Peter Slatin, 'A Broadway Showplace Returns to the Renaissance', *The New York Times*, 22 January 1995, 250).

PART TWO

THE SHOW

5 ACT ONE: BRAS, CARS AND UNITARDS

As audiences file into the Royal Shakespeare Theatre, they encounter a foreboding red hue from the filtered house lights. On Broadway, the interior walls of the Virginia Theatre have been freshly painted a deep black.

'Overture'

The show kicks off with a bold Overture. The orchestra – twenty-eight-strong in Stratford, twenty-three on Broadway – strikes up with a drumroll, and after a few seconds . . .

Stephen Dolginoff (audience member, Broadway)   Boom! The entire house is plunged into darkness. People screamed, because it was so effective. All they did was flick a light switch. I'd never seen anything like it.

Scott Briefer (audience member, Broadway)   There was no dimming of the house lights. I was, like, 'Whoa! Cool!' I was hooked.

James Noone (audience member, Broadway)   Even the exit signs went off, so the theatre was pitch black. The audience screamed every time I saw it. Half the time people were still trying to find their seats!

Dolginoff   And then the pulsing Overture starts, and it just sounds great. I just remember thinking, 'Oh, my God, this is gonna be so wonderful.'

The Stratford and Broadway Overtures are quite different (and both would evolve during their respective runs) – the former is an eerie soundscape of discordant notes and echoing screams, while the latter is a minute-long stampeding montage of melodies from the score to come.

Mark Silver (audience member, Broadway)   I'm sitting in the dark with my mouth open thinking 'This is *Carrie*! The musical! I just can't believe I'm sitting here!' It was a thrill. I'll never forget it.

Philip Argent (audience member, Stratford)   I remember a couple sitting in front of me, putting their fingers in their ears as the over-amplified orchestra made their first ear-splitting noises. They were clearly used to much quieter fare.

Dolginoff   I had literally no idea what I was going to see next.

As the Overture ends, a plain black scrim rises, and the audience glimpses designer Ralph Koltai's enormous box set for the first time. It was, perhaps, not the all-American high school setting they had expected.

Briefer   What we saw was a completely contained white space with a slightly plasticky sheen to it, which I thought was to protect it from the blood that was coming.

Argent   It had a plasticky, shiny surface which looked nice and easy to wipe clean.

Dolginoff   It looked so unusual. I remember thinking, 'Oh, there's gonna be blood all over that!' How wrong I was.

'In'

The female Ensemble are glimpsed in the midst of an energetic exercise routine led by the spirited Miss Gardner (Darlene Love). Some recordings feature a countdown of, '5, 6, 7, 8!' as the song starts.

Dolginoff   Darlene Love walks down through the girls, and the audience applauds for her, and she seemed to sort of acknowledge the applause!

The review in *Time* confirms that, bizarrely, Love 'breaks character to step forward and smile in acknowledgement of the audience's greeting'.[1] According to the *Daily News*, she is 'dressed like a hostess in a cocktail lounge'[2] in an all-white suit, gathered at the waist with a red ribbon. She wears red wristbands and immaculate white pumps, all of which seem unlikely attire for teaching an exercise class. She barks orders at the girls:

All right ladies, I wanna see sweat!
I keep on looking but I ain't seen it yet!
The more you suffer the tougher you get!
So come on, ladies, work, work, work, work!

Dolginoff   That reminded me so much of Debbie Allen.

---

[1] Henry III, 'Theater'.
[2] Kissel, 'Don't "Carrie" Me Back'.

As she prowls around the gym yelling lyrics like, 'I wanna see sweat!', Love's rallying character does indeed bring to mind Allen's portrayal of dance teacher Lydia Grant in *Fame*, particularly her well-recognized 'fame costs!' scene.

The routine – part cheerleading, part callisthenics – brings the girls to the front of the stage, where spotlights reveal that they are wearing short, white, ruffled skirts, tied at the waist with red bands to create a toga-like silhouette (Plate 10).

'I thought, right, aerobics, costumes for girls who are beautiful, who've got gorgeous figures, legs up to their armpits? Well, what could be nicer than little Greek sort of *chiton* things, but with an overlay of 'modern'. Like, leg warmers, and bandanas on their heads to keep their hair up,' explained costume designer Alexander Reid. 'But where there's a slight skirt on the doric chiton[3] I've turned that into shorts, cut high to show their legs, and bare midriffs in some places.'[4]

Critics would declare that the cast look like 'suburban aerobics instructors',[5] or might be better suited to 'an outer space version of *Grease*'.[6] The costumes, combined with Koltai's minimal, representative set, are the first suggestion that this will be far from a naturalistic piece.

The number ('In') features Allen's most intensely aerobic routine of the show; a relentless sequence of high-kicks, star jumps and cartwheels (Plate 9).

'The libretto dictates the style of the choreography, to a degree,' Allen told *TheaterWeek* in 1988. 'Then it's up to my fabulous imagination to come up with the rest. In the opening scene, they're in a gym class, working out, so that said to me... that it should be gymnastic – aerobic exercises in dance terms. That's where I started and I took it a step further.'[7]

Peter Michael Marino (audience member, Broadway)   It felt like someone had told Debbie Allen, 'We need you to fill this plastic void we've created with as many arms and legs as possible. Go!' You know, it was so distracting. But then you have to wonder, how were they doing those aerobics and singing at the same time?

Kenny Linden (Ensemble, Stratford and Broadway)   In Stratford, there had been 'booth singers'[8] for the girls doing the opening number, backing up their vocals. By the time we got to New York, there were no booth singers, so it was all up to them.

---

[3]The Doric chiton is a single rectangular piece of fabric, tied at the waist and draped/fastened at the shoulder, worn by both men and women in ancient Greece.
[4]*Theatre Craft*/Pirani interview tapes.
[5]Rich, 'The Telekinetic "Carrie," with Music'.
[6]Kuchwara, 'Broadway Musical "Carrie".
[7]Tony Vellela, 'A New Role for Debbie Allen', *TheaterWeek*, 21 May 1988, 24.
[8]Booth singers add to the sound onstage by singing in a recording booth offstage, which is helpful during particularly energetic, dance-based numbers.

Michelle 'Shelley' Hodgson (Ensemble, Stratford and Broadway)   It was a full-on exercise class. Trying to do jumps and sit-ups and hold the notes.

Kelly Littlefield (Ensemble, Stratford and Broadway)   It was difficult to sing harmonies while doing certain movements. Debbie did end up taking some stuff out and changing some of the choreography [in rehearsals] to allow us to sing better.

Sally Ann Triplett ('Sue Snell', Stratford and Broadway)   After the song, stagehands would have to fan us and bring us water. We could barely move!

As the song proceeds, Miss Gardner yells:

Shame on you, shame on you. Overweight's a sin!
Make it sore, Make it sore. Keep those bodies thin!

Rosemary Jackson (Ensemble/Understudy 'Carrie White', Stratford and Broadway)   When I think about the lyrics now . . ., oh my God, we were promoting the worst things on the planet! The opening number, I mean, by today's standards, you can't go up to a young person and say you need to be thin or the boys won't like you!

Indeed, Miss Gardner's 'encouragement' to lose weight might be dubious when examined through a modern lens, but the lyrics establish that these perfectly formed proto-*Mean Girls* are under extreme pressure to perform and conform as the leaders of this social microcosm, and provide context for Carrie's 'otherness'.

The song started life in the workshop presentation as 'Ain't It a Bitch', with similarly suspect advice from Gardner to her students:

Gardner:
   Men will never ask you out unless your body's tight!

Girls:
   What if she's right? What if she's right?

Indeed, the RSC's archive copy of the rehearsal pianist's libretto demonstrates the show's state of flux during rehearsals; there are at least eight replacement pages of lyrics glued together, demonstrating the regularity of changes during the process. One particularly entertaining (cut) verse from Miss Gardner goes:

In! Out!
Scream and shout!
Keep those buns in shape!
Grunt! Groan!
Pant and moan!
There is no escape!

Newsday's Linda Winer was no fan of the song's message, calling the lyrics 'hateful', and uncharitably describing "In" and the other school-based routines as 'unrelentingly charmless, slutty numbers'.[9]

'A lot of the dancing has a sexual edge,' Allen told the *Los Angeles Times*, 'but each piece is different in attitude. The girls in Carrie's gym class, for instance, want their bodies to be perfect, so their dancing is like that.'[10]

As the song progresses, the girls form a kick line upstage before breaking out once again into choreographed aerobics. Charlotte d'Amboise (Queen bee Chris Hargensen) gets an elaborate, high-kicking solo routine, centre stage.

Dolginoff I remember wondering, 'Which one of these girls is Carrie?' A door opens in the very back of the white box, and you see her slink out and just stand there. She's wearing a white button-down shirt. I remember her just sort of standing there, really stoic.

In Stratford, Carrie (Linzi Hateley) attempts (and fails) to join in with the energetic routine. On Broadway, she cowers shyly behind the other girls. 'Carrie's costume, at that point, is very boring,' said Reid. '[Her skirt] has a typical sort of old-fashioned length where all the rest have got sexy little short things.'[11]

As the song heads into its final moments, trapeze bars lower down towards the stage.

Noone The girls threw themselves onto these bars to make a pyramid, and it started to lift them very high up in the air . . .

Dolginoff The audience was really eating it up by now.

Technical drawings suggest that the bars lift the girls a dizzying seven metres into the air, with no apparent safety restraints. Carrie joins the bottom row of girls 'supporting' the pyramid, but nudges them and causes the pyramid to 'collapse' in slow motion. As the lights fade, the girls lie flat on the stage in a spiral formation.

Prayer / 'Dream On'

The lights flicker, revealing Carrie, who stands centre stage as taunting whispers of her name echo around her. She sings a short prayer, with lyrics that vary between Stratford and Broadway; the latter places more emphasis on Carrie's close bond with her mother, pre-empting Margaret's first appearance later in the Act. The prayer is set to a melody that returns shortly as the verse in 'Carrie':

---

[9]Winer, '"Carrie": Staging a Horror'.
[10]Harper, 'STAGE: Horrors!'
[11]*Theatre Craft*/Pirani interview tapes.

Stratford	Broadway
Dear Lord	*Mama*
Nothing I do is ever done right.	*Everything's better when you're near me.*
That's all that I hear.	*You're brave when I'm not.*
Oh, Dear Lord	*Oh, Mama*
I want to fade into the sunlight	*If I cry out I hope you hear me.*
And just disappear.	*You're all that I've got.*

The gentle melody is interrupted as Chris stands and slowly utters the immortal line:

Carrie. White. Eats. Shit.

The girls spring back into reality, surrounding Carrie and taunting her about her body, clothes and lack of social prowess. The school bell rings, and the stage transforms to a representation of the school's locker room.

Mark Bailey (assistant to Set Designer Ralph Koltai)   There was a large platform the width of the stage that rose to become the base of a row of showers. On it was a plastic screen the width of the stage, separating the actors from the audience, which had water running down it. Built into the screen were revolving panels.

Briefer   The girls seem to get undressed behind the translucent doors.

Carrie, shrouded completely in an oversized towel, makes her way through one of the seven pivoting polycarbonate panels to face the audience. Soon she is joined by . . .

Paul Clayton (audience member, Stratford)   Nubile girls wrapped in tiny white towels, wandering in and out of the shower . . .

Dolginoff   You could see their bra straps. I remember thinking how dumb that was. At least take the bra straps down under the towels! There had to be a better way to do that! It didn't look skilfully theatrical. It just looked like they had their underwear on the whole time in the shower!

As they reveal their secret hopes and aspirations ('Dream On'), the girls insinuate that pressure to impress the boys is at the root of their problems, including their dislike of their own bodies. One girl recalls her boyfriend's charming assertion:

But he says if I stop eating sweets
I can lose twenty pounds by June!

We hear the first mention of the upcoming Senior Prom (although diction or amplification problems led the *Times*' reviewer to mention that the girls are 'occasionally dropping a comprehensible word about the forthcoming prom')[12] and of Sue Snell's boyfriend, all-round good guy Tommy Ross ('Tommy told me he loves me!' Sue repeats throughout the song; 'Dream on!' the rest of the girls consistently reply.).

Carrie – emerging from one of the cubicles – gets a verse to share her feelings, but only the audience pays attention:

In my dreams, no-one ever hates me
In my dreams, I have lots of friends
Just one friend would be lovely
Momma's there, and her song awaits me
Momma's there, when the nightmare ends
Momma says that she loves me
Sometimes I dream that I could be strong
Maybe I'm wrong, but sometimes I dream I belong

She returns to her shower, disappearing from view behind the screen.

By the chorus, the rest of the girls have removed their towel wraps, revealing tiny, flesh-coloured bikini-like garments as they primp and preen. Some attempts had been made to convince the audience that the girls were, indeed, not wearing their underwear while they showered.

Hodgson   We were going into this big show destined for Broadway, so we assumed that we were going to get some kind of clever body stocking to make us look nude. We basically got chucked a load of flesh-coloured bras and knickers that they bought at Debenhams.[13] Just Debenhams' bra and knickers, nude colour! The girls of colour, the underwear didn't even match their skin. We were like . . . 'Seriously?' In the end Debbie stepped in and said, 'Let's just put them in white bras and knickers. Let's not pretend. Let's not try and hide it.'

Triplett   Our 'Dream On' costumes were made in this material that shrunk. They were just a little bit bigger than bikinis to start with. Every time we got to work we were, like, 'Oh, my God. My costume is so small!' And they just kept getting smaller and smaller!

Hodgson   They were so small, there was nowhere to hide the mic packs. Now, I've worn a mic pack in some strange places, but in *Carrie*, wow. They would go in our bras, or up our bum cracks, basically! At one point we had to

---

[12]Shulman, 'Carrie with Rock'.
[13]Recently shuttered mid-range staple of the British high street.

sit down and do the choreography balanced on one cheek! They were huge things. We were in agony!

It is clear from a comparison between early publicity photos from Stratford and the video from Broadway that more fabric was added to the girls' waists over time, protecting their modesty (and hiding their microphone batteries) but inadvertently making the 'clothes on in the shower' problem even more obvious (Image 5.1). 'Believability went right out the window'[14] was Barbara Cook's stark assessment.

Soon, the stretching and writhing of each girl synchronizes, as they 'dry themselves' in a line in front of the showers. According to Victoria Radin in the *New Statesman*, one of the girls repeatedly slides a towel between her legs 'like a seasoned stripper'.[15]

As the song concludes, the angst-ridden gyration is interrupted by a piercing scream.

Clayton   Suddenly, with an accompanying resplendent discord from the orchestra, her [Carrie's] shower cubicle glowed red on the inside.

Carrie – who has noticed her first period, and believes she's dying – reappears, and pushes her way through the girls before collapsing on the floor. On Scott

IMAGE 5.1 Dream On: The scantily clad Ensemble. Ivan Kyncl / ArenaPAL.

---

[14]Cook, *Then and Now*, 208.
[15]Radin, 'Blood Money'.

PLATE 1 Lawrence D. Cohen, Michael Gore and Dean Pitchford pictured in 2012. WENN Rights Ltd / Alamy Stock Photo.

PLATE 2 The RSC's youngest ever leading lady, seventeen-year-old Linzi Hateley in her RSC dressing room. ColourNews / Alamy Stock Photo.

PLATE 3 Darlene Love and the female Ensemble rehearsing 'In' at Stratford. Suzanne Thomas (photographer).

PLATE 4 Paul Gyngell, Linzi Hateley, Charlotte d'Amboise and Gene Anthony Ray aboard the *Carrie*-branded bus. Mary Ann Hermansen (photographer).

PLATE 5 Barbara Cook takes a break from rehearsals outside the Royal Shakespeare Theatre. Georgia Otterson (photographer).

PLATE 6 Tech rehearsals continue on the staircase set in Stratford. Cook is on the centre pedestal. Mark Bailey (photographer).

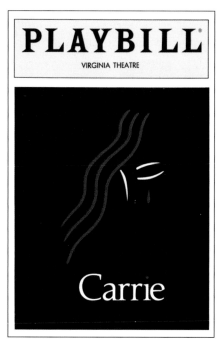

PLATE 7 *Carrie*'s Playbill cover. Used by Permission. All rights reserved, Playbill Inc.

PLATE 8 Cast member Mary Ann Oedy outside the Virginia on opening night. Mary Ann Hermansen (photographer).

PLATE 9 A high-kicking rehearsal for 'In'. Mary Ann Hermansen (photographer).

PLATE 10 Cast members in the infamous 'toga' costumes. Suzanne Thomas (photographer).

PLATE 11 The female Ensemble in the Stratford 'Do Me a Favor' costumes and (cut) wigs. Suzanne Thomas (photographer).

PLATE 12 Red laser beams emanate out from behind Hateley in 'The Destruction'. Mark Bailey (photographer).

PLATE 13 Hateley and Cook in their final moments on the epic staircase. Mark Bailey (photographer).

PLATE 14 A *Carrie*-branded bus on the streets of Manhattan. Mary Ann Hermansen (photographer).

PLATE 15 The *Friends of Carrie*'s illegal show jacket. Mike Borowski (photographer).

PLATE 16 Molly Ranson in 'The Destruction'. Sara Krulwich / *New York Times* / Redux / eyevine.

Wise's Broadway video, there is an audible guffaw of laughter when Sue Snell (Sally Ann Triplett) declares 'Carrie, it's just your period!'

Argent   I recall looking around at the audience members' faces as they started discussing Carrie's period. Jaws were hanging open in disbelief.

Bailey   Originally there was a more theatrical 'solution' to Carrie's first period. There was a section in the centre [of the shower set] that changed to a red liquid on Carrie's scream. It wasn't very successful, as the water diluted the red so it looked pink, also it stained the material of the screen, so the effect was cut for Broadway.

The girls whoop and holler with delight as they see their opportunity to attack. 'Hey everybody, Carrie's got the curse!' Chris announces, leading a chant as they toss her violently around the stage.

Hodgson   It was a hideous scene to do, because we've all been in a similar situation.

Linzi Hateley ('Carrie White', Stratford and Broadway)   There was no acting required. I can genuinely say that my whole performance was based on instinct, and reaction. As a seventeen-year-old who is still growing and learning, I think actually it was quite traumatic. I was playing the part and feeling the part.

Carrie's period and subsequent panic attack – followed by an aggressive slap from Miss Gardner – triggers the onset of her telekinetic powers, causing an overhead lightbulb to explode. John Simon, the reviewer from *New York* magazine, commented that this simple moment was 'more effective than the supposedly staggering conflagration she [later] wreaks at the Prom'.[16]
However, the effect was not always reliable.

Dolginoff   At the first preview it worked. You saw it pop, and there was a little sparkle effect. It looked really cool. I saw two more previews and then opening night, and I don't think it worked again until opening night.

Koltai had proposed an alternative surprise for this scene. 'I have a sheet of glass [that will] explode, but I'm not sure that's gonna work,' he said in a rehearsal interview. 'I've worked out how to do it in theory but it may not work! Let's see.'[17] With no sign or sound of this effect on the recordings, we can surmise it was not to the designer's satisfaction.
Plot-wise, one of the production's much-debated flaws is exposed at this moment. Without prior knowledge of the source material – and with special effects

---

[16]John Simon, 'Blood and No Guts', *New York*, 23 May 1988.
[17]*Theatre Craft*/Pirani interview tapes.

that may or may not work on any given night – there were very few hints as to Carrie's special power, particularly as many of the expository scenes were condensed before the Broadway opening. Her unusual abilities are put to 'minimal dramatic effect'[18] according to Simon, with the *Guardian* noting that the telekinesis was 'suggested by a few flickering electric shapes and apologetic thunder claps'.[19]

As the scene concludes, Miss Gardner chastises the girls and sends most of them away before trying to comfort Carrie.

'Her Mother Should Have Told Her'

In Stratford, a short song, 'Her Mother Should Have Told Her', follows Gardner's admonishment. Chris and Sue have their first spat about their treatment of Carrie, and the audience first learns of Sue's sense of guilt about her actions. By the end of the run in Stratford and certainly at the first Broadway preview, the song has been cut, with a few of its lyrics repurposed as a quick speech from Chris. Mysteriously, the song reappears in at least one further Broadway preview – as evidenced by audience recordings – then is removed again, testament to cast members' memories of the show being ever-changing.

In both versions, Chris has the final word, chanting Carrie's mean-spirited nickname, 'Scary White'. As she makes her way off stage the echoing taunts are interrupted by a determined cry from Carrie, who is now dressed in a frumpy, puffy white dress:

That's not my name!

'Carrie'

'I want' songs have long been used to introduce the heroine of a show, giving her the opportunity to directly tell the audience about her dissatisfaction with life and her desire to find something better. The lyricist Howard Ashman (*Beauty and the Beast, The Little Mermaid, Little Shop of Horrors*) summarized the trope when he said, 'In almost every musical ever written, there's a place – usually it's about the third song of the evening – where the leading lady sings about what she wants in life, and the audience falls in love with her, and then roots for her to get it for the rest of the night.'[20]

---

[18]Simon, 'Blood and No Guts'.
[19]De Jongh, 'Carrie On'.
[20]*Howard,* Disney+, Don Hahn (Stone Circle Pictures, 2018).

And here it is, about three songs in. This pacy and powerful *cri de coeur* ('Carrie') is all the more dramatic for its simple presentation, with the stoic Hateley spotlit centre stage. In the song – an impressive introduction to the vocal talents of the RSC's youngest ever leading lady – Carrie's suppressed rage and frustration spill out in a blistering anthem to loneliness and desire, interrupted by calmer, moving verses during which Hateley blinks away tears. Gore's music and Pitchford's lyrics sway between gentle, romantic visions and darker, revenge-driven imagery, creating ominous foreboding of events still to come:

> Sometimes their hatred is out of control
> God how they hurt me!
> Momma says suffering is good for the soul
> But they hurt me! They hurt me!
> And if I could, I'd bring them all
> Down to their knees!
> I'd make them sorry forever for teasing Carrie!
> Carrie! Carrie!

Hateley's memorable performance – concluding with her standing at the front of the stage, arms outstretched – is greeted with extended applause, evident on every recording.

Betty Buckley ('Margaret White', Stratford and Broadway)   I was backstage during Linzi's first number, and she stopped the show cold. Amazing. The audience went nuts.

Mary Ann Oedy (Ensemble, Stratford and Broadway)   That was the first time I ever saw a standing ovation in the middle of a show. It was so impactful.

Triplett   To think she was seventeen. It was incredible.

Briefer   The audience fell in love. She was breathtaking.

'Open Your Heart'

As the applause for Hateley subsides, panels on the sides of the white box set pivot, and Tommy Ross (Paul Gyngell) and the male Ensemble members enter as Carrie lurks at the back. A stilted scene follows, in which the boys awkwardly toss a basketball around, discussing who's taking who to the Prom. Some tease the dejected Carrie about her lack of date prospects. Tommy gives her a concerned look, asks if she is okay, then departs – Carrie looks longingly after him. Could Tommy be the 'Prince who could dance on air' we have just heard her longing for?

The set makes its first major transformation: a section of the back wall opens upwards, garage door-style, while a truck moves forward through the gap carrying a small 'house' set on a four metre-square platform. The house possesses a 'Shaker-type domesticity ... very sparse and simple, very elegant but very beautiful,'[21] according to Koltai. The back wall panel fully rotates – just in the nick of time – to become the wood-panelled wall of a living room, revealing Margaret White (Cook/Buckley) to a ripple of applause. This is, of course, the delicate scene change which 'threatened to decapitate this great Broadway star [Barbara Cook]'[22] at the first Stratford preview.

Buckley   They worked it out in New York, thankfully. I was always ready to run from that set!

Margaret wears a black, full-length, knitted cardigan or, as Frank Rich incomparably puts it, 'dominatrix black from wig to boots.'[23]

'The mother's in black of course, because she's a frustrated woman, sexually and religiously, she's also quite wicked, I think, sort of witch-like,' explained Reid in a rehearsal interview, who noted another reason for the design and fabric choice: 'Because Barbara Cook is quite big – she says she's not going to be by the time we get to Broadway – things have to be designed accordingly, shapes that are going to suit her. The knitted thing comes in there ... it's not glamorous but it's flattering ...'[24]

Cook's Stratford-edition Margaret is sitting on a wooden rocking chair, Buckley's Margaret is 'lying prostrate on the floor.'[25] The sight of Cook in the chair gives the impression of a much older, frailer Margaret; indeed, there were twenty years between the two actresses. Cook is described in one review as a 'softened-up, born again Christian mother, not at all the manic psychotic of book and film. She obviously finds time for a hairdresser.'[26]

Margaret begins to sing a soaring hymn ('Open Your Heart') 'with the purity, ecstasy and reverie-like devotion of a true believer':[27]

Lord, you have found me
A'wandering in the darkness
Light my way with your true faith
And I'll sing with joy of my new faith

Carrie returns home, sneaking through a door in the rear wall of the house set, which appears dwarfed by the shadowy panels of the larger surrounding box. Nervous about explaining what happened at school, she lurks nervously in a

---

[21]*Theatre Craft*/Pirani interview tapes.
[22]Jim Hiley, 'Couldn't Scare Less', *The Listener*, 25 February 1988.
[23]Rich, 'The Telekinetic "Carrie"'.
[24]*Theatre Craft*/Pirani interview tapes.
[25]Mandelbaum, *Not Since Carrie*, 4.
[26]Coveney, '"Carrie"/Royal Shakespeare Theatre'.
[27]October 1987 working draft script.

corner. Without so much as a glance in her direction, Margaret offers Carrie a hand and they sing the song together in a demonstration of their close but fragile bond and religious devotion, eventually embracing, the soft and soaring melody jarring with Margaret's alarming pleas to God:

Finally free of temptation
And the flames of Hell's devastation . . .

'And Eve Was Weak'

Carrie hesitantly reveals the shower incident to her mother. Margaret fixes her with a glare as the eerie notes of a solo French horn kick in. As Carrie pleads for understanding, Margaret spirals into a frenzy, violently slapping her daughter with a Bible,[28] sending her crumpling to the floor:

Go to the cellar and pray, woman!
Pray to heaven for your wicked soul!

'And Eve Was Weak' – particularly Buckley's blistering interpretation of it – is certainly one of the evening's more memorable and dramatic moments. Cook's Margaret is slower, and the rage contained within the lyrics does not translate quite as well to her floating soprano singing style.

Argent   Cook sang her fabulous heart out but looked like she'd rather be somewhere else.

Buckley's wiry Margaret paces furiously around the room, dragging Carrie towards a trapdoor and flinging it open. In Stratford, Hateley does most of the work to clamber down on her own, the audience politely ignoring the fact that she could overcome the rather slow advances of Cook with a good hard shove.

Buckley   Linzi and I had a physical fight every night during 'And Eve was Weak', chasing her around the stage and throwing her down into the basement. It was exhausting! We would go home from rehearsal every night

---

[28]Audience member Stephen Dolginoff recalled some fun trivia about the kind of seemingly inconsequential changes being made even as the show was playing in New York:

> At the first preview, Betty had a red Bible, and when she opened the cellar door, it was painted red on the inside. By the third time I saw it, she had a black Bible. But the cellar door was still painted red. The next time I saw it, black Bible, and the cellar door had now been painted black, but very poorly. They painted it right before, you could still see the red shining through. By the opening night. . . I was sitting far away, but could see the black Bible and a beautifully painted black cellar. So, these were the things that they were worried about, like what colour should the Bible be? You've got to paint that cellar door . . .

covered in bruises! It was really intense. I'll never forget the memory of throwing Linzi down into the trapdoor, and there would be this stagehand there to support her legs as she was scrambling to get out. It was a hilarious sight to see this big burly guy holding her up!

Scott Wise (Ensemble, Stratford and Broadway)   The first day they sang it, it stopped the rehearsal. Everyone started crying.

Charlotte d'Amboise ('Chris Hargensen', Stratford and Broadway)   That whole sequence is the best performance I've ever seen on a Broadway stage, ever. Betty and Linzi, they were both incredible.

Carrie scrambles for grip as she tumbles down out of sight. As the trap door slams shut, a jet of flame fires into the air from the corner of the room (though, reportedly, not at every performance, often leaving Margaret to look alarmed at an empty space).

With Carrie gone, Margaret launches into her final rage-filled lines:

Oh Lord, I've seen this power before
The flesh is weak and I implore
Father, don't forsake her
Father, take her
Cleanse and purify her
With the fire
And the power
And the glory
Forever
And ever
And ever
Amen!

Buckley   There are five verses in that song and it ends with me belting a G. I was amazed I had the breath left to do it! I did Debbie Allen's warm-up every morning, and she had me running wind-sprints to keep me strong enough to sing the material.

Buckley's performance is met with an extended standing ovation. In particular, Broadway audience members can be heard screaming their appreciation even before Buckley reaches the end of the song.

'Don't Waste the Moon'

At the forefront of many of the production's criticisms was the notion that *Carrie* felt like the uncomfortable merger of two different shows, 'one compellingly written and overpoweringly performed, the other so ditzily conceived and grisly staged that it deflates the first,'[29] according to William A. Henry III in *Time*. The experience of constantly lurching between the disparate settings and tones was 'rather like coming across a jive competition in a Trappist monastery',[30] making it hard for the audience to focus on the story and appreciate the show without being distracted to exhaustion or giggles.

> **D'Amboise**   You'd have a scene where Margaret's beating up her daughter, and then you're in a *Fame*-style scene within seconds. An audience member doesn't know how to deal with those feelings. You start to laugh!

Which brings us neatly to 'Don't Waste the Moon'. Four stacked rows of car silhouettes roll on to the stage from the wings, beaming wobbly but dazzling headlights into the eyes of the audience. As they come to a rest on stage, the wall panels of the set change, for the first time, to black (mechanically, 'the bottom half of the wall is lifted to reveal black behind; for the top half, black is flown in front. At the back wall, black sections slide in at each side to meet in the middle, masking the white behind.').[31]

The script explains that 'the latest teen horror movie is being projected to an audience of what appears to be empty cars – the kids in them making out like crazy, in various stages of undress'.[32] Indeed, in the dim light we catch glimpses of couples in a variety of exaggerated sexual poses.

'When the cardboard cars arrive, doubts about director Terry Hands' control of the evening's tone become exacerbated,' Ken Mandelbaum recollects in *Not Since Carrie*. 'So far, half of it is thuggish camp, half of it is gorgeous music theatre.'[33]

Considering the infamous expense and precision of the set, not to mention Hands' insistence on abstract scenery, the shaky cars of 'Don't Waste the Moon' look and feel somewhat out of place with what the audience has witnessed thus far. The cars are not only visually jarring – the automated scene change that brought the rows of cars on to the stage was prone to frequent malfunction, bringing the show to a crashing halt whilst stagehands manually pushed the set pieces into position.

Sue and Tommy emerge from their car, bopping to the (extremely catchy) tune ('Don't Waste the Moon') as she explains her distress about the shower incident to her nonplussed boyfriend. Their jaunty hip movements are somewhat incongruous to the angst-ridden lyrics.

The limbs of other couples emerge through the car windows, and some couples gyrate around the window frames, supported by strong metal bars. According to

---

[29]Henry III, 'Theater'.
[30]Shulman, 'Carrie with Rock'.
[31]*Theatre Craft*/Pirani interview draft.
[32]October 1987 working draft script.
[33]Mandelbaum, *Not Since Carrie*, 5.

the *Daily Express*, they resemble 'sex-mad Muppets.'[34] Another car (which on Broadway has been adorned with an orange and yellow fire-painted façade) is spot-lit to reveal Chris and her dimwit boyfriend Billy Nolan (Gene Anthony Ray's first appearance – receiving a welcoming cheer from *Fame* fans in the audience).

In Stratford, the villainous duo's vehicle is placed in the centre of the second row; on Broadway they have been repositioned to the stage left side of the bottom row, allowing d'Amboise and Ray easy access to the stage floor for a quick dance break. Dressed head to toe in demonic red, Chris is recalling the incident in the shower, attempting to get her ambivalent boyfriend to justify her cruel treatment of Carrie. The couple's interaction is laced with juvenile allusions to sexual favours and masturbation.

Linden 'Don't Waste the Moon' had some fantastic lyrics. They used to make me think 'this is so rude!' . . .

Chris:
You don't hear a word I say
Maybe 'cause your brain gets in the way.
I think you're the victim of an active gland!

Billy:
Oh yeah!

Chris:
Oh yeah!

Billy:
Oh yeah! You, what a twisted mind
Don't you know that boys are going blind
Cause they don't have someone who will lend a hand?

Chris:
That smarts

Billy:
My heart

Chris:
Don't start. See, boys like you.
Wham and bam and thank you ma'am.

Billy:
Me? That's not true.
Who do you think I am?

---

[34]Paton, 'What a Carrie On'.

Costume Designer Reid described the number as 'the sex bit. It's a bit like *Grease*, but if it had been done like *Grease*, they'd all have been wearing jeans and t-shirts and the usual.' Applying the classical overlay, Reid attired the cast in 'knitted stuff . . . the knitting suggests antique pleating. The girls have got miniskirts, or little shorts, or high boots, and the boys have got white sweaters.'[35] In contrast to Chris's dazzling red outfit, Sue is dressed in what Reid describes as 'sweety pink . . . a typical goody-goody colour.'[36]

Decked out in what we will soon learn is his preferred attire of head-to-toe black leather, Billy eventually flings the nagging Chris away, demanding 'Who the hell is "Scary White"?' – except at the Broadway opening night performance, where a mischievous Ray switched a word: 'Who the fuck is "Scary White"?' Their bickering hints at a more complex dynamic, but the surface of their toxic relationship is barely scratched during their fleeting appearances.

Rehearsal room footage shows an energetic Allen encouraging each pair of dancers to come up with a series of rapid-fire poses, hitting each beat of the song's dance break. The clips provide a fascinating glimpse into the process of creating the number, showing Allen building the routine by layering movement from each pair of dancers.

> **Joey McKneely** (Ensemble, Stratford and Broadway)   Debbie is going round each couple one at a time.

> **Hodgson**   She would say, 'You've got six counts of eight. Choreograph something!' And then you would have to show her and everyone else what you'd come up with. Then she'd put them all together.

Translated to the stage, the effect of each pair's bespoke, energetic routine based around each car (should we call it car-eography?) creates a wall of seemingly chaotic movement – pirouettes and high kicks, thrusts and grabs – as the song reaches its crescendo:

> *Don't waste the moon*
> *Now that the night is ours!*
> *Oh baby, don't, baby, don't waste the moon*
> *And the stars!*

Nonsense, but it wouldn't be *Carrie* without it.

'Evening Prayers'

As the cars shudder their way off stage and the audience is treated to a final, fading chorus, we experience another tonal shift representative of one review's claim that

---

[35] *Theatre Craft*/Pirani interview tapes.
[36] Ibid.

the show 'alternates between heavy doses of kitsch and would-be highbrow art'.[37] Indeed, 'Evening Prayers' is regarded as one of the most beautiful and poignant numbers in the show.

Lights reveal Carrie, kneeling in prayer, and Margaret sitting (in Stratford) or lurking in the shadows (Broadway). The subsequent staging was altered slightly between the two productions; in Stratford, the scene takes place on the 'house' platform. On Broadway, the pair are revealed in a vast space with mirrored wall panels; if we follow Koltai's logic that the set always represents a sort of 'dream space' in the eye of the beholder, perhaps this dark void is a representation of Carrie's state of mind as she prays in the cellar.

As Carrie reveals that she feels 'something shifting' in her mind, her mother prays to God for the strength to help her, promising protection from the Lord and offering up what passes as an apology ('Evening Prayers'). Hateley and Buckley, in particular, harmonize beautifully, singing:

You're the reason I'm alive
You're the only reason I survive
In my life there's only one thing true
I will always love you

While Cook remains relatively stationary, Buckley's emotive performance certainly adds nuance to the complex character. She lies crumpled on the floor, her voice tearful, soliciting sympathy from even the most hardened of audience members.

Buckley   Often an abusive parent will say they are very sorry and try to repent and all of that [as in 'Evening Prayers'] but they re-enact what they experienced as a child. I saw Margaret as someone who was frozen in time, like she was not a full adult, with this incredible pain and longing for love that translates to abuse.

They embrace and, according to the script, 'the enormity of their love is so overwhelming for Carrie that her power spills over: the flames in the candles literally rise, growing in height'.[38] Indeed, technical drawings for these candlesticks suggest they would have been over a metre in height with 28 centimetre gas-operated candles atop, but there is no sign of them in the video footage.

With some semblance of calm restored to the White home, Margaret sends Carrie to bed.

---

[37]Wolf, 'The Horror of "Carrie"'.
[38]October 1987 work draft script.

In the 1984 workshop presentation, 'Evening Prayers' was followed by a scene in the students' English class, recreating a memorable moment from the movie in which Carrie eagerly listens to Tommy read a poetry homework assignment out loud. The song, 'Dreamer in Disguise', was not included in the 1988 production but reinstated in the 2012 revival, where Tommy's character is fleshed out substantially (see Chapter 8).

Apologies / 'Unsuspecting Hearts'

In Stratford, a brief interstitial scene follows in which the boys list their Prom dates, as Carrie says her prayers in front of an enormous, fire-licked crucifix. According to technical drawings, it was 2.4 metres high and 1.8 metres wide and 'begins to bleed'[39] as she prays. The scene is cut in New York.

Soon, the wall panels rotate and the stage lights up in brilliant white, and the girls – back in their Grecian-inspired leisurewear – leap, high kick and cartwheel back into view. Low 'practice bars' rise up from the floor along the back and sides of the space. Miss Gardner enters, demanding the students apologize to the humiliated Carrie. Sue does so immediately, but Chris – as per tradition – leads a taunting chant of 'Suzy is sorry!' then yells that 'Carrie White eats shit!', calls Gardner a bitch, and is shoved to the floor by her (in a rather tamer retaliation than the stinging slap doled out by Buckley in the movie role.) Chris is banned from attending the impending Prom – the ultimate punishment in this world where the social calendar is everything.

A seething Chris begs the other girls to back her up, to no avail; interestingly, the students she calls out to for support vary throughout the Stratford run (and offer a fun reminder of the Ensemble members' real names).

After the gym showdown, Gardner – back in her white high-heeled pumps and glamorous toga dress – consoles Carrie and encourages her not to rule out finding happiness, and to consider going to the Prom ('Unsuspecting Hearts'). Carrie cannot comprehend that anyone would be keen to take her, but her teacher tries to motivate her nonetheless. In the workshop presentation, Gardner (Laurie Beechman) sings a song called 'It Only Has to Happen Once', but in the Stratford and Broadway productions, Love and Hateley sing a replacement number, 'Unsuspecting Hearts'.

Love's famously soulful voice attracts appreciative whoops from the audience, and she is matched by Hateley's soaring vocal in the final chorus as Carrie's self-confidence grows. The song is intercut with spoken encouragement, although this is largely focused on how Carrie could improve her own appearance in order to bag a date: Gardner recommends some lipstick and a new hairdo. In a 'fantasy'

---

[39]Ibid.

dance break, the panels pivot 180 degrees to their mirrored surfaces, the lights dim and the gym bars glow an icy-blue neon – a rare splash of a colour in the monochrome set[40] – creating a sort of otherworldly dream space for Carrie to briefly lose herself in the fantasy as Gardner playfully twirls her around the gym.

The now-placated Carrie shares a hug with her teacher, and they depart.

'Do Me a Favor'

In Stratford, a minute-long section of transition music recalls the discordant, metallic sounds of the Overture soundscape. Harold Wheeler's Broadway orchestration is faster-paced and rockier, and accompanied by a dance from the Ensemble couples.

The gym's white wall panels rotate to black, representing a location noted in the programme as 'The Night Spot'. In the script, this location is named 'The Cavalier', after the drinking den in the novel where Chris and Billy wait before doing their dastardly deeds at the Prom (and where they ultimately meet their ends).[41] In Hands' interpretation, of course, the location is more metaphorical.

From the darkness, the dancers come together to form a tight group, gyrating towards the centre of the stage.

Hodgson   Debbie was inspired by Bob Fosse . . . that amoeba style, moving together like a single cell . . .

From within the group, Sue and Tommy undulate towards the front of the stage, their hips gyrating as they sing ('Do Me a Favor').

Triplett   Sue comes through this sea of people who are doing this kind of wiggly dance. In rehearsals, as I came through in my leotard, I remember that Debbie Allen crossed her legs and said, 'You go girl!' Ahhh! It was so wonderful. I felt like I was part of her gang! You know, like I was a proper dancer!

Sue and Chris both need the titular favour from their respective boyfriends. Sue wants Tommy to take Carrie to the Prom, giving her a night to remember (little does she know). The earnest nature of their debate is somewhat undermined by the ongoing hip-swivelling.

Sue reaches the crux of her argument:

I've been thinking, 'bout how happy she would be
If only you'd take Carrie to the Prom instead of me

---

[40]Close-up photos of Love show she is wearing blue eye make-up, perhaps suggesting blue was intended as a recurring motif in Gardner's scenes.

[41]*Cavalier* is also the men's magazine for which King originally intended his short story.

Pausing briefly from his near-constant hip gyration, Tommy agrees to the plan in record time, considering that – in the eyes of the audience – he has only previously interacted with Carrie for the sum total of around ten seconds.

Meanwhile, Chris and Billy have whirled into position and she requests her favour: she has decided to take the opportunity to humiliate Carrie, and needs help gathering the pigs' blood with which she's decided to slather her. This duo are even more animated than Sue and Tommy, spinning, thrusting and pawing at each other's bodies and faces as Chris sings:

There's something that Carrie White will just have to learn
If she plays with fire then she's gonna get burned!
I want her to pay up for all that she's cost me
And make her good and sorry that she ever crossed me
You've got to help me!

D'Amboise It was my favourite number, because I didn't have to dance as hard as the rest of the show! And I could be sexy, and I loved the way it sounded. I loved working with Sally Ann, and the group effort of it all. I loved how it came together.

Triplett I've got such wonderful memories of it in rehearsal in Stratford. It was hard work, I really had to work to keep up with the others. But I loved it. I was getting fitter and fitter.

Carrie emerges from the crowd of dancers for Tommy's proposal, insinuating that the action has now transposed to her home (though the dancers remain). To disguise her split-second entrance, Hateley had to perform a few bars of the intense choreography behind the dancers, striding forward for her cue. Indeed, a close examination of rehearsal room footage reveals Hateley learning the moves at the back of the room.

We hear Margaret call Carrie's name from offstage, and she hurriedly accepts the proposal.

As entertaining and dynamic as 'Do Me a Favor' is, several pivotal plot points are buried in the midst of the frantic dance number and the layers of overlapping, often incomprehensible lyrics. There is little respite from the constant movement, so much of the already-complex character and plot development is swallowed up in a sea of rippling dancers. Considering his apparent propensity to alter or cut any material that caused confusion or attracted derision – and this scene was certainly flagged by the critics as one of the show's more *outré* moments – it is interesting that Hands considered the number 'locked' and not worthy of any significant changes between Stratford and Broadway.

The abstract 'empty space' of the set and unusual costuming certainly do not aid the audience's understanding. In an interview, Reid discussed his struggle to interpret Hands' ideas for costuming the scene: 'It was quite a difficult one to do. I can't tell you how many designs I did for it, different approaches to it. I hadn't quite grasped what he [Hands] wanted. He kept saying he wanted the costumes to be unusual, and I didn't know what he meant, and it was only after I got the boys established that I started to think of ways of doing the girls.'[42]

The final result was another memorable element of *Carrie* lore.

Triplett   I guess, costume-wise, we have to talk about the unitards.

Triplett and d'Amboise are attired in 'unitards': skin-tight dance garments designed to provide maximum flexibility, but not an item that brings to mind high school fashion of the late 1980s. It was a design choice which might have tested the imagination of even the most ardent classicists in the audience.

Kim Criswell (audience member, Broadway)[43]   It was just hilarious. All these people in colour-coded unitards. The ingenue girl is wearing a baby pink unitard, and the devilish girl is wearing a red one. What teenage group do you know that wears unitards to go to school? Colour-coded, just in case we missed who were the good guys and who were the bad guys!

'So subtle!'[44] scoffed the *Daily Express* with regard to d'Amboise's devilish garb.

With the good/bad colour-coding, we might assume that Hands was playing with the notion of Greek 'archetypes', stock characters from mythology representing universal traits (the hero, the villain, etc.), but there is little time for the audience to come to such conclusions.

'Everyone else pretends to be sexy in black,'[45] snarked Linda Winer in *Newsday*, referring to the dancers. The females are wearing 'all-over, black body stockings,' according to Reid, 'and their tops are draped [with] beads so everything is glistening.' The male dancers wear black leather jackets and trousers, emblazoned with metallic studs and red fabric stripes. The stripes are arranged in the form of the classical Greek 'meander' pattern, a line with angular spirals, arranged in such a way that suggests military armour (Image 5.2).

Reid said he looked to modern designers like Yves Saint-Laurent for inspiration. Other early ideas had included light-up jewellery and ultraviolet (UV) paint applied to the dancers' legs, which would glow under the stage lighting. Another cut concept involved the headwear of the female dancers. 'I want them to have brilliantly coloured wigs, with ponytails. There's a kind of feel there of the Furies,'[46] said Reid, referring to the Ancient Greek goddesses of rage and retribution.

---

[42] *Theatre Craft*/Pirani interview tapes.
[43] Criswell would, much later, play the role of Margaret White in the 2015 Southwark Playhouse, London, production.
[44] Paton, 'What a Carrie On'.
[45] Winer, '"Carrie": Staging a Horror'.
[46] *Theatre Craft*/Pirani interview tapes.

D'Amboise   Debbie, I think, stood up and said, 'Let's cut the wigs!' because she liked the way my real hair moved.[47] The designers were very futuristic about the whole thing. I would have had a blonde ponytail, Sue would have a black one and then everyone else would have different colours.

The space-age wigs were indeed duly cut, but even without them, the cast soon became aware of the audience's baffled reaction to their avant-garde aesthetic (Plate 11).

Hodgson   [We all went to] a cafe, and we sort of mutinied. We got Debbie along in our lunch hour and said, 'You've got to do something, because no one's going to know what we're doing or what we're wearing! This is not making sense! We need to wear our own clothes. Maybe, if we come in and we just costume it ourselves …!'

Briefer   I honestly believe that if they had re-done the costumes, the show would not have been treated the way it was treated. They were ridiculous. They were so inappropriate, and they set the tone all wrong.

D'Amboise   God damn, I wish I had kept my costume from that number.[48] At one point, I did have one of them, but I think I gave it away. I didn't even think… I should've given it to the Actors' Fund to auction or something, because it would have sold like crazy!

Triplett   I've got a huge picture of me wearing mine. It's about five feet tall, from the Front of House display. It's in my house in London! You know, my husband is very grateful for that unitard!

'I Remember How Those Boys Could Dance'

In Stratford and at the first few Broadway previews, the moving, wood-panelled 'house' truck (transporting Margaret, seated) is used for this scene. After a few Broadway performances, the house is jettisoned in favour of the vast, empty stage, with Buckley slinking towards Carrie at the end of 'Do Me a Favor' rather than calling her name from offstage, as had been the case in Stratford.

Carrie explains her intention to go with Tommy to the Prom, and the tension is palpable as she tries to justify the decision. Margaret's big pre-interval number ('I Remember How Those Boys Could Dance') starts by lulling the viewer into a false

---

[47]Allen was not one for letting the show's hair and costume design get in the way of her work: in a May 1988 *TheaterWeek* interview, she mentions a demand to cut one costume: 'It wasn't just me being bitchy, the cast needed to be able to dance' (Vellela, 'A New Role').

[48]One fan swears he saw a rack of show-used *Carrie* unitards at a charity flea market in the months after the show closed: without photo evidence, the sighting remains unconfirmed and the unitards' whereabouts unknown.

IMAGE 5.2 Male dancers in the original 'Do Me a Favor' leathers – note the Greek-inspired shoulder spirals and metal studs. Suzanne Thomas (photographer).

sense of hope; the opening bars have a light, floaty feel which feels almost optimistic. Perhaps Margaret will let her go, after all? No: the relative composure of the opening bars crescendos to an explosion of rage as Margaret recalls how she, too, had been seduced into a life of sin, warning Carrie that the same is likely to happen to her if she falls for Tommy's tricks:[49]

> *They'll make fun of you!*
> *They will break your heart!*
> *Then they'll laugh at you!*
> *Watching you fall apart!*
> *Don't you think that I know?*
> *Don't you think this has happened before?*

Cook's performance is, arguably, too restrained for such a famously brutal sequence: the *Observer*'s Michael Ratcliffe said that she 'takes the stage with a grand, contained, simple authority, but more opportunities for anger would be advisable before New York'.[50] Indeed, she appears to sing the song below tempo.

---

[49]In the novel, it is alluded that Margaret and Carrie's absent father Ralph – presumably one of the titular *boys* – struggled to live a sinless lifestyle.
[50]Ratcliffe, 'Strutting Their Stuff'.

Buckley – as she did in 'And Eve was Weak' – snaps into a blazing fury, prowling around the stage before eventually pouncing on Hateley and screaming the lyrics into her face.

Buckley   I wanted to make sure our work was very realistic, naturalistic.

Margaret flings open the cellar door once again, but this time, Carrie is having none of it. As a storm brews outside and the orchestra swells, Carrie uses her powers to slam shut the windows of the house.

In Stratford, where the action has taken place on the wood-panelled truck, we witness a *coup de théâtre* as Carrie realizes – for the first time – that she can control her telekinesis:

Bailey   The house set moved downstage, then Carrie stepped off the truck. The stage floor between Carrie and the house dropped away, leaving a void the width of the stage, and flames filled this space with the house apparently cantilevered above the flames. Meanwhile, Carrie's mother levitated from her chair to hover in the air, as the house did its reverse move.

With Cook suspended six feet above the flaming pit, Hateley turns to the audience, her outstretched hands now on fire too.

When asked in rehearsals how he would achieve the effect, Koltai stressed it would be done via fairly traditional means to avoid the concern of repeated technical problems. 'She will be lifted from below rather than [using] wires, but the audience won't see that,' he said. 'They won't know how it's possible that the house and the chair are going away. I'm quite looking forward to that.'[51]

Bailey   Terry cut this effect during previews on Broadway, and restaged the end of Act One so that Carrie and her mother played the scene on a largely bare stage with just a chair as a prop. The scene became a battle of wills, a big argument. I think Terry was turning back to his strength as one of the greatest directors of language, the basis of most of his work.

It would seem that Hands felt concerned that the focus on spectacle would distract from the powerful interaction between Buckley and Hateley, and so he simplified the final tableau of the first Act. Though Margaret does not 'levitate', flames leap from a trough in the stage, and Carrie's hands remain aflame.

The closing moments of the act are certainly breathtaking, even when glimpsed on a blurry audience bootlegs, but, as Mandelbaum quips in *Not Since Carrie*, 'by now, anyone unfamiliar with the Stephen King novel on which the musical is based, or the subsequent film version, wouldn't have the slightest idea what's going

---

[51] *Theatre Craft*/Pirani interview tapes.

on, or who the characters are, or even where the show is taking place . . . why are Carrie's hands aflame, and what just happened to the stage?'[52] 'There's no hint even that Carrie has telekinetic powers,' the *Financial Times* agreed, 'until, suddenly, at the end of the first act, her fingers spurt fire.'[53]

With her petrified mother looking on, Carrie sings a final, haunting refrain:

I am not afraid of you at all
I have nothing left to lose
I have power I can use
Nothing you can say or do
Will ever stop me again . . .

Margaret is left hovering (or, at least, frozen in fear in her seat). Carrie turns to face her, her hands finally extinguished, arms outstretched as if on the cross herself. Fiery-orange smoke engulfs the stage, and a black curtain falls.

Does anyone need a drink?

---

[52]Mandelbaum, *Not Since Carrie*, 5.
[53]Hurren, 'A Rocky Horror Show'.

6 ACT TWO: SHIT! LOOK AT ALL THESE PIGS!

Paul Clayton (Audience member, Stratford)   At the interval, my friend and I wandered out onto the balcony looking over the river and lit a cigarette. Neither of us knew what to say to each other. There were no words. We returned to our seats and sat down in silence. Suddenly, from behind us, we heard flat Yorkshire tones proclaiming, 'Eeeeh, I don't know, two and a half hours on the coach and then this . . .!'

If some audience members found the first act of *Carrie* bewildering, the first twenty-or-so minutes of the second would add a layer of other-worldly deliriousness.

A glance at the programme would reveal that the bare, black stage before them represented a location called 'The Pig Farm'.

'Crackerjack' / 'Out for Blood'

Often, the opening number of Act Two of a musical is fairly dispensable – a chance for the slower members of the audience to make their way back to their seats in the dark without missing too much of the plot. If you were late for 'Crackerjack' (or 'Out for Blood', as it came to be called after rewrites) you would miss one of Broadway's most infamous numbers of all time, and the scene which 'turns out, inadvertently, to be the funniest moment'[1] of the show.

Anders Eljas (Co-orchestrator, Stratford)   I worked, like, forty-eight hours with two hours' sleep to finish 'Crackerjack'. I was really happy with what I had accomplished. In those days, music was all written by hand; there was no

---

[1] Henry III, 'Theater'.

scoring on computer, so you could never play a full demo for the composer, you had to play some bits on the piano and verbally try to illustrate what would happen in the arrangements: 'When they stab the pig, this is what you will hear,' and so on. Michael Gore wasn't too happy with my explanation, and told me to re-write it. I felt really bad and showed the score to Michael Starobin, who said, 'But this is perfect! This is exactly how the second act should start. Let's go to the pub.' Over two pints he said, 'Now get some good sleep. Tomorrow, you go back with the same score, but change your story to what you think he wants.' Next morning I went to see Michael, and with a big smile said, 'I've been thinking about your wishes for the opening of the second act . . .' Luckily I managed to say the right things, and all of a sudden the score was just right. It worked pretty well!

With the 1984 workshop focusing only on the first Act of the show, the writers had never had the opportunity to properly test out the songs, scenes and structure of the second half before heading into rehearsals in London. This is reflected in the fact that there are significant changes between the Stratford and Broadway iterations of Act Two. Much later, by the time the 2012 'revisal' came about, the entire sequence of songs and interstitial scenes that kick off Act Two was almost entirely jettisoned in favour of new material, suggesting that the authors were never truly satisfied with the way the sequence landed.

Gore readily admits that he was never fond of the Act Two opener and how it was staged.

Michael Gore (Composer)   We spent most of our time out in the lobby while it was being performed.

The curtain rises and thunder cracks. The space is entirely black. Amidst the flaring synths, the male members of the Ensemble are glimpsed leaping through beams of light. In an interview, Ralph Koltai mentioned that he had loaned a small trampoline to Debbie Allen, who wanted to position it in the wings 'to give the dancers a flying start. But it's decided that's too dangerous.'[2]

The dancers form a wedge mid-stage, clicking their fingers and gyrating in another Fosse-like sequence. These are, according to the script, 'Billy's goons' who have gathered at 'Henty's Pig Farm'[3] though there are few clues on stage to signify this.

Bad boy Billy Nolan (Gene Anthony Ray), who, once again, 'seems to have wandered in from a TV show about leather gangs,'[4] strides forward to take his place at the apex of the wedge. Several members of this peculiar gang are topless, their oiled-up torsos complemented by a variety of black leather chaps, mesh

---

[2]Smurthwaite, '"Carrie" from Behind the Scenes'.
[3]October 1987 work draft script.
[4]Winer, '"Carrie": Staging a Horror'.

waistcoats and mohawk wigs. In front of them, a spidery Chris Hargensen (Charlotte d'Amboise) emerges from a long, rectangular trough in the stage – the same trough which burst into flames at the end of the previous Act – clad in a blood-red leather miniskirt and bikini top combo (Image 6.1). Breaking the fourth wall, she appears to address the audience in a style one can only describe as 'pantomime villain':

IMAGE 6.1 Charlotte d'Amboise and Gene Anthony Ray in full villain mode. Suzanne Thomas (photographer).

I believe in getting even, that's what I believe
And I just don't forgive and forget!
I don't take no attitude when I know I've been screwed
Carrie White's got a lot to regret!

James Noone (audience member, Broadway) They were clearly the bad couple, you know? She was in red, and he was all in black. Evil! I think it was supposed to be metaphorical, but it didn't work. They just looked cheesy.

For early audiences in Stratford, this scene ('Crackerjack'/'Out for Blood') may well have taken some time to decipher, particularly following the interval and without any sort of precursory explanation. Why is Chris emerging from the ground? Why is she suddenly addressing us directly? Why is she so angry? What are they all *wearing*?

By the time the show reaches Broadway, audience members begin to arrive forewarned and forearmed: they have heard all about this soon-to-be-infamous sequence. On bootleg recordings there are delighted whoops and cackles as it starts, and at one performance, an audience member is clearly heard exclaiming, 'Ooh! It's the pig number!'[5] as the dancers bound on stage.

Costume Designer Alexander Reid told an interviewer before previews: 'I saw the choreography [for this number] and it's wonderful, it's very, very good. Billy appears, and he's in white PVC with shorts. He [Ray] hates the fabric, because it cracks when he dances.' Early promotional photos confirm Ray's white costume, but plans clearly changed before previews started, as Ray's leather get-up is entirely black on video recordings. 'Chris is in scarlet PVC with an abbreviated mini skirt, a bra which has studs and things on it, and a sort of a bomber jacket thing, with her hair cut short, and little red boots.'[6]

Dean Pitchford (Lyricist) The boys were all wearing leather. Not just leather pants, but S&M-looking leather straps and leather vests. Very revealing. Not very American High School. Let's just say, it didn't look like these were kids pulling a prank . . .

Noone It looked like a club down in the Village.

Joey McKneely (Ensemble, Stratford and Broadway) We have these crazy Mohawk punk hairdos, like someone vomited *Mad Max* and *A Clockwork Orange* together, and we're dancing like maniacs, like banshees out of hell!

---

[5] This bootleg, generally believed to be from 14 May 1988, the fourth Broadway performance, is particularly fascinating because of the extremely vocal audience: one assumes that the voices we hear laughing and commenting on the unfolding action must belong to the bootlegger and his/her companions, because they sound so close to the recording device.
[6] *Theatre Craft*/Pirani interview tapes.

'This is where you get all the punks, with the Mohican hair, and funnily enough with all those straps of leather and studs and codpieces and tight jeans, and the Mohican hair, they tend to look like warriors. It could well be a plume of a helmet, with mesh masks covering their faces,' Reid explained. 'It's futuristic, definitely, but it has its roots in classical style, which you can't escape from.'[7] Reid chuckles and sighs wearily during the interview, as if he hasn't quite fully bought into the party line on the 'Greece' theme.

In Broadway's only pig-slaughtering number (to this author's knowledge), a scene which would 'haunt some theatregoers,'[8] Chris has persuaded Billy – along with his gang of unusually attired sidekicks – to slit the throat of a pig and collect its blood in a bucket as part of her extreme revenge plot. It's a complex piece of exposition to get across on stage, not aided by the show's placeless design and, in Stratford, 'an incompetent sound system,'[9] which apparently muffled the crucial lyrics about obtaining the blood and Chris's motivation for doing so.

> **Kim Criswell** (audience member, Broadway)   At one point, it all stops cold and he [Gene Anthony Ray] looks down and he says, 'Shit! Look at all these pigs!' The whole house started to giggle, but I don't think that's what they meant us to do . . .

Prompted by Billy's memorable outburst, the boys perform 'a frenetic, if confused dance'[10] comprised of exhausting-looking leaps and dives into and around the trench, as flames lick its edges from below: 'never were groins so resolutely swerved, or hips more aggressively swivelled,'[11] noted one reviewer. There are high kicks and bump-and-grinds aplenty with the gang 'supporting their leader in his gyrating codpiece':[12] *Back Stage*'s reviewer suggested Ray receive 'an award for the biggest padded crotch on the Rialto.'[13] Praise indeed.

Pre-recorded squeals suggest the pit is, in fact, some kind of subterranean pig sty, confirmed by the fact that 'no expense has been spared in bringing the audience some of the loudest oinking this side of Old McDonald's Farm,'[14] as Frank Rich recalled in his review. Koltai said in rehearsals:

> The idea is that the pigs are being kept underneath that trough, we just imagine there are thirty pigs down there, and just before the end of the scene – and we

---

[7]Ibid.

[8]Patrick Healy, 'An Outsider Gets a Nicer Date for the Prom', *New York Times*, 5 February 2012, available online: https://www.nytimes.com/2012/02/05/theater/carrie-a-huge-stage-flop-is-reinvented-by-mcc-theater.html (accessed 18 September 2022).

[9]Coveney, '"Carrie"/Royal Shakespeare Theatre'.

[10]Richards, 'N.Y.'s Hairy "Carrie"'.

[11]Hiley, 'Couldn't Scare Less'.

[12]Shulman, 'Carrie with Rock'.

[13]Schaeffer, 'Theatre Reviews'.

[14]Rich, 'The Telekinetic "Carrie"'.

haven't totally decided how we're going to do it ... well, we've all decided how we're going to do it, but we've all decided differently – that a pig is being killed in order to get the blood.[15]

The boys continue to throw themselves at the stage floor, bouncing back up as if partaking in a deranged push-up workout.

Criswell They're all dancing around, you know, in a pig blood frenzy. They just keep chanting about killing the pig and taking its blood. It was a lot to take in.

The mob chants:

Chop! Kill the pig! Pig, pig Kill, kill! Kill, kill! We'll make 'em bleed! Ooh! Here's his blood! Blood, blood! Get the blood, it's all we need! Out for blood!

Todd Graff (audience member, Broadway)[16] They would dive down into whatever that pit was supposed to be – I don't know why they were keeping pigs in a pit, but hey – and then you would see bodies leaping up over the periphery, and then going back down to kill the pig, and then they would spread blood over themselves ...

Kenny Linden (Ensemble, Stratford and Broadway) The [people in the] Stalls had no idea what we were doing because they couldn't see the pit. You could only see it if you were in the Circle or the Dress Circle. We were killing ourselves, working really hard. And all at the same time as chanting the funniest lyrics ever. That rap thing we did. It was just silly. We came off that stage feeling like we'd just run a marathon.

D'Amboise is rewarded with the show's most oft-quoted lyrical misfire – one which would go on to haunt the writers in reviews and retrospectives of this number for decades:

It's a simple little gig, you help me kill a pig,
And then I've got some plans for the blood!

Chris' declaration of war continues as the dancers – certainly earning their money – form a circle around her, pawing at her (are they supposed to be angry pigs? She pirouettes on, regardless) before commencing another round of leaping, thrusting and back-flipping as the unfortunate hog's howls of anguish boom out over the

---

[15] *Theatre Craft*/Pirani interview tapes.
[16] Graff, a member of the 1986 workshop cast, had been invited to Stratford late in the run to see the show by the writers.

sound system. The action is happening at such break-neck speed that it is hard to take everything in: 'apparently, a pig is sacrificed somewhere along the line, but I learned about this afterwards from King aficionados,'[17] complained *The Listener*.

Hands and Koltai had argued about how the pig massacre would be staged. 'I don't want to see a pig, I just want to convey the idea of killing a pig,' Koltai said in an interview. 'Terry seems determined that we're going to have a pig of some kind, I don't know how we're going to finish up . . .'[18]

Hands got his way, for the Stratford run at least. A life-size prop pig was built for a split-second cameo, and can be seen on video briefly poking up from the trough.

> **Mark Santoro** (Ensemble, Stratford and Broadway)   Yes. I had to wrestle the fake pig.

> **Michael Starobin** (Orchestrator, Stratford)   It was about six-feet long, made of latex, with floppy ears. A stagehand would lift it up and poke the head out of the open hole in the stage. The actor would punch the pig, the pig would come up again, he'd punch it again, he'd punch it a few more times . . .

The makers of the BBC's comedy series *Spitting Image* – known for its cast of exaggerated latex puppets of popular celebrities and politicians – had been asked to construct the life-size animal, but their estimate – £8,000 – was deemed too expensive: 'It would be cheaper to buy actual pigs and use those!'[19] laughed Koltai.

> **Jeremy Sturt** (Deputy Stage Manager)   I remember we had numerous complaints from the audience about the scene, what with the blood, and the squealing pig, and everything else. People were either fainting or their kids were getting upset . . .

> **Starobin**   The pig played Stratford, and though they brought him over to New York, it was decided they didn't want the pig on Broadway, so he was cut.

But the pig lives on.

> **Starobin**   I heard that they were going to throw it out, and I said, 'I want the pig!' And so, Anders [Eljas – Co-orchestrator] and I went to the Stage Door on 52nd Street and they brought the pig out to us. We hailed a taxi – not easy with a six-foot pig in our arms – and Anders helped me get in the back seat with it. I took the pig up to where I was living at the time, and I've kept it ever since. We used to put it outside on Halloween and dress it up. Nowadays, he's in rough shape. One of his ears has come off and there's a lot of general wear and tear . . .

It's true (Image 6.2).

---

[17] Hiley, 'Couldn't Scare Less'.
[18] *Theatre Craft*/Pirani interview tapes.
[19] Ibid.

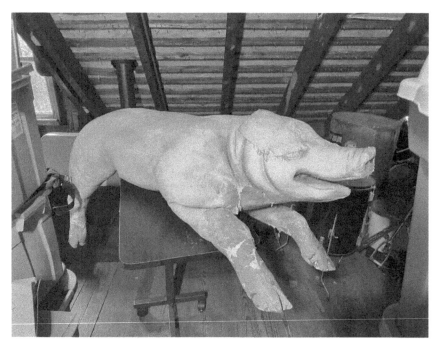

IMAGE 6.2 'The pig', now retired and living in the home of orchestrator Michael Starobin. Michael Starobin (photographer).

'Out for Blood' began life as 'Crackerjack', named after the American popcorn snack which traditionally came with a prize inside the box, a somewhat complex metaphor which seems to allude to the unpredictable nature of Chris and Billy's exchange-of-favours relationship:

> *You'll never know what your nickel buys*
> *When you grab a box of Cracker Jacks and open up the prize . . .*

According to Pitchford, Hands had long argued that Brits – less *au fait* at the time with the American snack market – just wouldn't get the reference, and so the song's lyrics and its title were duly adjusted.[20]

The number concludes with Chris lifted high by two dancers, her recently filled bucket raised triumphantly into the air as a final porcine squeal blasts out. Kudos must go to the extra-flexible d'Amboise, who has been thanklessly twisted and tossed around the stage by the 'goons' for an exhausting-looking five minutes, punctuated by a series of effortless-looking splits, spins and leaps.

---

[20]In fact, they were probably more likely to think of *Crackerjack*, a long-running British kids' TV show which had only recently ended and certainly featured no farmyard massacres. Interestingly, Sally Ann Triplett had been a presenter on the show in the early 1980s.

Bright red lights dazzle the audience briefly, perhaps a trick by Hands (in Lighting Designer mode) to distract them from the blood-soaked and panting cast exiting the stage. At their first Stratford performances, frozen in their split-second final tableau before making their exits, the cast get a clear view of the astounded faces staring back at them.

McKneely   There must have been 600 people with their mouths aghast. You could hear a pin drop. Not a clap, not a sound for what felt like ages. People were just shocked, mortified by what they had just experienced. We all stood there in the wings going 'They're not clapping, nothing's happening! We're awful! This show is awful! We're going down!'

Ken Mandelbaum recalled: 'When the number ends,' he says, 'a few applaud dutifully, but most look at the stage or each other with their mouths open, just like the audience at *Springtime for Hitler*, the show-within-the-movie in *The Producers*.'[21] With 'Out for Blood' quickly gaining notoriety by the time of its arrival on Broadway, the American reaction is palpably different, with screams and cheers the second the sequence ends. The bootleg-maker quietly mutters a single word as the delirious applause rolls on: 'unbelievable . . .'

'Crackerjack'/'Out for Blood' was certainly a bold statement from Hands and Allen on how the rest of the show would pan out: 'Were the rest of the evening as consistent in its uninhabited tastelessness, *Carrie* would be a camp masterpiece – a big-budget excursion into the Theater of the Ridiculousness,'[22] recalled Rich.

Graff   I mean, my hat goes off to it, because it was so brave in its single mindedness of 'No, we're not listening to anybody! This is what this show is!'

Unlike the pig, all that leather met a sudden end.

Linden   When we came off stage after the final performance, they took our leather jackets off us and shredded them. I was, like, 'I wanted to keep that!' The American wardrobe union was so powerful that they had to destroy our costumes as soon as we came offstage, because they had a rule about remaking them if they ever did the show again.

Mary Ann Oedy (Ensemble, Stratford and Broadway)   They made sure to take everything: every costume, every shoe, everything. I remember thinking, 'If it's closing, why can't we keep our leather jackets? Why can't we keep something?' I wanted to keep my custom-made boots, they were so gorgeous. But everything had to go.

---

[21]Mandelbaum, *Not Since Carrie*, 8.
[22]Rich, 'The Telekinetic "Carrie"'.

'Dream On reprise' / 'Heaven (White Star)' / 'It Hurts to Be Strong'

The white walls of the set return as the girls enter, dressed head to toe in white tracksuits, tied at the waist.

In the Stratford iteration, they recap the current situation for anyone in the audience who has lost the plot, which is most people: to the tune of "Dream On", they explain that Tommy has asked Carrie to the Prom, and they simply can't believe it. The girls mock Sue (Sally Ann Triplett's) claims to be doing the right thing, but she claims not to care. Tommy (Paul Gyngell) enters through a pivoting panel, checking with Sue to see if she still wants to go through with her plan for reconciliation. Frustrated not to go to Prom with his girlfriend, he leaves. On Broadway, the 'Dream On' reprise is cut, replaced with a spoken scene which passes quickly: Tommy doesn't appear (or at least speak; there's no known video of Act Two on Broadway to check against).

In Stratford, Sue is left alone to sing a song known as 'White Star' (but actually listed in the programme as 'Heaven'), an introspective number in which she struggles to come to terms that she has surrendered her boyfriend to Carrie for the evening.

Sally Ann Triplett (Sue, Stratford and Broadway)   I think one of the funniest things that has ever happened to me on stage was with Paul in Stratford. He was supposed to leave me on stage to sing my song ['White Star'] – he turns upstage, and he goes to the back. He's feeling around this vast expanse of white but he can't find the door to get out; you had to push it in a certain place, and it would sort of spin out and off stage. And he was going like . . . [feels around madly for the exit]! It was the biggest laugh that Carrie ever got. And all through this I had to sing my ballad!

Linden   This multimillion-pound set with these big spinning doors didn't work! We used to have to give them a good hard shove to get on. We were, like, 'You spent a million on this!' And we would have to shove them hard just to get off stage.

'White Star' is a precursor to the more familiar 'Heaven' song reprised by Tommy in the Prom scene: in this production, the two numbers are effectively variations of the same song, creating a melodic link between Sue and Tommy.

Triplett   They didn't write it for about six weeks. Honest to God, every day they'd be, like, 'and this is when Sue will sing her song . . .' We were in the middle of teching the second act, and we were getting closer and closer to the moment, then one day Dean Pitchford came running down the aisle waving a single sheet of music, like he was in *42nd Street* or something. So, I finally got my song the day before we were due to tech it!

By the time the show opened on Broadway, 'White Star' was cut and replaced with the moving 'It Hurts to Be Strong', in which the focus changes to Sue's anxious but determined stance to make things better for Carrie, despite her having to come to terms with being banished from her friendship group:

I had a perfect childhood
I always felt at home in a crowd
I did the things a child would
Sang along but never too loud
Then I made a choice
By raising my voice
Now I'm all alone in my song
You know how that feels?
It hurts to be strong

Triplett   I guess they wanted to make Sue a bit tougher, a bit stronger, a bit more self-willed.

In 2014, Triplett starred in *The Last Ship* at the Neil Simon Theatre on West 52nd Street, directly opposite the August Wilson (formerly Virginia) Theatre. Going to see a show there on her night off, Triplett experienced *déjà vu* in the lobby.

Triplett   As I went in, I looked to my left and I saw the piano – or rather, the spot where the piano would have been – where I was taught 'It Hurts to Be Strong'. It's incredible that the memories came back. The full circle of everything.

'I'm Not Alone'

Pitchford   We realized we'd never seen Carrie enjoy her powers. It had always been a matter of fear and dread to her that she had them. In the run up to rehearsals, Michael and I wrote a song for her called 'I'm Not Alone', during which she's using her powers to get ready for the Prom.

'There is a scene which doesn't exist in the Stephen King [novel], where she just simply uses her power for pleasure,' said Hands, who was keen to add some levity for Carrie. 'I very much wanted the show to be about what might have been.'[23] The number also acts as a timely reminder of her telekinetic ability.

---

[23] *Theatre Craft*/Pirani interview tapes.

Pitchford   Terry had this idea that he would activate all these moving effects and magic tricks. It wasn't quite what we had imagined for the number.

'I'm Not Alone' was certainly a welcome moment of calm for Hateley after being pummelled by both parent and peers in the first Act, but, after the incomprehensible mayhem of 'Out for Blood' and Sue's moving solo, the audience's patience is tested by another severe tonal shift as the 'Disneyesque'[24] number begins. The scene 'completely convulsed part of the first night [Stratford] audience,'[25] according to the *Express* review, as Carrie's clothes and accessories spring to life under her telekinetic control and frolic around the stage of their own accord. A floating powderpuff causes Carrie to 'a-choo!', a pair of shoes do an awkward little tap shuffle, and her homemade dress – incidentally, not the same as the one she actually wears in the Prom scene – swishes about the stage of its own accord to twinkly woodwind accompaniment.

Peter Michael Marino (audience member, Broadway)   At this point we could take anything, really. I loved it!

Mark Bailey (Assistant to Set Designer Ralph Koltai)   Strangely, in contrast to the 'high tech' minimalist overall design, some elements of the show were decidedly low tech, almost naïve, including the 'black light' sequence where Carrie danced with her clothes and hairbrush . . .

'Black light' is the technique often employed in pantomime or children's magic shows in which brightly glowing items – lit by ultraviolet lights – are moved around by performers dressed entirely in black against a black background, giving the appearance that they are floating in the air. In an interview recorded for *Theatre Craft* magazine, Hands referred to it grandiosely as a technique made popular by the 'black theatre of Prague,'[26] becoming somewhat prickly when asked for a definition: 'You are doing an interview for a magazine of crafts and things . . .? Well, I don't know, just ask somebody in the office. It's an old European technique and anybody can tell you about it . . .'[27]

In interviews, Koltai discusses having to (begrudgingly) make adaptations to his set in order to accommodate the show's various illusions, designed by magician Ali Bongo. 'There isn't such a thing as magic,' he said. 'Magicians don't perform magic, they perform tricks, and tricks require certain technical requirements . . . magic is illusion coupled with engineering.' Koltai talks about his disappointment in having to create a neutral, black space in order for the magic tricks to take place,

---

[24]Kramer, 'Bloody Awful'.

[25]Paton, 'What a Carrie On'.

[26]The technique is indeed popular in several theatres in Prague, where it was honed using modern lighting techniques, though its lower-tech version has been around for centuries.

[27]*Theatre Craft*/Pirani interview tapes.

and having to place a piece of black carpet on his glossy floor so as not to reflect the crew involved in bringing the effects to life: 'I literally had to cheat a bit ... I've had to take the scene where most of the magic happens out of the house that we've got used to, and create another environment. I can't redesign the whole show for one piece of magic, so I've had to introduce a black ambience where you imagine that it is Carrie's space for that moment.'[28]

As a demonstration of Carrie's newly found (but thus far, rarely witnessed) powers, 'I'm Not Alone' is closer to the much-later bedroom-cleaning antics of *Matilda* than, say, Sissy Spacek's unnerving mirror-shattering scene of the *Carrie* movie. 'The musical's one protracted attempt to show Carrie's sway over inanimate objects has to do with her preparations for prom night,' wrote the *Washington Post* about 'I'm Not Alone'. 'Puppetry has its uses, although advancing terror is not one of them.'[29]

> **Bailey**   It was pretty terrible and out of place in the context of the show. I am not surprised people found it laughable.

The song has the inadvertent effect of killing any accumulated tension and granting the audience permission to indulge in laughter just as the story heads towards a climax intended to be grave and disturbing.

> **Bob Sembiante** (audience member, Broadway)   They [the audience] had lost control, and things were funny that shouldn't have been. Poor Linzi Hateley. She deserved an award just for getting through that number without laughing ...

The frivolity doesn't last for long. As the sentient dress swoops its way off stage into the wings, Margaret White is back once again to spoil Carrie's fun.

'Stay Here Instead'

In a final attempt to get her daughter to abandon her sinful Prom plans, Margaret tries to bargain with Carrie in a short but increasingly menacing song ('Stay Here Instead'):

> *Aren't you aware how people deceive?*
> *They'll take you and break you*
> *And then they will leave you, Carrie!*

In Stratford, Cook solicits an involuntary laugh from the audience 'in an otherwise humourless evening'[30] when she earnestly commands Carrie to hand

---

[28]Ibid.
[29]Richards, 'N.Y.'s Hairy "Carrie"'.
[30]Steyn, 'Period Pains'.

over her dress so they can burn it together. Again, Cook's performance is slower and more maternal than Buckley, who delivers the song with a pacier, steelier edge. Cook's final plea of, 'Don't go!' is accompanied by a grand, orchestral sweep, whereas Buckley whimpers the line against a more ominous underscore.

Undeterred, the newly determined Carrie leaves for her big night, leaving her dejected mother alone on the dimly lit stage.

'When There's No One'

The Stratford programme, printed before opening night, lists a song called 'Once I Loved a Boy' at this point in the show. The song was never performed, replaced at the last minute by 'When There's No One'.

> **Gore** 'Once I Loved a Boy' was a favourite song of mine. It was written to be a pop style aria, à la 'Vissi d'Arte' from *Tosca*.

Luckily, an audio recording exists of Cook rehearsing the song. It is beautifully sung in her soaring, quasi-operatic style, and the crackling effect of the much-copied recording combined with the simple piano accompaniment gives one the sense of listening to an old record from the 1920s. In it, Margaret provides more details of the youthful love affair with Carrie's father which led to her pregnancy:

> *He had a touch like fire*
> *I only prayed I could resist*
> *And, well, alright, I swallowed all of his lies.*
> *And one night, I lost myself in his eyes*
> *And I loved him*
> *I loved him.*

Her lust turns to sinful shame as she sings to her absent daughter:

> *You were my only crime.*
> *All of the world could see my sin.*
> *I feared so long that the evil might come again,*
> *If I'd been strong, I might have ended it then,*
> *But I loved you,*
> *God help me I loved you.*

She ends by resolving to finally 'cleanse your soul in paradise', setting in motion the show's climax.

> **Pitchford** 'Once I Loved A Boy' had more of an unstructured shape, more of a story unspooling. We wrote that song before we cast anybody in the show,

and then we got Barbara. And of course, when you have somebody like Barbara in your show, you write to her strengths, and that began to gnaw at us. Barbara was hoping for a big 'eleven o'clock number' that spoke to what her character was thinking at that moment, rather than recalling the past. We had one of the greatest stars in the history of Broadway, and we needed to give her something more than beating her daughter up and throwing her in a closet.

Gore   At a piano in one of the upstairs dressing rooms in Stratford, Dean and I wrote the new song, 'When There's No One', while the cast was rehearsing downstairs. We played it for Terry and Barbara, and their reactions were extremely positive. Michael Starobin immediately orchestrated it and the song went into the show.

A big second act number had become a key bargaining chip in the increasingly high-stakes negotiation with Cook to remain with the show. 'I said, give her [Margaret] a song during which she makes the decision to kill her [Carrie] and we see what her thoughts are,'[31] she recalled in her autobiography.

Pitchford   We wrote something that she could float in that incredible, inimitable style of hers. We have, at that moment, her announcement that she is going to kill her daughter, but what we didn't have is the gut-wrenching decision process. Because she truly loves her daughter, but she just can't let her live:

Was I so foolish to think I could pray
When there's only one chance I can save you?
I gave you life, I can take it away
Let the shadows descend like a knife!

Cook, however, was not impressed. 'It was a lovely song, but it didn't touch on what I had asked for,' she said.[32]

The audience-shot footage of Cook performing the new number is distant and grainy, but, luckily, 'press reel' footage of Buckley's version exists. Close up, we see her cheeks wet with tears, and she is attired in what looks like a kimono over a low-cut silk negligee. Many have questioned why this religious zealot would own, let alone wear, such a revealing garment.

Betty Buckley ('Margaret White', Stratford and Broadway)   I was barefoot, and wearing what was meant to be my former Prom dress.

Indeed, Margaret's wardrobe appears to grow subtly more unhinged as she descends into madness throughout the show, and hers is one of the few costumes without an apparent nod to the Hellenic aesthetic.

---

[31]Cook, *Then and Now*, 208.
[32]Ibid.

Linden It was just a stunning song. I used to scoot down to the front of the stage in the wings to watch Betty do it. She would be crying every night. I thought 'This is just amazing. It's amazing.'

Noone The audience immediately stood up as she finished singing it. I mean, it was beautiful. Every time she came on stage, your hair stood up on end.

Although written specifically for Cook, "When There's No One" would later become a concert staple for Buckley, and the song features on her studio albums *Children Will Listen* (1993) and *Betty Buckley's Broadway* (1999).

A recording also exists of the original workshop Margaret, Maureen McGovern, performing the song.

Lawrence D. Cohen (Book writer) After the show closed, Michael [Gore] called Maureen and asked her to go into the recording studio with him and record the song so he had a version for posterity. It was a simple piano/voice recording, with Michael playing the piano and Maureen singing. It was beautiful.

Before long, this quiet and ominous break in the proceedings is over. A bell tolls, and it's Prom time.

'Wotta Night'

'Wotta Night' sees the Ensemble couples from 'Don't Waste the Moon' reunited for a fast-paced, poppy dance number which, according to Frank Rich, 'looks like the sort of cheesy foreign-language floor show one flips past in the nether reaches of cable television'.[33]

The couples wear baggy-looking formal wear, a 'wonderland of white satin and gold lurex',[34] according to the *Times*.

'The original idea had been to finally break the red, black and white theme and introduce a swirl of colour in the finale,' explained Reid.

> Terry said, 'let's try multi-colour for the last scene,' which is in fashion just now. [People] are wearing all these puff-ball things, in brilliant blues and cerises and magentas and reds, all mixed up. I thought, well, American high school proms are usually white, with the corsage and all that – I was weaned on all that through American musicals – so I checked on it, and they definitely wear white.[35]

---

[33]Rich, 'The Telekinetic "Carrie"'.
[34]Wardle, 'What a Carrie On . . .'.
[35]*Theatre Craft*/Pirani interview tapes.

IMAGE 6.3 Ensemble member Suzanne Thomas in her Prom costume. Suzanne Thomas (photographer).

He recalled Allen being generally agreeable to all of his designs until she saw his original tight-fitting designs for the Prom:

> When Debbie saw them, she said, 'are they gonna move?' Because they were very much figure-hugging, and the legs came out from the waist … I got a

friend to do a prototype, and we got one of the girls to come in and test it, and she was right, so we went back to the more classical designs. So, they're all chiffon and layered, so that when they move they swing out … the sort of classical costume you see in Ginger Rogers Fred Astaire films, you know, that kind of feel (Image 6.3).[36]

The set is, according to the script, 'transformed into Heaven [as] we come in on a spectacular dance number'.[37] The side panels of the set rotate to mirrors. According to the working script, an enormous star would be brought on stage by two cast members and raised to the ceiling, emphasizing the 'heavenly' theme of the Prom. In addition, technical stage drawings reveal that four enormous spherical 'planets' were planned to be trucked into various positions around the stage.

Bailey   I had forgotten about the giant mirror balls! I think they were Terry's idea so he could bounce light off them for the Prom.

Some of the spheres would be lit from within, creating an eerie glow which could change to red during the scene's climax. By the time the show opened in Stratford, the only survivor of these plans was a single oversized mirrored sphere which rotated on a platform upstage left, reflecting pins of light across the stage and the audience.

Peter McKintosh (set design student)   It was the most astonishing thing, the biggest mirror ball you have ever seen in your life, bigger than a person, and it was just sitting in the corner of this white box on a little base that turned it. It wasn't even hanging in the air. It was a stunning visual effect.

Linden   Debbie just said, 'That's gotta go,' and she had them remove it. As the stage-hand was wheeling it off the stage, he said, 'That's £20,000 of set going off …' I just thought, 'You can buy a flat for that!' because you could then!

'Unsuspecting Hearts reprise' / 'Heaven' / 'Alma Mater'

Tommy enters in a white suit and, unusually, gleaming white sneakers, alongside his date for the evening, the newly transformed Carrie White.

Even in the final days running up to the first Stratford preview, Reid was frustrated by Carrie's Prom costume after being asked to make it as simply (and cheaply) as possible. 'It doesn't work with Carrie at the end,' he said.

---

[36]Ibid.
[37]October 1987 work draft script.

I'm not quite sure if it's a practical problem, as she's got to get blood all over her, but Terry – for some unknown reason – said, 'Right, Carrie should be in a dress which looks as if she's made it herself. She's got to look pretty, but she's the only one that doesn't fit in.' It's a very simple dress made of white cotton with little puff sleeves … I mean, she'll look sweet in it, but it's not like all those elegant ones that are around her.

With Carrie's dress looking so different and clearly un-Grecian, Reid felt that Hands had made a rare compromise in quality and theming:

I said that to Terry and he said, 'it doesn't matter, make a point of that'. I said, 'In other words, you're saying that the dress has got to be made every night in a fabric that's cheap!' But his point was that all these girls are from madly rich families, and she isn't. He can find a rationalization if he really needs it![38]

He laughs with the interviewer.

Miss Gardner (Darlene Love) – wearing a distinctly toga-like off-the-shoulder gown – reassures a nervous Carrie with a quick, powerfully sung reprise of 'Unsuspecting Hearts'. Tommy then encourages Carrie to the dance floor, where – as other couples slow-dance in the background – he sings his verse of 'Heaven'.

'We have a whole prom sequence where you see Carrie fall in love with Tommy, which I just finished fine-tuning,' Allen told *TheaterWeek* just before Broadway previews. 'We see her actually get comfortable enough with him that she has a good time at the prom. And she believes it's all wonderful and that it's all true – before the nightmare happens – and it's done with dancing and singing. If they're not singing it, they're dancing it.'[39]

It is heavily insinuated that Tommy has fallen for Carrie, too, despite the audience witnessing only a couple of brief, awkward interactions between the two. In the workshop production and the early scripts, there are extended scenes where, as in the novel and the movie, Tommy visits Carrie at home to reluctantly persuade her to come to the Prom, and slowly realizes she is more than the 'pig' the other kids see. In 'Heaven', though, he essentially professes his love for her:

Two hearts
That's when true love starts
It starts when you feel the way I do . . .

Tommy suggests that they vote for themselves as Prom King and Queen, and a hesitant Carrie is quickly persuaded to say, 'what the hell!' Poor forgotten Sue – who,

---

[38] *Theatre Craft*/Pirani interview tapes.
[39] Vellela, 'A New Role'.

without much explanation, has slipped into the Prom to observe – starts to question her decision to hand him over for the evening, imagining what it would be like to dance with him with her own verse of 'Heaven'.

'Heaven' was originally sung as an octet, with the distinct voices of eight characters singing their parts around the stage, crescendoing into an epic, synchronous finale. The writers had aimed for a layered, choral sound – amplifying the 'heavenly' feel – but felt that the resulting sound became too complicated to follow, and so the song was simplified after previews in Stratford. The working draft script of the 'Heaven' octet demonstrates its complexity: it is written across several pages taped together, divided into eight columns laying out the overlapping lyrics for each of the component singers during each part of the song.

Before long we welcome back our nefarious duo, Chris and Billy, who are, of course, banned from the big bash.

Stephen Dolginoff (audience member, Broadway)   Charlotte [d'Amboise] comes out and she's wearing a black leather bustier with studs.

Chris growls 'I'm ready to vote!', once again seeming to break the fourth wall, and members of the Broadway audience cheer loudly.

In the early Stratford performances, the votes for Prom King and Queen tie: Carrie and Tommy are level-pegging with 'Matthew Dickens and Cath Coffey' – the real names of two Ensemble members. The 'work draft' script reveals the two alternative finalists were set to be known as 'Dave Majors and Laurie Tyler'.[40] The script was eventually simplified so the announcement simply reveals that Tommy and Carrie have won by a single vote. Of course, Chris has rigged it. As she hears her name read out, Carrie can't believe her luck.

Noone   Some gold capes were draped on them [Tommy and Carrie], and then they sort of paraded upstage . . .

The newfound lovebirds make their way to be crowned Prom King and Queen – their crowns are entwined with Grecian-style laurel bay leaves, of course. The rest of the students proudly sing the 'Alma Mater' school song, which shares a melody with 'Open Your Heart'.

'The Destruction'

In the novel and the movie, Chris has rigged the bucket of blood high in the rafters above the winners' podium, and with a swift yank of a rope, she sends its contents splashing down on to the humiliated Carrie, triggering her supernatural massacre.

---

[40]October 1987 work draft script.

The 'blood drop' scene in the movie is often used as an example of great film-making: De Palma builds the tension over several minutes, with tense music and repeated close-ups of Chris's steely gaze and twitching fingers as she prepares to soak Carrie.

The writers of the musical had envisioned a similarly tense and shocking conclusion, as illustrated by the visceral stage directions in the original script:

> She opens her eyes wide and they're glowing, literally glowing, in the darkness. And extending her arms in front of her, she flexes, and lasers come out of her fingers, flying over the audience's heads and slamming two side theatre doors shut. In the orchestral section that follows, the dream becomes a nightmare as Carrie unleashes her full arsenal of supernatural powers. Utter pandemonium ensues as she seals off the gym, trapping everyone inside like fish in an aquarium. In a blaze of special effects, music, lighting and dance, she enacts her terrible revenge against classmate and teacher, friend and enemy alike. At the height of this spectacular holocaust, Carrie walks through the fiery gymnasium, the stage blazing like Valhalla behind her as she exits.[41]

Dolginoff   We're obviously expecting something really spectacular to happen because it's the highlight of the movie. Everybody knows it's coming.

The music cuts. Chris runs to centre stage, grabs Carrie, and yells out:

Now Billy, now!

Billy runs on from the opposite wing holding a bucket. In early publicity photos, it is clearly made of plastic, the sort you might pick up from a local hardware store (Image 6.4).[42] In videos of later performances, it has been swapped for a galvanized metal version. He places the upturned bucket over Carrie's head, and a trickle of thick, goopy liquid oozes out. The moment 'is so poorly staged it gets laughs', according to Ken Mandelbaum.[43]

Triplett   Linzi, bless her, had to kind of push the bucket onto her face, and then when she took the bucket off, it looked like she had loads of blusher on . . .

Philip Argent (audience member, Stratford)   The bucket was jammed on her head, and a few dribbles of stage blood leaked out.

Charlotte d'Amboise ('Chris Hargensen', Stratford and Broadway)   It was just like a red glob. Like a blob, a little blob. And then she would have to kind of smear it on herself. It was so bad. I remember being so embarrassed by it.

---

[41]Ibid.
[42]Perhaps sourced from the same Stratford emporium as Barbara Cook's iconic sledgehammer?
[43]Mandelbaum, *Not Since Carrie*, 8.

IMAGE 6.4 The big moment – d'Amboise, Hateley (under plastic bucket) and Ray kick off 'The Destruction'. Ivan Kyncl / ArenaPAL.

The surrounding cast attempt to amplify the horror of the slow trickle with exaggerated gasps and surprised gestures.

McKintosh   I couldn't believe my eyes when I first saw it. I mean, is that it? This is the climax? This is the moment that every single person who knows this story is waiting for, and that's how you deliver it?

'And the pig's blood that we are all waiting for?' asked *Time Out*'s critic. 'No dramatic drop, just a pail plonked on the poor girl's head.'[44] John Simon in *New York* described Hateley being 'bedaubed slowly and carefully, as if a makeup person were powdering a star between takes of a movie'.[45] *The Stage*'s review commented that 'the pig's blood did not look much like blood of any kind'.[46] 'Surely someone might have found stage blood (porcine or human) that doesn't look like strawberry ice cream topping,'[47] an exasperated Rich chimed in.

Dolginoff   I remember thinking, 'Oh, that must be just for tonight. That's part of why we were delayed a half an hour, a problem. Whatever the blood thing usually is, it's just not on tonight.'

---

[44]Edwardes, '"Carrie" Review'.
[45]Simon, 'Blood and No Guts'.
[46]Kerensky, '"Carrie"'.
[47]Rich, 'The Telekinetic "Carrie"'.

But it was not 'just for tonight'. A trifecta of concerns had forced the creative team to settle for the less-than-satisfying solution: that too much liquid would damage Hateley's clip-on microphone, stain everybody's gleaming white costumes, and coat the stage (and possibly the first row of audience members) in sticky, slippery liquid.

Linzi Hateley ('Carrie White', Stratford and Broadway)   There was so much blood going over me that the microphone sound was being distorted. Martin Levan had his work cut out to make the sound work! You want this amazing visual image, but at the same time, the audience had to be able to hear me! Otherwise, it just wasn't going to work. I remember the taste of it, I loved it! It tasted like toffee apple![48]

Martin Levan (Sound Designer, Stratford and Broadway)   It was hard to prevent and was usually a bit 'hit and miss' although I have to say that the backstage mic techs were incredibly inventive at finding solutions.

Hodgson   Stupidly, we're all wearing white. Again, a fundamental problem ... has anyone thought about that?!

Santoro   Our costumes were turning pink. When the blood hit the floor we could not go near it or roll in it ...

In addition to the practical reasons for not completely soaking Hateley from on high, Hands was reluctant to compromise his artistic vision with an epic horror-movie style drenching, preferring that the audience should focus on Carrie's emotional transformation and not what he considered a cheesy special effect. Later, he reflected: 'I'd been trying to replace a splosh with a moment of humiliation, but they didn't want it in sophisticated, character terms. They didn't want humiliation. They wanted a bright, clear impact ...'[49]

Understandably, Hateley – lightly sponged with red food dye – felt awkward having to subsequently perform a full telekinetic meltdown. Attempts were made to intensify the effect. Night after night, she was doused with an array of different substances to try and better replicate the effect of blood. Hands flooded the stage with deep red lighting. Hateley's costume was fitted with snaps down one side, and she was fitted with an even bloodier version underneath; amidst the commotion, d'Amboise would rip off the top layer and throw it offstage – on the Stratford bootleg video, the moment is clearly visible.

By the final performance, and with nothing to lose, cast members took matters into their own hands.

---

[48]In one online photo of Hateley signing playbills at the stage door, she is sticking her tongue out to demonstrate the red dye that has permeated it from so many dousings.
[49]Tookey, 'Flop!'

Hodgson   We told them [the crew] 'Water it down!' When he [Ray] threw the blood at Linzi, it was with such force that she nearly fell backwards, and we were all splattered. But the thing is, that's kind of what everyone wanted. We were slipping and sliding everywhere, covered in red. The walls had blood up them. Everything. Linzi was literally shivering, covered head to toe. It was incredible.

A translucent scrim – described by Mandelbaum as looking like 'a plastic shower curtain'[50] – drops downstage like a guillotine, creating a barrier behind which the excluded Sue – ejected from the gym after being discovered by Miss Gardner – can watch the unfolding massacre. As Carrie's murderous rage commences, discordant lines and lyrics from other parts of the show illustrate Carrie's spiral into meltdown. Hateley described her approach to the intense scene, saying that:

> she has so many complicated feelings all going on at the same time … just a couple of days ago I began to feel that although she has the ability to move things, when she is hurling things about and killing people she is inflicting pain on herself as well. I think we have to show that Carrie is physically and emotionally drained and injured each time those powers are unleashed.[51]

Hands, in his role of Lighting Designer, threw everything he could at the finale. An arsenal of lighting effects illustrate Carrie's destruction of the gym, illuminating the theatre like a rock concert using laser beams and state-of-the-art, computerized, moving lights, rarely used on Broadway at the time.

'With the new computers, you can rhythm it [lighting] to be both the pulse of the show as well as a means of directing focus,' he said in an interview during rehearsals. He listed the laser equipment – sourced from a specialist company in Cambridge – as 'a couple of Kryptons and an Argon … they're very expensive, and very temperamental'. The Kryptons would project red beams, moving at high speed to create a 'flame environment': 'I felt that the one way in which lasers have not really been used recently is as scene-painting light,' said Hands. 'You can make it, with smoke, into a suggestion of fire which the audience's imagination will then pick up – hopefully.' The Argon would add green beams to the red to produce white 'bolts' from behind Hateley, giving the appearance that they originate from Carrie herself (Plate 12).[52]

Linden   In Stratford, they were allowed to fire the laser beams directly at us because we didn't have any health and safety rules! We all got to do these

---

[50]Mandelbaum, *Not Since Carrie*, 9.
[51]Ledford, 'Linzi Hateley's Date'.
[52]*Theatre Craft*/Pirani interview tapes.

amazing deaths when Carrie hit us with a beam. When we got to Broadway, they [the Union] said we couldn't do that – we could use the laser beams but they couldn't hit anyone. So even though the laser beams completely missed us, we still had to die dramatically!

'The laser will be kept under the stage, in its own sort of concrete and rubber pit, because they can be unstable,' Hands said in rehearsals. He described a plan to use fibre-optics to make the lasers appear as if they were actually coming from Carrie's body or from a prop given to her at the Prom ceremony, such as a sceptre. 'We haven't quite established yet how we'll do it,'[53] he said. Presumably the effect proved too complex, as it is not visible in the videos.

Gil Benbrook (audience member, Broadway) Our seats were in the front of the balcony, and as we were being seated the usher told us that there would be two gentlemen who would need to get access to some controls situated next to us during the second act. It wasn't until the moment when they asked to get by us, that we realized they were controlling the lasers during the destruction!

For many reviewers, the display was a damp squib, with Rich informing readers that the pyrotechnics 'wouldn't frighten the mai-tai drinkers at a Polynesian restaurant'.[54] It was a 'reasonable hullabaloo with laser beams, smoke pots and showers of sparks',[55] according to the *Washington Post*, but nothing more than 'an old dud of a strobe-and-laser show',[56] in *Newsday*'s opinion. John Simon of *New York* magazine was not impressed either, declaring that: 'the supposedly staggering conflagration … is nothing more than the laziest of laser shows, for which a provincial rock concert would blush'.[57]

Benbrook I do distinctly remember that the lasers were very wonky and not very elaborate, and that the guys who operated them right next to us literally had what seemed like a single joystick that they moved up or down to point the lasers either out towards the top of the audience or down toward the stage.

As the cataclysm concludes, there is an exhausted silence, and Carrie is left standing alone.

However, the show's biggest (and priciest) *coup de théâtre* is about to begin.

Bailey The piece of stage that Carrie was standing on started to rise, and as it did so, the ceiling of the gym started to lower, revealing that the other side of it was a huge staircase.

---

[53]Ibid.
[54]Rich, 'The Telekinetic "Carrie"'.
[55]Richards, 'N.Y.'s Hairy "Carrie"'.
[56]Winer, '"Carrie": Staging a Horror'.
[57]Simon, 'Blood and No Guts'.

As the staircase begins to descend to the stage, a square hole in the structure aligns perfectly with the plinth upon which Hateley is standing, and she glides seamlessly through the massive structure.

According to technical drawings, the staircase is 10.35 metres wide at the front, 4.6 metres wide at the top with each of its 36 steps 0.25 metres deep. A roller system at the back of the stage allows it to pivot downwards and backwards in its descent towards the stage deck. The hole through which Carrie's podium seamlessly glides is 2.3 metres square. A second lighting rig has been constructed above the structure to illuminate the final minutes of the show.

According to the *Evening Standard*, the gleaming white staircase 'cries out for a chorus of Busby Berkeley dancers'.[58] The *Washington Post* agreed it was ripe for a kick-line, declaring it 'worthy of a latter-day Ziegfeld'.[59]

Koltai said that he had imagined the spectacular set piece at the very beginning of his design considerations, letting the staircase and its technical requirements dictate his vision for the rest of the show: 'The audience have to leave the theatre with their mouths open, or we've failed,'[60] he said.

'In the 1980s, people expected big entertainment,' writes Jessica Sternfeld in *The Megamusical*. 'Big sets, big songs, big stories.'[61] The staircase was perhaps an attempt by Koltai and Hands to leave audiences with the sort of memorable, spectacular scenic moment seen in the likes of *Les Misérables*, where the height of late 1980s engineering was employed to make an enormous set of barricades rotate on to the stage, or *Starlight Express*, where in London an entire roller-skating rink had been assembled around the theatre auditorium. 'It requires some engineering expertise, it's fairly sophisticated,' Koltai said. 'It's not something you would do for any little two-hander.'[62]

Understandably, it had been one of the most technically challenging aspects of the show to create.

Simon Opie (Production Manager, Stratford and Broadway)   The staircase needed to be light but strong, so was made out of formed aluminium painted white, the mechanics necessary to move such a load with lighting equipment installed on the underside, the coordination of the hole for the platform, the rising of the platform itself and above all ensuring the safety of the performers – this was an epic but extremely demanding finale.

Noone   It was breathtaking. I mean, it just stopped your heart when this thing came down. It was stunning.

---

[58]Shulman, 'Carrie with Rock'.
[59]Richards, 'N.Y.'s Hairy "Carrie"'.
[60]Smurthwaite, '"Carrie" from Behind the Scenes'.
[61]Sternfeld, *The Megamusical*, 174.
[62]*Theatre Craft*/Pirani interview tapes.

Benbrook   It was met with gasps from the audience members around us.

Triplett   I mean, wow, it looked amazing. And I got to watch the whole thing.

Triplett, as Sue, is trapped behind the translucent scrim as the staircase descends. While it slowly falls into place, the recently laser-zapped cast are left to perform their death throes.

Linden   It got to about a third of the way down, and Debbie said, 'Oh, you've all died. Can you keep dying until the staircase drops? Just do it all again!' We all had to die several times.

The Ensemble duly repeat their death throes, or in the words of Mimi Kramer's *New Yorker* review, 'the characters turntable about confusedly'.[63] 'If you haven't seen the movie, you don't have a clue [what's happening],' said Joel Siegel in his ABC News review. 'Everyone on stage is writhing with looks of pain on their faces, but everyone in the audience had that same look . . .'[64]

At the top of the staircase, transported there by means of a backstage elevator, appears Margaret White, who begins a slow climb down towards Carrie.

Buckley   At one show, I was at the top of the staircase and someone yelled, 'Betty Buckley, come on down!' The energy was crazy!

Sembiante   I remember the gasp of the audience as you started seeing her come down that giant white staircase. What is this going to be? Where are we?

The staircase has been variously interpreted as a physical representation of the school's entrance – a memorable scene in the movie sees Carrie slowly descending the steps as the school burns behind her – or the collapsing gymnasium ceiling. There is an obvious 'stairway to heaven' metaphor, not to mention more than a passing resemblance to a grand Greek temple.

Sturt   Of course, it was painted brilliant white. In Stratford, Barbara Cook, standing at the top, just couldn't see the edges of the stairs. So, she quietly said to Terry, 'I can't see anything! This is impossible!' (Image 6.5.)

Appreciating Cook's plight, Hands asked the set builders to add a white metal handrail down the centre of the staircase, allowing her the opportunity to descend without the risk of a fall. Koltai, seemingly displeased that his very expensive, very metaphorical staircase had been blemished with a crude safety measure, made his own modifications.

---

[63]Kramer, 'Bloody Awful'.
[64]cold144, *Carrie the Musical – Opening Reviews*, YouTube, 4 January 2009, available online: https://youtu.be/S191a99wUc8 (accessed 5 May 2022).

IMAGE 6.5 Barbara Cook begins the long descent down the staircase (with the assistance of a handrail) at the end of Act Two in Stratford. Ivan Kyncl / ArenaPAL.

Sturt   Overnight, he painted it red. So, you now had this enormously brilliant white staircase with a red handrail running down right through the centre of it. Amazing.

Bailey   I honestly don't remember when [the railing] was added, or if it was there from the start. I would have thought it would have needed to be part of the initial build for security and safety, but maybe not. It was a pretty huge staircase so I can't imagine we would have gotten away without one, but I wouldn't have put it past Ralph to try. It wasn't really in Ralph's nature to make a design decision out of a fit of pique, but if it had to be there it is very likely he would have tried to make a feature, rather than to hide it. Adding a strong dynamic line to a feature was something Ralph often did in his work.

Hands didn't appreciate the paint job.

Bailey   Just before the final preview, Terry watched the show from the seat that Frank Rich would be sitting in. At the end of the show, he told me that the red handrail would have to be repainted a different colour before Rich saw the show. So, we had to schedule a paint call to repaint it. I did wonder if, with all that was going on with the show, this was the big change needed to ensure a favourable review, but I had to do as I was told!

There was a further change to the staircase between venues.

Bailey   From a design point of view, one big change between Stratford and Broadway was to paint the ceiling [the underside of the stairs] black, which Ralph resisted. Ralph felt that this was being done to accommodate the lighting, rather than for aesthetic reasons or to help the production.

In rehearsals, the ceiling issue had obviously been preying on Koltai's perfectionist mind: 'it's white, well it's white at the moment ... it may change', he said. 'Terry is worried about it reflecting too much light, but by the time he's got all his lighting gear on it, I don't think you'll see the white ceiling.'[65]

The writers had grown frustrated that such an enormous amount of focus and resource had been placed on the finale's design at the expense of fixing the show's overarching issues.

Pitchford   So much preparation was done for that final reveal. Everything else was pushed out of the way in order to make one moment happen.

'Carrie reprise' / finale

Margaret – having made her way down the staircase to Carrie's plinth 'like Lady Macbeth on her way to a mad tea party',[66] according to the *Daily Mail* – plunges a dagger into Carrie's back (Plate 13). Her pleas of, 'Baby, don't cry now ...', lead to 'one of the show's bigger unwanted laughs' at opening night in New York.[67]

---

[65] *Theatre Craft*/Pirani interview tapes.
[66] Steyn, 'PeriodPains'.
[67] Rich, 'The Telekinetic "Carrie"'.

Carrie retaliates by using her powers to stop her mother's heart. This method of dispatching Mrs White is drawn straight from the novel, and is rather more reserved than Piper Laurie's memorably orgasmic death scene in the movie, caused by a barrage of flying kitchen knives that impale her on a wall. Once again, anyone unfamiliar with the book struggles to comprehend the subtle process taking place. 'Miss Buckley dies, inexplicably, on a vast staircase that ludicrously descends and is never used or, for that matter, identified – she just sort of keels over after stabbing Carrie, which draws embarrassed laughter from the audience,'[68] observed the *New Yorker*, while *The Stage* described the moment as 'incomprehensible'.[69]

Sombre closing notes play as Carrie stumbles down the last few steps to the stage floor, where she is met by Sue – the lone survivor. The 1987 'work draft' edition of the script includes stage directions for a curious adjustment to the ending: we see Carrie in Sue's arms and 'on this final image, as Carrie reaches out toward *us* with her hand – – – CURTAIN.'[70]

For Hands, it was perhaps a step too far towards 'interactive horror', with the director selecting a more reserved final tableau: Sue embraces the exhausted Carrie, and weeps as she dies in her arms.

Fade to black.

Bows

Hateley   The lights went out and there was a mixture of boos and cheers. I was just, like, 'What is going on? Do they like us? Do they hate us? What is it?'

Buckley   The whole house was booing in unison. I'd never heard it before in all the years I had been a performer. I remembered my freshman theatre studies course in college and the stories of audiences at Jacobean plays starting riots and thinking, 'My God, this is a bona fide theatrical riot!'

Hateley   And she held my hand in the dark. And I looked at her . . .

Buckley   She said, 'What do we do?' because she's trusted me through this whole thing, and I said, 'Linzi, we've gotta get up!'

Hateley   The lights went up. And as I stood up, literally the entire audience erupted and stood on their feet for us.

Buckley   There was an instant, overwhelming standing ovation. It flipped in a second. Such a visceral reaction.

Pitchford   The two of them, centre stage . . . what else could your reaction possibly be? I'm getting chills thinking about it. You couldn't cheer louder or

---

[68]Kramer, 'Bloody Awful'.
[69]Kerensky, '"Carrie"'.
[70]October 1987 work draft script.

throw enough roses on that stage for those ladies and the performances they had just given.

With the staircase dominating the stage, the rest of the cast were left to file along a narrow gap in front of it, a clumsy manoeuvre which often led to an awkward dip in the cheering.

Linden   We were all off in the wings and we just had to trail on in a straight line from the edge because there was nowhere else for us to go.

In Stratford, Cook – nervous of slipping in the darkness – had remained in place halfway up the staircase until several other cast members could assist her down to join Hateley for a shared bow.

Thanks to their villainous performances, and perhaps due to the pantomimic atmosphere that had developed, d'Amboise remembers the crowd booing her and Ray's entrance.

D'Amboise   Screaming and then booing. I was, like, 'Is that a boo?!' I remember calling my mom going, 'Well, I think they're booing when I bow! I think they're booing me!' I will never forget that feeling. Oh my God, it's horrible. It would only be a few people. It was just enough to hear. It was kind of weird.

Hateley   I remember walking to the dressing room after the show and leaving a trail of blood behind me. Slipping all the way up. There were only a few showers for the girls. I was, like, 'Please let me have mine first!'

PART THREE

THE LEGACY

7 ARE YOU A FRIEND OF CARRIE?

Linzi Hateley ('Carrie White', Stratford and Broadway)   I didn't want to talk about it. I couldn't even listen to it. It took me a long time. Whenever I heard any *Carrie* stuff, the emotion in me was so uncomfortable, because it was so raw, and it was part of me. I spent a lot of years trying to either apologize for it or justify certain things about it. I was always proud of the work I did on it, but I was almost afraid to ever say that because there was so much negativity.

Dean Pitchford (Lyricist)   We [the writers] didn't come together for a long time. We didn't talk about it. We couldn't face it. To be honest, for a long time, I didn't even want to hear the word *Carrie*.

Hateley   I was fortunate that I wasn't blamed for it. I was picked up by Cameron Mackintosh, who basically said, 'Here you go, here's *Les Mis*. Come to the West End . . .'[1] So, *Carrie* did help to put me on the theatrical map.

The Holy Grail

In December 1988, the United Kingdom's *Telegraph* Saturday magazine supplement dedicated an entire issue to 'The Inside Story of Theatre's Biggest Flop', a multi-page *Carrie* obituary liberally scattered with quotes from Shakespeare's tragedies. A glossy supplement in one of the country's best-selling weekend papers was testament to how much the show's failure was settling into the public's consciousness, and perhaps the first suggestion that *Carrie* would not go quietly into the night.

---

[1]Hateley replaced original Eponine Frances Ruffelle just a few weeks after returning to the UK. Interestingly, a prerecorded scream by Hateley was still in the production as recently as 2021.

Though many theatregoers had missed their chance to experience *Carrie* first-hand, they had certainly heard a lot about it.

Mike Borowski (*Carrie* fan)[2]   I wasn't old enough to be in the city seeing shows when *Carrie* was on. But in my freshman year of college, I became involved with a group of friends who were obsessed with trading recordings of Broadway shows, and of course, *Carrie* was the Holy Grail.

In 1991, three years after the show closed, a small advert appeared in the back pages of *TheaterWeek* magazine: ARE YOU A FRIEND OF *CARRIE?* it asked in bold black and red type, followed by a postal address for an apartment in New York's West Village.

Jimmy Donahue (*TheaterWeek* magazine staff)   *TheaterWeek* was a weekly magazine featuring interviews, reviews and industry gossip. It was such a fun place to work because it was independently owned.

Edited by John Harris, the *TheaterWeek* staff also included columnist and *Not Since Carrie* author Ken Mandelbaum as well as future *New York Times* theatre critic Michael Riedel.

Borowski   If you were a *Carrie* fan, you knew this magazine. I was a summer intern there in 1991. Jimmy was also obsessed with the show. We'd get together and play the tapes of different versions. He placed the ad.

Donahue   I recently searched for the address from the ad on Google Maps, I thought maybe it was Mike Borowski's apartment. Nope! Mine!

Jon Putnam (*Carrie* fan)   When I saw the 'Friends of *Carrie*' ad, it felt excitingly clandestine … a coded invitation that only a select audience would recognize. I mailed a response immediately.

After an anxious wait, a letter arrived:

```
Thank you for expressing an interest in CARRIE. We're
sorry it has taken so long to get back to you, but the
response has been overwhelming! The purpose of the ad
was to find people interested in purchasing CARRIE
memorabilia. Because of the enormous amount of mail
received – from as far away as Spain and England, and
from 15 different states – we realized there existed a
great interest in, but no network for CARRIE fans . . .
```

---

[2] Borowski now works on Broadway as a press agent.

In exchange for a $20 cheque or money order, respondents could be furnished with a list of fellow fans – a sort of unofficial database of those keen to discuss and trade merchandise, photos, unsanctioned recordings and gossip. The letter goes on to list some of the treasures available for the Friends of *Carrie*[3] to acquire: the now-rare souvenir issue of *TheaterWeek* (Image 7.1), a silver pendant from Tiffany's given to cast members as an opening night gift, or a bound copy of the show's score.

IMAGE 7.1 A much-desired *Carrie*-themed special issue of *TheaterWeek*.

---

[3]Undoubtedly a thinly veiled nod to Friends of Dorothy, a slang term for gay men.

As the list of fans grew, so did their desire to own something tangible that proudly demonstrated their passion: no official merchandise for the show had survived, and the supply of leftover promotional posters and Playbills was growing scarce.

A Broadway trend saw many musicals creating limited edition branded jackets, given to cast and crew members to celebrate their opening night.

Borowski   I mean, they were the coolest thing in New York City. If you were walking down the street and you saw a dancer walking by with her *A Chorus Line* jacket or, you know, some amazing-looking singer in his *Phantom of the Opera* denim, it was like seeing a Hollywood star. No one had *Carrie* jackets, not even the cast and crew of the show.

Donahue   We approached the lady who made most of the jackets for other shows. The only condition of her making them for us was that – being unofficial – we could not make a penny of profit off of them. All in all, I think no more than twelve were made.

At $250 each, the unofficial *Carrie* jackets weren't cheap but they were durable – Borowski boasts that his is still in top condition (Plate 15) – and they spread the show's logo and strapline far and wide. The legend of *Carrie* had received another boost.

Borowski   We'd get stopped all the time by people wanting to talk about the show. It was just kind of fun, you know, when you're young and you think you're kind of superior! I mean, it's ridiculous now to think that we actually did that.

Members of the public who spotted the jackets and found themselves curious to listen to songs from the show would have been disappointed when making enquiries at their local record store. With the cast quickly scattered by the show's sudden closure and funding withdrawn, plans for an official cast recording had been quickly abandoned.

Gil Benbrook (audience member, Broadway)   I would often find myself at Tower Records checking the 'C' listings in the cast recordings section to see if one happened to have been made. You have to remember, this was long before the internet, so there wasn't really any way to know if a cast recording existed unless it was mentioned in a magazine like *TheaterWeek* or you found it yourself.

Hopes were raised in the 'On Stage' column of the *New York Times* in 1989, when it was reported that a group of Wall Street investors had come up with the funds to record the songs using a mix of Broadway and pop music stars. 'The wonderful thing is that the theater really does offer an afterlife,' composer Michael Gore commented in the article. 'The music can stand on its own.'[4] Picking up the story, the *San Francisco Examiner*'s *Showbiz* column snarkily refers to the plan,

---

[4]Enid Nemy, 'Possible Disk for "Carrie"', in 'On Stage' column, *The New York Times*, 5 May 1989, 62.

saying it would delight 'buzzards who feast on the carcasses of Broadway flops'.[5] Alas, the recording was never made, and the mysterious Wall Street 'Friends of *Carrie*' are not mentioned again.

Lyricist Dean Pitchford believes the prospect of a retrospective album was never likely.

Pitchford   Had we gone to the studio in '88 and preserved the show, that would be one thing. But to come back later and perpetuate the mistakes on vinyl or cassette tape would have been unthinkable.

Hateley   My biggest regret to this day is that we didn't do a cast album. Of course, had that happened, maybe people wouldn't have the same sort of fascination with the show. But it's a bloody shame that it didn't happen.

In the mid-1990s, a handful of songs from the show gained a wider listenership after Betty Buckley released 'When There's No One' on her 1993 album *Children Will Listen*, and Hateley recorded 'Carrie' for 1994's *Sooner or Later*.

In 1996, Buckley staged an AIDS fundraising concert at Carnegie Hall, and – to the delight of fans – invited Hateley on stage to perform the title track and their harrowing duet 'And Eve Was Weak'. Hateley has described the concert as a moment of closure, giving her the chance to perform on a New York stage for the first time since the show closed.

Later, in 1999, Broadway performers Alice Ripley and Emily Skinner, who had starred together in *Side Show* the previous year, sang 'Unsuspecting Hearts' on their album of the same name.

Once fans had exhausted these authorized tributes to their favourite show, the most ardently flop-curious could find a way – with a little digging – to hear the rest of *Carrie* through more nefarious channels.

The bootlegs

In his book *Understanding Fandom*, Mark Duffett defines the notion of fandom as 'a sociocultural phenomenon largely associated with modern capitalist societies, electronic media, mass culture and public performance'.[6] If *Carrie*'s fandom had originated with the audience members who saw it first-hand, it would snowball thanks to the fan-driven exchange of one of Duffett's elements, electronic media.

Since portable recording equipment was invented, small but dedicated communities of theatregoers have illicitly recorded Broadway shows, trading their 'bootlegs' in secretive groups.

---

[5]Gerald Nachman, '*Showbiz*', column, *The San Francisco Examiner*, 21 May 1989, 17.
[6]Mark Duffett, *Understanding Fandom: An Introduction to the Study of Media Fan Culture* (London: Bloomsbury, 2013), 5.

A quick online search using the right keywords brings up a plethora of high-definition recordings of any new Broadway show one might care to watch, filmed secretly on phone cameras and distributed to the world in seconds. In the late 1980s, however, technology was more primitive; camcorders and tape recorders were expensive, bulky and noisy, and needed regular tape and battery changes. Bootleggers had to disguise their equipment in increasingly creative ways; posts on online message boards talk nostalgically about avid traders booking out entire sections of Broadway theatres, surrounding themselves with friends to hide their recording equipment from prowling ushers.

The next challenge was in reproducing and distributing the tapes: without professional mastering equipment, fans would resort to simply making copies of copies, with the quality degrading each time.[7] Fans would discuss their collection – as well as the tapes they wanted to trade or acquire – by letter, phone and, eventually, online. Occasionally, a flurry of excitement would ripple through the community with the announcement of a newly released or freshly discovered recording of a particular performance. Collectors would crave rare recordings featuring unusual quirks such as lyric changes, on-stage slip-ups or the first appearance of a particular performer.

For such a short-lived show, there are a surprising number of 'unofficial' audio and video recordings of *Carrie*, of varying quality levels. They provide a unique and fascinating record of a legendary show continually in flux, proving first-hand that audience reactions oscillated wildly throughout the show's life: something that would have been impossible to gauge from a studio recording. Even now, fan forums exist solely to speculate over tiny differences at performances just days apart.

In the early days after *Carrie*'s sudden demise, a thriving network of bootleg trading sprang up.

Benbrook After the show abruptly closed, I made it my life's mission to find out anything I could about it. A year or so later, my friend sent me a small package; inside was a cassette tape with the label *Carrie* – Live and Illegal! He had somehow found a bootleg copy of the show. I was in heaven! I devoured that tape and practically wore it out. It was only the songs from the show, so none of the dialogue scenes were on it. However, knowing this recording existed made me actively seek out a more complete one. Shortly after this is when I stumbled upon the *TheaterWeek* ad, and it connected me to other fans of the show.

Putnam I had always assumed that the most ardent *Carrie* fans never saw the show, but Gil had seen it on Broadway and was every bit as passionate

---

[7]Bootleg communities developed their own quality rating system: A+ for the highest grade, stumbling down to C, D or even E for the worst (but often rarest) recordings.

about it as I was. Unlike so many collectors, he believed in sharing the wealth. He sent me a video of Act One on Broadway, and then a video of a full Stratford performance and some rehearsal footage. He acquired a lot of material over the years, and he shared it all. Someone else put me in touch with a friend who allegedly had a video of the Stratford production. I called the guy. I was prepared to pay any amount, but he told me that he couldn't make me a copy, that the video had been given to him on the condition that he not share it with anyone. I offered to fly him to Chicago to show me the video, but he refused!

Pitchford   Once, in the late 1990s, I was in a theatre bar in the Times Square area called Charlie's. The waiter came over and he said, 'I have to tell you, I am just such a huge fan of *Carrie*.' I remember this so clearly. I said, 'How do you know the show?' and he said, 'Because I have a pirated recording of it. You don't?' First of all, it's not something that I sought out – you know, can I get a recording of that show that I can't bear to revisit? – but by that point, enough time had passed to talk about it. He was amazed that I did not have a recording of it. He was telling me about how his friends get together to sing the songs!

Pitchford had received his first in-person validation that there was a groundswell of love for the show.

Pitchford   He said, 'I can make a phone call and arrange for you to get a copy.' So he went away and he came back and he said, 'On Thursday, go to One Shubert Alley.' It's a Broadway-themed gift shop. 'My friend works there and he will have it behind the counter for you.' I went in there and I said, 'Are you so-and-so?' and he said, 'Yes, are you Dean?' and he reached behind the counter for a plastic shopping bag containing two cassettes. They were actually very nicely done. He had prepared a J-card to wrap around them, and inside was a running order of the songs. It all felt very illicit. I walked out of there looking over my shoulder!

Hateley   One bootleg recording landed in my hand, and I stuck it in the tape machine – which tells you how long ago this was – and I got about as far as the end of 'Carrie' and was like, 'I can't do this.' Even now, if I hear it, there's something that it does to me. It's not that I'm uncomfortable with hearing it anymore, but it just strips me bare. It just takes me somewhere . . . You know, it was such an early stage in my life, and to have something as extreme as that happen to me . . . it's stayed with me to this day.

Mary Ann Oedy (Ensemble, Stratford and Broadway)   When I was touring with *Smokey Joe's Café* and *Chicago*, I would have fans at the stage door with *Carrie* paraphernalia for me to sign. One of them gave me a bootleg DVD of the show. It even had a little slipcover, personalized with my name.

In his 1999 *Playbill* column, theatre writer Ken Mandelbaum summarized the bootleg recordings that any *bona fide* Friend of *Carrie* should have in their collection: 'hardcore fans must have live recordings with both Buckley and Barbara Cook, as well as the Cook rehearsal, the Maureen McGovern workshop, and demos'.[8]

Mandelbaum himself had been a key contributor to the amplification of the *Carrie* mythos. If bootleg recordings of *Carrie* fed its underground fan community, his 1991 book of musical flops, *Not Since Carrie: Forty Years of Broadway Musical Flops*, was its public storefront. The catchy title and memorable cover shot of a grinning, blood-soaked Hateley – an out-take from a promotional shoot – positioned the show as a sort of wacky farce and is, arguably, most responsible for perpetuating the show's chaotic reputation. Mandelbaum dedicates his opening and closing chapters to *Carrie*, sandwiching descriptions of hundreds of other musical flops, an early proponent of the theory that no other Broadway disaster had, or ever would, compare to this one.

> **Joe Iconis** (*Carrie* fan)[9]   *Carrie* came into my life at a very young age, and it never left. When I was young, I educated myself by reading every book about theatre and how it was made that I could get my hands on. I remember going to Barnes and Noble and looking in the theatre section, and one day I saw *Not Since Carrie*. I started reading about the show and imagining what it could be, and I just became obsessed.

Iconis – not satiated by multiple readings of Mandelbaum's tome – began to seek out recordings. The case study of his teenage *Carrie* obsession is useful to demonstrate a typical fan's voyage of discovery in the show's 'wilderness years'.

> **Iconis**   I was constantly internet sleuthing, trying to find whatever information I could get my hands on. How do I get hold of *Carrie* stuff? The Holy Grail was a video, but I was, like, 'I'll take anything!' I finally found the well-known audio of the final Broadway performance, and I think I paid cold, hard cash for it, because it was owned by a person who was not interested in trading. They said, 'I will sell you this *Carrie* audio for,' you know, probably 'one hundred dollars!'

It was an expensive habit for a pre-teen.

> **Iconis**   I remember trying to save up, and having to ask my mom for money and having to lie about it. You know when you watch movies and see high school kids lie about needing money so they can buy drugs or booze? Well, I

---

8 Ken Mandelbaum, 'Stage Views', column, *Playbill*, exact date unknown, 1999.
9 Joe Iconis is now a Broadway composer, best known for creating the show *Be More Chill* and his macabre-infused concerts.

was a middle-school kid lying to get money for my *Carrie* audio bootlegs! I would put cash in the mail and get the cassette tapes back. I remember being in my bedroom one night, and my Uncle Walter had come over for dinner. I had a big Italian family, we were always around each other . . .

At the family dinner, Joe had his mind on just one thing.

Iconis I was holed up in my bedroom listening to *Carrie*, and I would go downstairs and, you know, let myself be kissed by aunts and uncles, and I would have a few bites of pasta and then run back upstairs, listen to the songs, go back downstairs, have some chicken, back upstairs, listen to the songs . . .! I was just so excited. I could not believe that I was finally getting to listen to this thing that I had read so much about and had fantasized about for years. I truly remember being, like, 'Oh my gosh, this is not what I thought it was gonna be at all.' It didn't sound like musical theatre. It was amazing. I was just totally blown away. The absolutely maddening joy of receiving the video cassette of Act One of *Carrie* on Broadway, well, there's just no other feeling. It'll never be topped!

Iconis had to take things a step further.

Iconis Of course, I did what any enterprising young bootleg collector would do. I used that one video as leverage to get other videos. I was very brazen online, like, 'I have this video of *Carrie*. How cool is that?' And also 'What can you give me for it?' Not fully understanding the Internet. I mean, I was probably a freshman in high school at this point.

Then things took a surprising and, frankly, terrifying turn.

Iconis I got a call one day from Betty Buckley's attorney! At my parents' house! 'Hi, this is Betty's lawyer. Am I speaking to Joseph Iconis? So, . . . you've got this illegal videotape. I'm going to need you to send me every copy you have or we'll be pressing charges!' [laughs nervously] It was the most frightening thing. My first 'the Internet's real, this isn't a joke' moment, you know? Betty Buckley has found me on suburban Long Island, and can sue me because of this videotape! So I, of course, made a copy of the tape and then sent that to the lawyer, and kept the original!

Luckily, things came full circle in the Iconis-Buckley escapade.

Iconis Betty, a few years ago, truly out of the blue, messaged me on Facebook. She said, 'Oh, I really like your music, I just want you to know. Maybe one day we'll get to work together.' No way, this can't possibly be happening! I can't *not* work with Betty Buckley! You know, I don't have any of my own show posters on the walls of my apartment. But the one – literally the one – framed show poster that I have is *Carrie*, and I've had it since I was in high school. Suddenly, Betty Buckley is singing this song I wrote just for her, in my apartment, in front of that poster. So that was how Margaret White entered my life! I have not yet actually told Betty that story. I've spent so much time with her, but there's just never been a time where I can be, like, 'This is such a funny story . . .', because there's still part of me that doesn't want Ms Buckley to be angry at me for trading that videotape!

Some *Carrie* videos are not 'bootlegs' in the traditional sense. There is professionally filmed 'B-roll' of some numbers shot for press use[10], and snippets of rehearsal footage filmed by news crews, not to mention the documentary footage commissioned by the RSC and producer Friedrich Kurz.

One popular video of the Broadway production was made by cast member Scott Wise who – with only twenty-four-hours' notice of the show closing – decided he couldn't miss the opportunity to capture it for posterity.

Scott Wise (Ensemble, Stratford and Broadway)   We just had to have a record of it.

Jeremy Sturt (Deputy Stage Manager, Stratford and Broadway)   He came to me and said he had one of those old video camcorders. He asked, 'Do you mind if I film the show?' And I said, 'Well, from where?' He said, 'Up where you are, because you've got the best view.' I was on the gantry with the follow-spot operators.

Unlike most musicals, Sturt was 'calling the show' from the back of the house rather than the wings, due to the unique walled-in design of the set.

Wise   I took my huge video recorder, taped it to a pole in the spot booth, and turned it on.

The result is a fixed but distant view of the final performance – or rather, half of it. Wise pressed record before going backstage for his half hour call, and by the intermission, his camera battery died. Act Two – including the dramatic finale – was not captured. No (known) film of the entirety of *Carrie* on Broadway exists.

The most popular audio recordings of the show are the so-called 'soundboard' tape recordings of both closing performances. These recordings come from live feeds of the on-stage microphones, usually piped to the dressing rooms backstage, and are rumoured to have been rescued and leaked by members of the crew. The professional equipment used means that these recordings – particularly the Broadway audio – are much clearer, and as close to a cast recording of the original production as we can hope to get.

Benbrook   The Broadway soundboard recording is the one that I've listened to hundreds of times over the years.

---

[10]Some of these 'press reels' show only a few seconds of a particular number: many fans live in the hope that longer sections may still exist in a dusty cabinet somewhere.

While many fans traded their bootleg recordings for the love of it, the rarity of the *Carrie* tapes and the uptick in requests from inquisitive collectors also generated a booming black-market economy. By the end of 1988, some *Carrie* bootlegs were reportedly changing hands for hundreds of dollars.

As the analogue world turned to digital, free internet hosting soon changed the model. As Duffett acknowledges, YouTube and similar services 'have facilitated fandom for independent, lost and obscure cultural phenomena that might formerly have gone undiscovered'.[11] Indeed, free web hosting brought the various *Carrie* bootleg iterations to a new generation of musical theatre aficionados.

> **Robbie Rozelle** (Unofficial *Carrie* site webmaster)   I grew up loving two things: musical theatre and the novel *Carrie*. When I discovered that both of those things had come together, I went online to find out as much about it as I could. But, of course, there was very little at that time. So, I created a website with images of the show that I found. I went to the local library to hand-type the reviews from Stratford and New York and I put them online. It truly was when the Internet was just sort of coming of age. The website was built in, I think, Geocities[12] at first, before we got a URL of our own.

Rozelle's site rapidly expanded beyond text and photos to include audio and video recordings.

> **Rozelle**   It was such a legendary show that people wanted to help bring it to a bigger crowd online.

The site grew in popularity after a mention in an article in *Entertainment Weekly* magazine.

> **Rozelle**   I was a subscriber and I did not know this was happening. I opened it up and there it was. Visits to the website just flew up, it just went sky high. The way that people obsessed about that show in the early days of the internet is a phenomenon that can't truly be explained, but I definitely got to live through it in its heyday.

After many years without a full video recording of the show, a film of the entire Stratford production appeared online in the early 2000s. It is an archive recording made by the RSC, shot on a single camera from the back of the auditorium and labelled as the 3 March 1988 performance.

> **Craig Hepworth** (*Carrie* fan)   I live not too far from Stratford, so one day I phoned the RSC and I said, 'Do you have a copy of *Carrie*?' and they were, like, 'Oh, we've not heard anybody ask to come and see that one, ever.' I was

---

[11]Duffett, *Understanding Fandom*, 14.
[12]The free web-hosting service which was popular with fandoms in the 1990s.

amazed. So, I booked to go and view the show with a couple of friends. We got there and we signed in, and they took us into a room and rolled in this old TV with a video recorder. I remember watching it and thinking, 'Oh my God, this is not what I expected it to look like.' I was just thrilled and fascinated by it.

However, Hepworth was on a secret mission.

Hepworth   I had brought a blank videotape with me, and I decided that if I got the opportunity, I was going to leave with the *Carrie* tape and leave them with the blank one. And I did. I switched the tapes and I ran through Stratford panicking that they were going to be chasing us down the road. I got home and I copied *Carrie* and then I sent them the copy back, which I know is very bad. But I really wanted to keep hold of the original, and it was just sitting there! I ended up sending it out to the fan sites, so people could finally see the show in full. I didn't realize the video would go on to be such a huge deal. But, yeah, I still have the master here. It's a simple video, and doesn't have a case or anything. It just has '*Carrie* 1988' written on the side.

Though Hepworth's Robin Hood-esque antics surely cannot be endorsed, fans of the show were grateful for his extraction of the footage. Viewing figures – and interest in the show – soared.

By collecting recordings over the years and eventually curating them online, fans effectively acted as the show's unofficial archivists. Anyone can now watch the infamous production for free at the click of a mouse, a state of affairs that the early collectors – scrabbling to fit their crackly recordings onto two cassette tapes – find mind-blowing.

Putnam   In the 1980s and 1990s, the idea of having such a bounty at one's fingertips was unimaginable. Fans had to work doggedly and patiently for each 'gain' – a new recording, a new video. We treasured them because they were so hard-won.

As home editing technology improved over the years, many fans enhanced the recordings, with some going so far as launching an online petition to have the Broadway closing night recording saved in the US National Recording Registry as a record of national importance.

Staging the unstageable

Requests to remount the show kept coming, but the writers consistently rejected them, a move described by the *New York Times* as 'a rare act of artistic exile.'[13]

---

[13]Healy, 'An Outsider'.

Hateley   I understood how the writers just weren't prepared to go there for a long time. When you've given so much of your time and attention to something, and it's so cruelly taken away, that's hard to face.

Perhaps the very fact that permission to stage *Carrie* was unobtainable made it all the more tempting for those keen to do so. Indeed, some directors took matters into their own hands, believing that begging for forgiveness later was easier than getting permission first.

Kaily Smith ('Chris Hargensen', 1999 Stagedoor Manor production)   Stagedoor Manor is a performing arts training centre in upstate New York. It's a theatre camp. But – at least when we were there twenty years ago – it was a very serious theatre camp. We were treated like adults and professionals.

Jeffrey Murphy (Director, 1999 Stagedoor Manor production)   I just thought, 'We should do *Carrie*, it's the perfect show for Stagedoor!' It's got all these great female leads and a female ensemble with as many guys as you can throw into the mix. I had actually been thinking about doing it for a long time, but there were no rights available.

Smith   I went for nine summers. I did *Carrie* in 1999, my second to last year there, when I was sixteen. And Julie, who played Carrie, has been my best friend since we were eleven.

Julie Kleiner ('Carrie White', 1999 Stagedoor Manor production)   I was an outcast at school, and Stagedoor was my home. Well, maybe I wasn't the *total* outcast that Carrie White was, but when you were a theatre kid back in those days, and there was no *Hamilton* for everyone to relate to . . .!

Murphy   I got hold of a pirated CD of the show. An audio of the whole performance. A friend and I sat down and typed up all the dialogue. We had the score, and we fiddled around with a couple little things here or there, changed some stuff that we wanted to change, and then we started rehearsal.

A week or so into the process, the camp's administrator appeared at the door. She'd received a worrying phone call.

Murphy   Connie came in to me and said I needed to go talk to [camp owner] Carl. They had found out. He called Michael Gore and Larry Cohen and said, 'Look, I will give you however much money to whatever charity you want if you'll let us do the show.' And they said yes.

Todd Graff, who had played Tommy in the 1984 workshop, had enjoyed five summers at Stagedoor Manor himself, and maintained strong links with the camp.

Todd Graff ('Tommy Ross', 1984 workshop)   I went there for three summers as a teen and I worked there for two. When they decided they wanted to do

Carrie, it had never been done except in the notorious Broadway version, but they didn't care! They just did it.

Michael Gore (Composer)   Todd phoned me to say, 'I don't know if I'm supposed to tell you this, but Stagedoor is doing a production of *Carrie* this weekend.'

Graff   I didn't tell them so the camp would get in trouble, but just because it was so hilarious, classic Stagedoor! To Michael and Larry's credit, they said, 'Oh my God, we want to see it!' not 'Oh my God, we're going to shut it down and send cease and desist letters!' So, they went and they watched it, the first time they'd seen the show since Broadway closing night.

Gore   Because it was being done at a theatre camp and not for profit, Larry and I drove up the hour and a half to see what a new stripped-down version performed by *real* teens would look and feel like. Amazingly, it brought us back to 1984 and the initial reading we'd done.

Murphy   They loved it. They said, 'This is the way we always wanted to see it done, with real kids, real teenagers.' I remember they said, 'Where did you get the girl who plays the mother?' I said, 'Well, she's one of the campers.' They said, 'I don't believe it!' Because Vivienne ... well, you'll see this at a lot of Stagedoor productions, these teenage girls transform into women on the stage, and she was quite convincing as a thirty-five-, forty-year-old woman!

Vivienne Cleary ('Margaret White', 1999 Stagedoor Manor production)   I've also sounded like this since I was eleven.[14]

Murphy   They both came to see the show and they were very, very positive.

Smith   I'm pretty sure that was the night that I blacked out on stage and forgot my lines and jumped half a song. Oh, yeah. It was a traumatic moment for my sixteen-year-old self!

Cleary   I was singing 'Open your heart, let Jesus in!' and I had these prop pamphlets to hand out to people in the audience. I turned around and realized I was looking directly at Michael Gore, who was smiling at me, and we're both holding onto each side of this pamphlet. I froze, and inside I was going, 'Aaarrgh!' but I'm sure I kept it together because he didn't start laughing at me! But I do remember I held on to that pamphlet a little too long. I was just like this seventeen-year-old loser, musical theatre freak, and I almost touched Michael Gore! We touched the same piece of paper, at the same time!

Kleiner   I was covered in blood when I saw them, and I remember being freaked out, excited. I've got this picture of him [Gore] where he's hugging me and he has this beaming face. I remember him saying how excited he was to

---

[14]She declares in a deep voice.

see the show featuring kids, because of what kids bring to it: this feeling of being an outcast. I remember him saying, 'Oh, we're so excited, we're gonna do it again!' He was thrilled.

Cleary   They were so gracious when they met us backstage. That vibrating energy of, you know, twenty-five kids waiting for them to speak to us. I'm sure that must have been a lot, but they took time with each of us to say how great we all were. To a bunch of overly nervous teenagers, that was incredibly kind.

Gore   Flaws in the show notwithstanding, it was infinitely better than what $8 million had bought. This was our first glimmer that there might be, someday, somewhere, another life for our show.

The Stagedoor production was filmed and later joined the other *Carrie* videos on YouTube – the first full recording of the show in over a decade.

Smith   When videos started popping up, we were, like, 'Oh, that's so funny, who would have posted that?' And to this day, people still say to me, 'Carrie White eats shit!'

Cleary   I was approached in audition waiting rooms for like ten years after the show. This chorus boy, he must have been nineteen or twenty, heard me talking to somebody and warming up, and he said, 'Erm, were you in *Carrie* at Stagedoor Manor?' That's the first time I heard about the video!

Kleiner   I remember going on YouTube and people were commenting on my performance! I was a kid! Later, I would go to Broadway auditions, I was even cast in a Broadway tour, but none of it mattered, because as soon as people saw *Carrie* on my resumé, that was all they wanted to talk about.

Cleary   I would say, until the *Carrie* revival happened, it was a claim to fame!

A 2000 unlicensed student production at Emerson College in Boston – also released on YouTube – mashed together cut scenes from the movie with songs from Stratford and Broadway in an attempt to even out the disparate sections of the story. Another version – the first non-English production of the show – took place a year later at a high school in Holland. Friedrich Kurz attended the production after bumping into the father of one of the student performers at a party. 'I explained the history to [him] and asked if tickets were still available that evening,' Kurz wrote in his autobiography. 'He took us with him as guests of honour. The school had actually managed to create a respectable, in parts impressive, staging of the piece. I congratulated his daughter on her performance. I avoided the teacher who was responsible. I would otherwise have had to deal with questions, how he had obtained the performing rights . . .'[15]

---

[15]Kurz, *Der Musical-Mann*, 20.

The school recorded the show and even released an unofficial cast album. Though intended for the young performers' parents, it did, of course, give *Carrie* fans the chance to hear new recordings of their beloved songs – this time, in Dutch.

Life's a drag

For those keen to witness a musicalized, stage adaptation of Stephen King's tale live on stage, there were other – unsanctioned – options.

David Cerda (Creator, *S'Carrie The Musical*)   I wrote *S'Carrie* in 1998. It was the first musical I've ever written. It's a tribute to the film, more than anything else.

Cerda's 'drag parody' proved so popular that it led to three separate productions.

Cerda   When we first opened it ran for eighteen months, late night in Chicago. It was a huge hit, and got a great review in the *Chicago Tribune*. We did it again and tried to make it bigger. We had a little more money and we realized it was a great production. It was fun, but we found that it worked better on a low budget, and so I did another version, sort of closer to the roots of the original. I finally got a 'Cease and Desist' when we did it for the third time. People started being interested in it, and I think somebody may have notified the people associated with the musical.

Drag queens have long mined the more over-the-top aspects of Carrie White's story for their own material, with many playing off the musical's reputation as a 'camp classic'.[16]

Cerda   There have been other *Carrie* musical parodies by little theatre companies throughout the United States. There's *A Very Carrie Christmas!* There's *Carrie* this, *Carrie* that. It's a big part of our pop culture. I think this story, for any gay teen, really resonates. I went to school exactly at the time it's set, in the late 1970s. The way the high school girls behaved, it was so spot on. I don't know if they were that cruel, but if they had had access to pig blood, I would have had some thrown on me, you know?

Drag/*Carrie* crossovers seemed to crescendo at the end of the millennium, with *Entertainment Weekly* reporting that Varla Jean Merman, the drag alter ego of

---

[16]Undeniably, many people adored (and still adore) the original *Carrie* for its 'camp' value. Jacques le Sourd, a writer for the Mamaroneck *Daily Times*, declared the musical to be 'high camp. Monumental kitsch. Mega-trash. I loved it.' Indeed, the story's positioning of its protagonist as a sort of tragic antihero – combined with the diva-like qualities of her mother – appealed greatly to those with an appreciation of camp. The casting of 'gay icons' like Barbara Cook and Betty Buckley (not to mention a gang of topless, oiled-up male dancers) certainly added to the show's 'camp' legacy.

actor Jeffery Roberson, had joined Buckley on stage in her cabaret show at New York City's The Bottom Line club, performing excerpts from the musical.[17]

Director Joshua Rosenzweig and writer Erik Jackson were two of the creatives determined to reassess and remount the musical with their own unique spin.

> **Joshua Rosenzweig** (Director, *Carrie* play, 2006)   I've always been obsessed with *Carrie*, the story. I saw the musical on Broadway. I remember it being the craziest mix of, like, really awful, but with these really amazing moments. But I was a real *Carrie* purist. I remember asking 'Why isn't it set in the 1970s?' I remember leaving the show with my friend and saying, 'This needs to move downtown. That's all they need to do, right? They need to understand that they're dealing with really high camp.' Not making fun of Carrie – it needs to be respectful – but it needs to have a real rough edge around it, in my opinion, to work.

> **Erik Jackson** (Writer, *Carrie* play, 2006)   We genuinely loved the musical. We just thought it had been ill-served by the humourless Broadway production. We thought the way to make people realize its value was to come at it from an entirely new angle: embracing the camp and heightening the humour, rather than trying to play it 'straight', so to speak, and not trying to replicate what basically didn't work the first time around.

Rosenzweig and Jackson later founded 'Theatre Couture', a fringe theatre company dedicated to staging well-loved musicals but with a twist: a drag queen would play the lead role. Desperate to stage *Carrie*, they appealed to the writers for permission.

> **Rosenzweig**   We wrote to Dean Pitchford and to Larry Cohen and to Michael Gore, and we just kept hitting walls. Eventually, we said, 'Maybe we'll just do a bootleg version of it.' But it was really hard to get hold of the music, and the score is very complicated. It's not your simple sort of show tunes, some of those songs are really, really complicated pieces of music. We were working in the club vernacular, and so it wasn't something that we could just hand somebody and be like, 'Hey, transcribe this for me.' We kept running into roadblocks, but finally, we somehow found some connection to Michael Gore, and he agreed to a meeting.

> **Jackson**   He was very kind and considerate but remained unmoved by our pitch. He believed that, one day, people would recognize that it had just gotten the wrong production or opened at the wrong moment. While we agreed that the piece had stellar elements and was at times quite moving, we explained that we thought it would benefit from the addition of humour. But Michael

---

[17]Gregory Young, 'Noises Off', column, *Entertainment Weekly*, 4 July 1998.

wasn't keen on seeing a troupe of drag queens and downtown oddballs putting a *Rocky Horror* spin on his work!

Rosenzweig　It became clear pretty quickly that the writers were terrified of being burned again. What I could glean from the conversation was that they were looking for a sort of 'redemption production'. They felt like they had this masterpiece that just was mishandled and misproduced. The people they were talking about who they thought should be playing Carrie and Margaret, you know, were opera singers, because they just wanted the music to soar. We were thinking of having our frequent collaborators, the drag queens Sherry Vine, and Jackie Beat, play Carrie and her mother. They both can sing, but they can't sing like *that*, right?

Sherry Vine (drag queen)　Obviously, we're men and we can't sing like Betty Buckley, so we were like, 'Okay, we'll lower the key,' and they said, 'Absolutely not. If you can't sing it the way it's written, you can't sing it.' And that was the end of it.

Instead, they pitched a new, non-musical, drag-led take of the story directly to Stephen King, and were surprised and delighted to be granted permission. The result, *Carrie: A Period Piece* was staged off-Broadway in 2006.

Jackson　Our aim was 'heartfelt camp'. The idea was to play up the absurdity and let the humour fly, but to find anchor points of true emotion. We let the audience laugh along at Carrie's initial humiliations but then worked to humanize her so that that derision subtly turned to compassion. By the end of the story, as Carrie embraced her power and agency, our audiences fully empathized with her. We loved the notion of having audiences think they were coming to a silly drag show and then pulling the rug out from under them when they actually started to feel something.

Vine　It was packed. Everyone was coming to see it. I thought it would run for years! But the sad ending is that it ran a month. When the financial crash of 2008 occurred, it essentially wiped out a lot of the off-Broadway scene. You either needed to do a show with a $10 budget or a $10 million budget. There was no more middle. But it was a great ride while it lasted!

A catalyst

Despite the failure of the original production – or perhaps, in part, because of it – something about *Carrie* was keeping the show alive in the imaginations of fans around the world. Each time somebody discovered Mandelbaum's book, or stumbled on another bootleg recording, the demand for a re-assessment of the show swelled. Rozelle, busy managing his fan site, remembers the levels of interest reaching critical mass by the mid-2000s.

Rozelle   I would get an email every day. I want to do *Carrie*, how do I get the rights? Can I get a script from you? Can I get this? Can I get that? Obviously, I had no connection to the show other than having just created this sort of one-stop shop so people could find out about it.

Lawrence D. Cohen (Book writer)   We were receiving tons of requests from stock and amateur companies as well as colleges and high schools that wanted to do productions. However, we were so unhappy with the show that we rejected all the offers. At one point, one fan actually released a petition to get signatures *demanding* that we make the rights available!

Pitchford   We would talk about it whenever we met, but we just couldn't bring ourselves to revisit it. There was so much that we did not want in the show. We had watched it go off the rails and we couldn't call it back.

A chance meeting almost led to a new, endorsed production.

Pitchford   I was in London in 2006 working on *Footloose* when I walked into the elevator at the Covent Garden Hotel and bumped into producer Jeffrey Seller. I'd known him and his producing partner Kevin McCollum[18] for quite a while, and we got to talking about the vague possibility of reviving *Carrie*. Back in New York, Kevin and Jeffrey joined me, Michael and Larry for dinner. During the course of the evening, I basically sat there and listened. I let Michael and Larry talk about the history of the show, and why things didn't work, and what their approach to a revival would be. And I realized that I didn't agree. I found myself thinking, 'I can't do this again. I can't go back and have this experience all over again.' The next day, I called them and I said, 'You can continue with another lyricist of your choosing, and I will step away and we can negotiate whatever parts of my material stays in. But I can't go back there.'

Pitchford realized he had not fully processed what returning to the show might feel like.

Pitchford   At that dinner, I was waiting to find out how things were going to be different now than they were before, and my conclusion was, they're not. We're going to go back to work on this and we're going to hash it out the way that we've always hashed it out. I had not yet realized what we needed was an arbiter. A dramaturg. I needed a fourth set of ears and eyes in the room. We all backed off from it at that point, and I called Jeffrey and said, 'Forgive us for rattling your cage, but we're not going to move ahead with this.'

---

[18]Seller and McCollum together produced *Rent*, *Avenue Q* and *In the Heights*, and Seller produced *Hamilton*.

But a 2009 article by *New York Times* critic Charles Isherwood struck a chord with Pitchford.

Pitchford   Isherwood was instrumental in getting the show redone without knowing it. One Friday – I didn't know this was coming – I opened the paper and there on the front page of the 'Weekend Arts' section of the *New York Times* was a massive grid of squares with screenshots. Isherwood's premise in this column was that for years we'd had no access to some great lost performances – people could only say, 'Oh, you should have been there.' But now that we have the Internet we could experience them again, so he'd revisited them all to see how they held up. All of the performances were operas, except the bottom right corner of the grid, which was Betty Buckley and Linzi Hateley doing 'And Eve was Weak'. He wrote the most rapturous review of that scene. He said, 'This completely floored me. I did not expect to have this reaction. Perhaps this show should be re-thought.' He elevated what he saw in that grainy, black and white video to the level of some of the greatest performances in opera history. That was when Michael and Larry and I got on the phone and said, 'Maybe something is happening here.'

Over the course of two decades, *Carrie* had gone from being an obscure in-joke with an underground cult following to being well recognized by a new generation of musical theatre fans. Now, even industry experts were recommending a critical reassessment.

Pitchford   In order to get it to a place where we would be happy to have *Carrie* back on stage, we would need to roll up our sleeves and do an enormous amount of work. But we needed that fourth set of eyes. We needed a catalyst to pull us together. And in 2008, we got that catalyst.

8 CANCELLING THE CURSE: REVIVING *CARRIE*

Stafford Arima (Director, off-Broadway)   I guess it was August of 2008. I wrote an email to my agent saying, 'I have this dream to do a one-night only concert version of *Carrie*.' I had this inexplicable fascination with this musical, and I thought that doing a concert version would be kind of cool. There was something about it that kept gnawing at me. Fast forward: I met Dean Pitchford in Los Angeles that October.

Dean Pitchford (Lyricist)   He said, 'I was in the audience for *Carrie* in New York. I was a teenager, my mother bought us tickets.' He had seen a Saturday matinee, and he still had the ticket stub.

Enthused by the lengthy meeting, Arima soon proposed something more than a one-night staging: a full re-examination of *Carrie* through a particularly contemporary lens. A slew of media reports about school bullying, online harassment and increasingly violent incidents in schools had dominated the news landscape throughout the 2000s.

Arima   I started to think about my own experience in high school. There were a few odd racial slurs here and there, and other kinds of crazy things about the fact that I was the 'theatre person'. But I never feared for my life, nor did I fear that I could say something and get killed for it. Something had definitely shifted in recent years. I started to think about Carrie White. She was bullied, too, in high school. Her 'out of sortness' or 'otherness' had a lot to do with who she was, how she presented herself, how she fit in or didn't fit in. And her otherness, in a very Stephen King kind of way, was her telekinesis.

Talking through how he might approach the task of remounting the show, Pitchford recalls being impressed by Arima's focus on how the story could work on stage, rather than how it hadn't.

Pitchford He didn't start putting Band-Aids on the original production. He didn't talk about how he wanted to take a scalpel to it. He approached it like the show had never been staged before. I called Michael and Larry, and I said, 'Stafford is working in New York, you should have breakfast with him. I think we might have a like-minded soul in the room.'

Lawrence D. Cohen (Book writer)   Having seen and enjoyed Stafford's production of *Altar Boyz*,[1] we agreed to meet. Purely by coincidence, what with all the requests by theatres and high schools to perform the show – we, as authors, had actually been talking about revamping the show so a new, approved version could be made available for licensing. Meeting Stafford was kismet; we immediately got along and his genuine passion for *Carrie* was clear. Working together seemed like a good fit.

Arima   As we started to converse, it came out that they were thinking about the show and that enough time had passed to consider re-looking at the material. So, there must have been some kind of serendipitous energy circulating that inevitably brought us all together.

Pitchford   We realized that we had found somebody to whom the show mattered as much as it mattered to us.

Relieved that Arima had no intentions of remounting a production with any physical similarities to the doomed 1988 show, the writers put three key questions to Arima: 'How would you handle the telekinesis? How would you handle the Prom? How would you handle the blood?' Satisfied with his overarching response that 'less is always more', they agreed to start the process of re-examining the show with him.[2]

Pitchford   The first thing I wanted to clear up was how we should leave the audience feeling at the end of the show. I don't think that we could have talked about that enough. I had the idea that we could – if we wrote it correctly – move an audience because of Carrie's plight. But there was no precedent for that . . . not in the book, the movie nor our first stab at the musical. So, agreeing to that objective, we rolled up our sleeves and we went back to work in 2009.

The writers soon realized that their passion for the story had been so drained by their experiences with the tumultuous 1988 production that they had forgotten how much they had enjoyed the early development process of the show.

Pitchford   We found those early discussions with Stafford as exciting and as challenging and as galvanizing as it had been in the beginning, and to be

---

[1] Arima's production of the musical comedy about a fictitious Christian boy band played from 2005 to 2010, making it the ninth longest-running off-Broadway show of all time.
[2] Healy, 'An Outsider'.

honest, we felt less encumbered by a lot of other projects. I did not hesitate to move to New York for long stretches of time to work with Larry, Michael and Stafford.

A *Carrie* for today

By now, producers and investors had realized the value of attracting a younger generation of theatregoers to their shows, and the stories told on Broadway stages had broadened to reflect the younger audience demographic. Recent well-received shows like *Wicked* (2003), *Spring Awakening* (2006) and *Legally Blonde* (2007) had not only showcased the trials and tribulations of young adults in high-profile, award-winning productions, but had actively reached out to them in promotional campaigns.

Arima   Broadway had become more accepting of a younger subject matter. Now, it seemed to be a draw rather than a negative. So, there was obviously a desire to update the piece, but not so much that the students were talking specifically about, you know, Instagram, because it really was important to keep a timelessness of it. It would quickly feel dated if we had thrown in those references.

Cohen   We were all clear that we didn't want it to be a 'period' piece, pardon the expression. To make the story resonate with modern audiences, we added some small creative touches, cell phones and social media, the addition of a gay student with a crush on Tommy, and so on. But the key to *Carrie*'s longevity was that like all the best fables, it lived and resonated in the now – whenever that now was.

One key aim was the reinstatement of realism, with a strong desire from the writers to root the show in the real world of the young people whose story it told. There would be no abstract costumes, classical staging devices or esoteric references in the new *Carrie*.

The team set about shaping up the show for an industry reading, re-engaging commercial producers Jeffrey Seller and Kevin McCollum. Cohen began work on a revised book, revisiting his original movie screenplay and introducing a framing device inspired by its memorable final scene, in which Sue Snell – the sole survivor of Carrie's murderous rampage – suffers repeated nightmares, essentially re-living the trauma on a loop forever.

Pitchford   Larry made the magic happen. He's the one who pulled the show apart at the seams and put it back together again. When we released the idea of doing it linearly, it allowed us to go back to a granular level. We looked at the messaging, the way in which all the kids were going to be caught up in this. That – in a way – all the kids were like Carrie, they were all dealing with their own private hell. We gave all the characters names and established relationships between them. They were more than the faceless gang they used to be. A real turning point came when we came up with the line 'What does it cost to be kind?' It was not just a story about vengeance, instead, it was a case of somebody seeking to understand otherness.

With the altered narrative structure and messaging in place, the next major challenge was tackling the show's score. Many of *Carrie*'s songs had been mocked for years, whilst others were lauded as some of Broadway's most compelling.

Pitchford   Those adjustments to the structure and the characters meant that certain songs didn't work anymore. We wanted to endow all of these characters with much more humanity than we had given them originally, and a lot of that came from what we had them singing. And, of course, some of the songs were written in such a 1980s vernacular that they simply felt out of place in a contemporary score, and needed to be rewritten or cut altogether.

Arima   There was always this – perhaps constructive – piece of criticism that had been attached to the score about these two worlds, that the score had a mother–daughter world and a kids', student world. They wanted to find a way to bridge that gap: even though I would defend the original score and say they are two different voices, and perhaps what makes that score so unique is the fact that it wasn't created in a homogenized way. But I can understand why the desire to meld the worlds a little bit more cohesively was something that they were excited to explore. There was a very rigorous, creative magnifying glass that went over everything. I went through the entire script, page by page, line by line, song by song, and asked a lot of questions. I was curious to know the background of why certain songs were in there. I didn't call it a revival, but a 'revisal'.

Michael Gore (Composer)   There were some numbers all three creators wanted to jettison. All in all, we ended up replacing over 50 per cent of the score with new material.

Pitchford   The songs that we wrote for Carrie and Margaret, for the most part, stayed the same, we just made slight nips and tucks. But the material written for the students was almost all redone. I found myself writing for these kids again, but this time I was in my fifties!

Re-casting *Carrie*

Casting for the reading began in October 2009. For the first time since 1987, the writers found themselves searching for performers to bring Carrie's world to life.

Bernie Telsey (Casting Director, The Telsey Office and Co-Artistic Director, MCC Theater)   Our office was asked to cast a reading of it.

Molly Ranson ('Carrie White', off-Broadway)   I was busy getting into the Halloween spirit, watching my favourite scary movies, when I was asked to audition for Carrie. I was, like, 'Carrie? The Musical? That sounds like a crazy idea!' As I learnt the music, I thought , 'Whoa, this is interesting. This is cool.' I loved the movie – Sissy Spacek was so amazing in her portrayal of that role – and I just like playing weird people. So, I got really excited about it, I knew it would be a fun role to do. I auditioned with an Avril Lavigne song, 'I'm with You'.

Telsey   She sounded so pure and so vulnerable and so innocent.

Ranson   I remember the writers all looking at my resumé and giggling. They said, 'Oh, you played "Mother" in *Ragtime* in high school!' I was, like, 'What? Why is that funny?' I didn't know that Marin Mazzie was going to be in it.

Mazzie – who had been nominated for Tony and Drama Desk Awards for originating the *Ragtime* role – had signed up to play Margaret White.

Telsey   Marin was revelatory. Obviously, she was somebody whose work we all knew, but she had not been seen in this kind of role before.

Arima   The casting of Margaret was key. There was no desire to – from the authors' perspective or mine – recreate a Barbara Cook performance or a Betty Buckley performance, even though they both created stunning versions of Margaret that have been etched into our brains. That character is a kind of walking entity of love. And sure, she might have some idiosyncratic behaviours that are questionable. But at the end of the day, it's all about her love of God and her love of her child. Marin understood that, and she wanted to bring to life a very three-dimensional Margaret. I remember, we would always say that if you saw her in the Whole Foods, probably at the organic section in her Birkenstocks, that you'd go up to her and you'd have a great conversation with her, and probably even be excited enough to invite her into your home, and she'd bring a great apple crumble.

The first reading

In October 2009, the *New York Post*'s Michael Riedel soon announced that a 'six-figure workshop' presentation of the musical would be staged the following month, noting that its producers must be 'supremely confident, bordering on cocky'[3] to revive such an infamous flop, before going on to recap the highlights (or lowlights) of the doomed original.

---

[3]Schulman, 'Is "Carrie" the Worst Musical?'

The presentation took place on 20 November, led by Mazzie and Ranson supported by Sutton Foster (Miss Gardner), Jennifer Damiano (Sue) and Diana DeGarmo (Chris), with musical direction by Stephen Oremus.

Opening with the cast circling Sue as they sing an increasingly ominous version of the Lord's Prayer before segueing into Sue's opening flashback, the reading introduced the show's new 'flashback' narrative structure. It retained the pace and energy of the 1988 production – even with intercut narration and minimal orchestration – whilst introducing more introverted and contemplative lyrics and themes. This was particularly noticeable in 'In', which maintained the upbeat tempo of the original but delved into more substantial subject matter than concerns about hair and parties.

> **Gore**   In particular, we felt that a major part of Act Two needed to be substantially rewritten. For all intents and purposes, it became an almost completely new act.

The songs 'Dream On', 'Don't Waste the Moon', 'Out for Blood', 'I'm Not Alone', 'It Hurts to Be Strong', 'Wotta Night' and 'Heaven' were all removed and replaced with new numbers, while the remaining songs were reimagined with updated lyrics and structures.

> **Pitchford**   The workshop was thrilling. The most emphatic response was from Bernie Telsey, who had cast the show but was also one of the founding artistic directors of MCC Theater, a leading off-Broadway theatre company. After the presentation, he said, 'Oh my God, this is stunning. Can we do it at MCC?'

MCC was, at the time, based at the 198-seat Lucille Lortel Theatre.

> **Telsey**   To this day, I still remember sitting there at the edge of my seat. I was blown away, emotionally. The score and the stakes of the story just engulfed me. I thought, 'Oh, my God, I want to do this at my theatre.' But it couldn't be a reality, because we were there to see a reading of a potential *Broadway* production, at that stage.

> **Pitchford**   All of their performances were done in a tiny, intimate theatre in Lower Manhattan. And our thought was 'What?!' We were thinking about Broadway. We were thinking about twenty-four pieces in the orchestra, special effects, a big cast. So, our first response was no. But as we began talking about it in more depth, it became clear that we could really benefit from throwing all the cards up in the air, tightening our belts, and trying it with as few people as we could, with as tight an orchestral setting as possible, and really focusing on the characters.

> **Bob Lupone** (Co-Artistic Director, MCC Theater)   I could see the appeal of doing it. It's an iconic musical, with a halo effect around it. When thinking

about producing a show, we always question whether it has a 'third act', meaning, will it send us off into the night talking about what we've just seen? This show had that. But we're an off-Broadway company. We can't spend $15 million on a musical, right? Well, I'm a firm believer in the idea that, you know, big Broadway producers and corporations solve problems by throwing money at them. Artists are more interesting. I've literally starved artists of budgets, and they've been far more creative than if they had lots of money. So, the challenge became: how can we do this big story on a shoestring budget?

Pitchford   By this time, I had done Footloose many times. It had been done on Broadway and had national tours go out, and productions around the world had been staged in all kinds of configurations, big and small. I had seen ways in which it could be collapsed and expanded. It made me realize that if we went straight back to Broadway with *Carrie* and did the same sort of thing we had done in 1988, in the same size configuration, the same sort of house, we would not have changed the rules. We thought, 'Let's change the rules. Let's see what happens.'

Telsey   And lo and behold, the three guys and Stafford were all, like, 'Well, that's what we want.' It became this great marriage.

Lupone   And what happened as a result was very creative, and that was the *raison d'être* for it.

Changing the rules

With a firm decision to reinvent the show on a smaller scale, Seller and McCollum – primarily interested in developing Broadway shows – amicably departed the project, with MCC taking on full responsibility for the ongoing development process.

The November 2009 *Carrie* reading had been well received, but there was a lot still to do to re-align the show with the new 'compact' vision and its simpler, character-driven approach.

Arima   We knew that the sound of the show – through orchestrations and vocal arrangements – was going to be key.

Mary-Mitchell Campbell (Musical Director, off-Broadway)   Bernie Telsey and Stafford Arima reached out to me about working on it. I was already a fan of the writers and was somewhat familiar with the score; I knew of the fate of the original production, but I was interested in seeing what would happen with a new take on the material. I worked with the unbelievable AnnMarie Milazzo who arranged all the vocals. I shaped the music for the production, taught it, and eventually conducted the run along with Paul Staroba, my associate. We also had Adam Wachter play a pivotal role of keeping up with all our changes and offering fantastic musical suggestions throughout the process.

AnnMarie Milazzo (vocal designer, off-Broadway)   I didn't know the show. I'd heard lots about it, but I'd never checked it out. It was awesome. It was some parts opera, some parts musical theatre.

Campbell   AnnMarie and I had done *Next to Normal* together, so I was already familiar with her unconventional process.

Adam Wachter (Assistant Musical Director, off-Broadway)   AnnMarie doesn't read or notate music; she records her own singing using audio editing software, one vocal part at a time, and layers each one. My main job prior to rehearsals starting was to transcribe all of her insanely brilliant arrangements. I would solo out each vocal part's recording individually, listen to it, and then write it all out as sheet music for the actors to read and sing.

Gore   AnnMarie is a unique talent.

Arima   She was tasked to create something that could be timeless, that we could hear in 2032 and not have it feel like it was something created in the mid-2000s.

Milazzo   I thought the idea of getting inside these kids' heads was really interesting. What's going on in there? What happened before they got to school? What's driving the story, from their perspectives? That's where the new version of 'In' came from. The students would go into their private moments and then they would break out and be singing the song as a group.

Campbell   We wanted to bring the opening number into a more current style and sound, so we spent a great deal of time working on 'In'. We really focused on the sound of the voices we had in the room, and made lots of specific adjustments. This is why the vocals to this show are so complicated!

Milazzo and Campbell aimed to use the infamous opening song as their starting point to create a new signature sound for the show, transforming it from its 1980s Broadway styling to something more reflective of the darker, introspective themes of the original story.

Gore   Some of our most fun and creative times were working with these two incredibly talented women. They had a very unique collaborative style together, and it was immediately apparent and exciting how right the sound was that they'd come up with for each number. They proved to be fantastic assets to the show and in particular, to the music.

Arima   I remember a very exciting moment when AnnMarie played her demo track for 'In'. She had layered in all of the tracks, twelve vocal arrangements, all on top of each other, playing all the parts.

Milazzo   Presenting it was very nerve-wracking!

Arima   I think the future of the show depended on how we all responded to this new arrangement, specifically Michael. He's such an incredible writer – flexible, and bizarrely intuitive – but also very protective, as he should be. To allow someone to just go off and play with his song says a lot about him as an artist. So, although this wasn't an audition, it kind of felt like one, because any of us could have responded either way. Milazzo pushed play, I looked over at Dean, and soon there was a tear running down his cheek. I could sense that it wasn't tears of sadness, but tears of joy. The track ended, and Michael said, 'Play it again, please.' After we heard it the second time, they all gave a thumbs up.

Milazzo   We didn't change the DNA of anything. The writers were just amazing at diving in and going, 'Yeah, we're going to do something that's *Carrie*, but it's gonna be a little different.' I think they had enough distance, so they were, like, 'let's get in there and see what could happen'.

The music in the 2009 workshop had been performed with just a single piano and basic percussion; the 1988 production had used a full-scale orchestra. Gore settled on something in between, suited to the intimate off-Broadway space of *Carrie*'s new home, MCC's Lucille Lortel Theatre.

Gore   We ended up choosing to go with a band of seven instruments: two keyboards, bass, drums, two guitars and cello. I turned to Doug Besterman, who had orchestrated some of my film scores and was comfortable in both the orchestral and pop worlds. Doug found a beautiful tone to integrate both the high school pop songs and the operatic Margaret/Carrie material with this instrumentation.

Doug Besterman (Orchestrator, off-Broadway)   I was completely unfamiliar with the original production and didn't really know any of the songs, but I did not hesitate to get involved with this version of the show. The authors were very enthusiastic about the new version, in particular about Stafford's concepts, and I felt we were going to create something that was unique and separate from the 1980s version.

Readings and labs

Though the 2009 workshop presentation had been invite-only, fans were thrilled when the news got out that *Carrie* might finally be returning to New York. On 5 October 2010, it was officially announced that the slimmed-down 'revisal' would be staged during MCC's 2011–12 season, and that a second reading in November would 'allow the writers to test a new draft of the script as they work to remount the production'.[4]

---

[4]Adam Hetrick, 'MCC Tests Carrie, with Marin Mazzie, Aaron Tveit and Molly Ranson', *Playbill*, 9 November 2010, available online: https://playbill.com/article/exclusive-mcc-tests-carrie-with-marin-mazzie-aaron-tveit-and-molly-ranson-nov-9-com-173412 (accessed 13 December 2022).

In 2011, two exploratory 'labs' were organized to continue developing the new material, helping to shape up the new songs, vocal arrangements and scenes. Each lasted two weeks and concluded with a presentation for the wider design team and producers.

Wachter   In the February lab, we worked through all of Act One, plus three numbers from Act Two: 'You Shine', 'When There's No One' and the Epilogue. The focus was primarily on AnnMarie's newly arranged teen group numbers, but we also did the Carrie and Margaret material. This lab featured Molly and Marin, of course, and added Annaleigh Ashford as Chris, Stark Sands as Tommy, Christy Altomare as Sue and Eric William Morris as Billy.

Christy Altomare ('Sue Snell', off-Broadway)   The first time I auditioned for the show was when it was just a reading [in 2009]. I had gone in for Sue Snell and I decided to sing the song 'True Colours', because I always try to pick a song that really conveys what the character's going through. The one thing I hadn't anticipated in my early twenties is just how high the key was! It was super high, and I don't think it came across well. So, I didn't get it that round. For the next audition, I sang 'Some Things are Meant to Be' from the musical *Little Women*. At one point, I remember sunlight streamed through the window just as the song crescendoed. It was like it was meant to be!

As well as honing the score and book, the labs allowed the team to start establishing a choreographic style for the show which would bind cohesively with the show's orchestration and scenic design. It would be far from Debbie Allen's 1988 high-kicking, aerobic approach.

Matthew Williams (Choreographer, off-Broadway)   My job encompassed a fair amount more than just choreography. Stafford was very collaborative and allowed myself and a sort of a 'quartet' team – which consisted of myself, my assistant, Jen Rapp and his assistant, Todd Underwood – to each contribute lots of ideas.

Unlike the original production, with its Ensemble made up of highly-trained dancers cast mainly for their movement skills, the focus in the revival would be on more subtle, gestural movement tied closely to the new sound of the show.

Williams   That word 'gestural' was a really key word that Stafford and I used back and forth about how we were going to go. I watched a lot of Ballet Preljocaj, led by Angelin Preljocaj, a choreographer from France. There was a really fascinating piece that he had called 'Haka'. I looked at videos of some incredible Japanese choreographers: precision movement pieces, incredible, gestural styles. Some Canadian and European choreographers. The show that we definitely got likened to, in terms of movement, is *Spring Awakening*, with Bill T. Jones' choreography. That was inspiring to me.

Lupone   The choreography was so good. It sort of lifted the story and made it current, you know, in a wonderful way.

Williams   By the time the writers had seen the choreography they were already used to the music and the sound, so they were sort of on board with the general style of everything. They were very complimentary and happy with what was presented. Dean, having been a choreographer and dancer, always had useful feedback. So, you know, if I presented something, it would go through a couple of filters, Stafford and Dean.

The second lab would focus on a particularly key moment of the story, reinventing the show's dramatic finale using the refreshed movement vernacular.

Wachter   In May, we focused on the rest of Act Two, including, of course, the Prom and Destruction. At one point we tried a new opening scene for Act Two that only existed for maybe a day and then was never seen again! It was a flashback to Margaret giving birth to Carrie, and stones were raining down on the house. She had a knife and she was going to kill the baby, but then the police arrived and stopped her. I think everyone was a little bit, like, 'What's going on?!'

Ranson, Mazzie and Altomare were joined by some new faces.

Wachter   Derek Klena joined as Tommy, Jeanna de Waal came in as Chris, and Ben Thompson was Billy. Karen Olivo played Miss Gardner – we also spent time working on her material – and Louis Hobson was the Adult Male, a new role which included a male teacher called Mr Stephens.

Jeanna de Waal ('Chris Hargensen', off-Broadway)[5]   I remember my sister came with me to the Telsey office for an audition. At that stage it was just the development lab.

De Waal was asked to perform a work-in-progress version of a new song written for the show's antagonist, 'The World According to Chris'.

De Waal   I mean, the song was crazy, wasn't it? It was like the school bitch, in song form! I remember just going in and sort of being as bold with the choices as I could be.

Derek Klena ('Tommy Ross', off-Broadway)   At the time I was a sophomore at UCLA. I remember putting myself on tape in Los Angeles. I did a few of Tommy's scenes and his 'Dreamer in Disguise' song.[6] I remember one scene in particular was when Tommy asked Carrie to the dance, and I actually filmed it

---

[5]De Waal would later play Princess Diana in a flop from more recent times, *Diana: The Musical*.
[6]Restored to the show for the first time since the 1984 workshop.

in a doorway with my acting coach! I felt like I was really right for this role, because – like Tommy – I had a sports background, but I also had this other life where I was pursuing theatre. I was very much that *High School Musical* kid!

Klena was called to New York for a week of callbacks.

Klena   Mary-Mitchell prepped me for the creative team, because they were very particular about how they wanted certain songs to be sung. And it all worked out.

Pitchford   The labs were full of extraordinary performers from Broadway and beyond. Bernie was able to pull in very high-profile, talented people to take part, and they held our material up to our faces and challenged us. It was very flattering. In the deepest points of the process, I would find myself reminding myself that so many people, all of whom had really high standards, had listened to our work and agreed to sing it. Barbara Cook had done it. Betty Buckley had, and now these great, new performers were doing it, too. That kept me going.

The new class

On 1 August 2011, some of the new material was presented for the first time at an MCC fundraiser entitled *Revisiting Carrie*, staged at the Lucille Lortel. Tickets quickly sold out, with guests treated to performances by Ranson and Mazzie as well as a stirring rendition of 'In'.

Pitchford   The place went berserk! This was the first time we were performing parts of the show outside a rehearsal room, in front of an audience that wasn't invited. So, the response to our opening number lifted our spirits enormously!

At a Q&A at the end of the event, one audience member informed the panel, 'I was one of the original dressers. I got a lot of overtime washing blood out of costumes!'[7]

A press announcement in November revealed that Ranson (Carrie), Mazzie (Margaret), Altomare (Sue), Klena (Tommy), de Waal (Chris) and Ben Thompson (Billy) would star in the revival, reprising their workshop roles. They would be joined by Carmen Cusack as Miss Gardner,[8] Wayne Alan Wilcox as Mr Stephens and a small Ensemble cast of six named supporting characters.[9]

---

[7] Staff writer, 'Post-Mortem on the Bloody Mess that was "Carrie"', *Variety*, 4 August 2011, available online: https://variety.com/2011/film/news/post-mortem-on-the-bloody-mess-that-was-carrie-1118040857/ (accessed 5 May 2022).
[8] Now with the forename Lynn.
[9] Not, alas, the names of the 1988 Ensemble, as they had been promised.

Pitchford   In 1988, all of the school kids were like a faceless mass of uncaring, haranguing adolescents. Now, every one of the characters had a name and a personality. We wanted a company of living, breathing, interacting, named characters, all with their own inner turmoil. Changes like that made such a difference to the show, and made us feel so much more excited.

Klena   I got the offer to be in the show about a month after doing the lab. I made the decision to take some time off school and come to New York to do the show. A little over ten years later, I'm still here today, I never finished school. My mom reminds me of that frequently!

The cast was encouraged to build their characters from the ground up, and to discard preconceptions built on previous interpretations of the roles.

De Waal   My approach was that Chris is the 'it' girl of the school, the girl with the rich dad who gives her all the things she wants, but none of the love and attention she needs. So, she has a bit of a void and a sadness in her. Like most bullies, she deals with her own lack of self-love by inflicting pain on others, so she goes after Carrie. She has a bad boy as her boyfriend, and she finds that thrilling. The idea of pouring pig's blood on a young girl seems really fun to her.

Klena   Tommy is this seemingly golden boy, the Prom King, and his girlfriend is the would-be Prom Queen. You know, that ideal couple. He's always been put on this pedestal. He ends up taking Carrie to the dance, and it turns into this magical evening where Carrie really sees a different part of Tommy, and Tommy sees this girl that Sue saw a glimpse of when she was getting bullied. That she is special, and just misunderstood. I think they connect in that way, as people that are just trying to find their own way in life, and are just regularly misunderstood.

Reflecting the show's new mantra, 'what does it cost to be kind?', new cast member Carmen Cusack was interested in exploring the character as a sort of substitute mother for Carrie, and was drawn to the show by a personal connection.

Carmen Cusack ('Miss Gardner', off-Broadway)   I found Carrie to be an incredibly relatable role to the young girl in me, as my background growing up was a highly religious one. Pentecostal in fact. We went to church three or four times a week. I would often watch people fall to the floor in convulsions, speaking in another language – what they call speaking in tongues – and I remember feeling very isolated and scared as a young girl in this atmosphere. Not really knowing what to make of it all. And certainly not being encouraged to ask questions or share my doubts and distaste on the matter. I was brought up in fear. Fear of God, fear of authority. All of it seemed to be based in fear. Hence, I am no longer religious! It was a lot of brainwashing and took years for me to reprogram my thinking. So, I felt very connected to this piece and what Carrie was going through. Miss Gardner was that adult I wished I had had in my life while navigating the challenges of adolescence.

With the full cast in place, journalist Patrick Healy was given access to rehearsals for a *New York Times* preview, and was struck by the change of tone in the new version. 'This *Carrie* is as serious as a hostage-rescue mission, which approximates how its creators – the same men who kept it under lock and key all those years – see their task.'[10]

Altomare The writers wanted the story to be taken seriously, as it should be, as if these are real people that are going through pain, and they wanted the audience to be able to see themselves in these characters, because how else are you going to react to any piece of art if you don't see the reality and the humanity in it?

De Waal They wanted a real exploration of a girl's struggle in high school with this unique gift. They really wanted it to be a coming-of-age story.

Ranson I think it was the first time that I really felt like I was able to contribute to the creative process of a show. Obviously, the writers had the final say and it was their material, but they were so open to hearing my interpretation of it, and so respectful of my opinions. It was a very empowering experience to be able to feel like I was able to have a say and to contribute my voice to it. (Image 8.1.)

A new home

It was soon time for the newly-assembled *Carrie* company to move into the Lucille Lortel Theatre. The intimate theatre, on Christopher Street in the West Village, presented unique challenges for the freshly-assembled creative and technical teams.

Kevin Adams (Lighting Designer, off-Broadway) It wasn't built as a theatre. It was built as a horse stable, I think. There's no space off-stage for lighting and equipment, which is really hard for a musical. You have to put a big cast in dressing rooms that are very small. But, you know, there are a lot of those kinds of spaces in New York City and you just have to make do the best you can. And sometimes you can make really beautiful work, and the space itself features a little bit.

---

[10]Healy, 'An Outsider'.

IMAGE 8.1 Molly Ranson (with levitating Jesus) in rehearsal. Stafford Arima (photographer).

Wachter   The seven-piece band were placed in a disused storage closet off the balcony's lobby that the sound department converted into an acoustic booth, and ran hundreds of cables to and from. We rarely ever saw the cast during the run of the show! They lived behind the stage on a different level of the building and had a different stage door entrance, while we musicians would just walk through the lobby and go up to our little storage closet and play.

Besterman   Everything was piped into the main space, so to speak. Our sound designer, Jonathan Deans, took very good care of things, and I remember being very happy with the sound – but there were some challenges there for sure.

David Zinn (Scenic Designer, off-Broadway)   I told the guys when I started working on the show that I really loved what I'd seen of, and what I've heard about, the original set design. I loved how bold the choice was. I'm someone who has been privileged enough to work on the premiere productions of a lot of musicals, and I know what happens: you take a first strong swing at the material and sometimes it's a triumph, and sometimes it's not. But you've got to take a swing. Ralph Koltai was a deeply serious, thoughtful designer and I think he gave it his best shot. The 'tone' of this musical is complicated – there's humour, there's a lot of drama. It's hard to know what set best serves a piece like that. I fully understand why they did what they did, and admire it.

Adams   Our show had to be so minimal. The bigger context is that it's off-Broadway and that means smaller budgets. How do you fill that space without a lot of money, and without much labour?

Zinn   Stafford's vision was smaller scale, more intimate, more human, less 'mythic'. I think doing it on a more intimate scale was probably appealing to the writers because you can focus on the performers, and be true to them. I had worked on a couple of shows with MCC and had wrestled successfully with that space, which is small and architecturally idiosyncratic. It forces you to make choices that aren't super fussy, and I like that. I think it was really helpful for all of us, there was no way this could feel like the original version.

Like the original production, the revival anchored the world of the show in a single space, the school's gymnasium. Koltai had interpreted the space metaphorically, turning it into an abstract white box. Zinn used a more literal representation of the setting as it might appear post-destruction.

Zinn   We had this grey, ashen, burned-out school which also felt like it could be the architecture of the theatre. Everything happened in the context of that. I like events that exist in spaces that don't necessarily describe every location, I think it forces us to use our imagination and I think the tension between the space you're seeing and the space that the 'scene' is taking place in can be exciting. I'm not sure it worked for both worlds of the show, but I don't think that's a problem. Not that I wouldn't be interested in seeing a version that was rooted in the difference of those spaces, or one, even, that was set entirely in the house. But as I said earlier, you pick a context for what you think is right for the show overall and give it your best shot.

Altomare The set was sort of one big foreshadow of what it was going to become later on, which was really eerie.

Zinn We had one big set of metal double-doors directly upstage, the doors that Carrie slams closed as she destroys the gym and traps everyone inside. A little bit of a sense that this space might be a memorial: some candles were burning, if I remember. But clearly you were walking into a place where something bad had happened. Everything lived within the context of that, with other locations being suggested fairly simply with chairs, a table and so on. (Image 8.2.)

A particularly memorable scenic element was the use of high-definition projections to suggest other locations and moods.

Sven Ortel (Projection Designer, off-Broadway) I made storyboards that pre-visualized the look for most of the scenes well in advance, a 3D version of the set so that I could play with it. I shared everything I was doing with the rest of the creative team as I was transforming David's unit set to suggest many different locations. Sometimes that just meant adding a bit of texture, at other times I was projecting scenic elements.

Williams Projections obviously don't take up space, they just need surface. The idea was not to crowd and to cram a lot of physical elements into the

IMAGE 8.2 David Zinn's model box of the set. David Zinn (designer/photographer).

space. Everything was meant to be quite flexible and have a small footprint out of necessity.

Ortel   The goal was to hide the technology and make it about the story, but that was tricky in such a small space because it's harder to make a projector disappear or to be quiet. I had to project around the performers, otherwise they would block the projected imagery and get hit by it, which was quite complicated at the time and not cheap, as it required more gear.

A night you'll never forget

On 31 January 2012, for the first time since 1988 – in an official capacity, at least – *Carrie* returned to the stage. A guest of honour was Piper Laurie, who starred as Margaret White in Brian de Palma's *Carrie* movie.

Klena   Across the street there was a little rally, a group that gathered to cheer the resurrection of *Carrie*. That was cool. We realized the show had a special type of following and a special type of support. Our audiences were super-charged. No-one really knew what they were going to come and see.

Gore   The audience response was gratifying, especially at that very first preview which felt that they were rooting for us and welcoming us back.

Lupone   There was the cult following who knew every line of the script and would sing along or comment. That was part of the show. It was like seeing the *Rocky Horror Show*, you know, they were committed, they came in costume. They did their whole thing, which was great. There were others who were less dedicated but had heard of the legend of *Carrie*, and were intrigued to see what we'd done with it. Everyone was there for a good night out.

The audience would certainly witness a very different production to the heavily mythologized 1988 original.

The show

The new *Carrie* is bookended by short scenes in which Sue is being aggressively questioned by unseen interrogators; soon, she is joined by the 'ghosts' of her schoolmates, and it becomes clear she is recollecting the night of Carrie's destruction, with the action 'flashing back' to the start of the story. The structure is reminiscent of both the movie's final flashback, and the novel, in which the story is partially told through testimonies and documents about the incident. The narration device returns at several other key points in the show.

Altomare   From very early in the process, they had had a vision of these moments where the story would jump back and forth, with Sue patching together the story for the audience. There would be moments where she would be a complete wreck, and then in a second, she'd be back in the school having a great day. Throughout the workshop process, the exact positions of the flashbacks shifted a few times. They'd add one, or cut one, trying to find the perfect shape. I remember at one point Stafford said that maybe she'd even have a straitjacket on, and she'd be at the state asylum. Eventually, we landed on Sue explaining to the authorities what had happened; she's exhausted and she's tired of answering the same questions over and over again. It was really cool and fun to play.

As Sue concludes her expository speech, she steps back into the action as the introduction to 'In' begins. The new opening number – now grungier, slower and *sans* aerobics – had received a full makeover, signalling to the audience that this was not the high-kicking *Carrie* they'd heard about or seen in grainy YouTube clips.

Telsey   It was a whole new everything. It just brought you right into the story and you knew the kind of show it was going to be. I still say it was the best opening number ever. I loved it.

Cohen   One of my most vivid memories was watching 'In' onstage for the first time. It felt light-years different in tone, and truly emblematic of our reworking of the show. It was so moving and exciting – for the first time matching up with what was in our heads – that I started to cry. I stood there thinking of everything that my fellow authors and I had been through, our insanely rocky journey that led up to this point. It was now all worth it. I was frankly overcome with emotion, as were my colleagues.

Klena   AnnMarie had tried different lines on different people to see how we could make these really cool, chaotic arrangements using all of these incredible, young rock voices to elevate the material that was already there, and also make it more contemporary. It just set the tone for the show.

Pitchford   Stafford made a really, really brilliant observation, that in the original production, 'In' was only sung by the girls. He pointed out that the boys are equally troubled. You start realizing that all of those people are pushing their own private boulder up a hill. So, the song now has both the girls and the boys. Suddenly, it's not just some nameless girls bitching about having split ends or not having a date on a Saturday night. I looked back and was kind of embarrassed, in retrospect, by how I sold out the kids with that number in 1988.

Klena   There are all these different groups that don't necessarily reflect the same stereotypes nowadays. The song established the hierarchy at the school, and it kind of took us through our characters and their internal struggles and having to put on this façade to try to fit in.

'In' also gave the audience their first glimpse of *Carrie*'s new choreographic style.

Klena   I remember we probably went through ten to fifteen different versions of 'In', physically. It was always a tough tightrope to walk, you know, because we wanted to establish the show as something different, we didn't want anybody to mistake it for camp. I think we found a version of the movement that was really satisfying in the end. Keeping it youthful, but also jagged and edgy and uncomfortable, because that is how Carrie views most of the world at that point, and how she feels in it.

Ranson gets the opportunity to showcase her vocal talents with the title song, 'Carrie', now featuring refreshed lyrics giving Carrie more agency and control over her own destiny, doing away with her longing for a boyfriend and awarding her with a more independent outlook:

I might take a chance
I've always wondered how
Or maybe I'll dance
And try hard to laugh more than I do now
And the world will open its eyes
And for once the whole world will recognize
Carrie!

The audience is introduced to Marin Mazzie's Margaret in 'Open Your Heart', her contemporary clothing lulling them into a false sense of security before the blistering 'And Eve was Weak', two largely untouched songs familiar and beloved to long-term fans of the show.

Soon after, 'Don't Waste the Moon' is replaced by a catchy new number, 'The World According to Chris'.

Pitchford   The song sows the seeds of the rift between Chris and Sue, and so it had to be unrepentant. In 1988, the kids were given boppy, fun, frothy things to sing and react to. In 2012, the school characters were all treated with much more gravitas.

Chris sarcastically sings:

Ew, Sue, I can see you're feeling bad
Boo hoo!
So we clobbered Carrie, and that's too damn bad!
This is why you gotta love my dad!
He's got the right idea!
My daddy taught me who's on top and who's below

And now it's time I let you know
The world according to Chris!

De Waal   Chris is explaining to Sue why she thinks it's okay to be a bully. She really drums up the energy of the whole group of kids, and they all sort of end up in a frenzy. It was cool, because I remember really being given permission to do anything I wanted on the stage. One night, I remember climbing up a wall and jumping off!

Pitchford   She's spewing these things right in the face of her best friend, and the audience is having such fun that you don't realize that you're witnessing the beginning of the end. Chris is getting such reinforcement from everyone that she doesn't care, and she lets the chips fall where they may.

The song builds to a crescendo as Chris is egged on by the students, before they all depart, leaving her alone on stage.

Pitchford   She says what's on her mind and the hell with everybody else, and she's left alone as a result. She's the queen bee, the party girl at the top of the song and by the end, the stage is empty and she made her bed, and she's now going to have to lie in it. She's more than the two-dimensional villain we used to know.

Like most of the songs with Carrie and her mother, 'Evening Prayers' is retained, shortly followed by a scene in a class at school – led by the new character, Mr Stephens – adding some character development for Tommy.

Gore   We chose to restore Tommy's classroom poem song, 'Dreamer in Disguise', which had been in our initial reading in 1984 but never ended up in the 1988 production. We always loved the song and chose to put it back, and also reprise it for the moment with Tommy and Carrie at the Prom.

Tommy sings:

The things I dream
The things I feel
There's more to me than I reveal
And cuz I shine in quiet ways
I'm someone you don't recognize
I am a diamond in the rough
A dreamer in disguise

Todd Graff ('Tommy Ross', 1984 workshop)   I hate to think that my butchering of that song in the workshop is why they cut it out of the show for decades, but I imagine it didn't help that I blew it and it got very tepid applause at the end. I retired from acting pretty soon after that with good reason!

Graff was not the responsible party.

Pitchford   Terry Hands had cut it in line with his concept of the show. He thought the show should focus on the women – Sue and Chris, mother and daughter, the gym teacher – and he thought that giving Tommy a number, as short as it was, really distracted from the forward momentum. It was things like that that were 'big gulps' for us. Tommy is an enormous agent of change in the story. He had an enormous part in the tragedy of it all. As soon as we started discussing the revival, we knew we wanted to bring it back.

Though Tommy's poem provokes derision from his classmates, Carrie is mesmerized and meekly voices her appreciation, making their surprising connection at the Prom notionally more realistic.

Klena   It was Tommy's 'I Want' song, and it felt like you wouldn't understand him without it. Tommy being this misunderstood person was a strong and necessary move for this new iteration of the show. The song illustrates that there is a lot more that he wants to pursue, but he's afraid to take that step, like so many young people are.

Pitchford   When Tommy asks her to the Prom, she says, 'Why are you doing this?' and he says, 'Because you liked my poem.' It's a very potent arc of the story. You know, the bonding at that level transcends soft touches and longing looks into each others' eyes.

Klena   We were careful to never suggest that he is having genuine feelings for Carrie. I think they develop a mutual respect that didn't exist at the beginning of the night. The Prom is an awkward evening. It's not a comfortable night out. Carrie has never experienced something like this, she has no idea how to act. She's terrified and excited. Tommy is feeling the exact same way. What am I doing? How is this going to look? Is this really how you want to end your school career? We found little lines and moments where Carrie sees Tommy and Tommy Carrie, solidifying the deeper understanding between the two of them. Yes, there is an understanding that this is uncomfortable. She knows it's not genuine. She knows that he's doing her a favour, basically. But in the end, that's okay, because she knows it.

Tommy's solo is followed by one for Sue, 'Once You See'. It was the third attempt at an introspective, contemplative number for the character, after 'White Star' was cut in Stratford and replaced with 'It Hurts to Be Strong' on Broadway.

Gore   'Once You See' became a window into Sue's interior evolution from mean girl to good girl with a conscience. She realizes what she had done to Carrie, and vows to make it right.

Sue sings:

For years you look
You look at someone passing by
And then one day you see her
One day you finally see her . . .

While Sue's moment of self-reflection had previously taken place near the start of Act Two, here – in line with her role as the show's guide and storyteller – she begins to realize the error of her ways much earlier. Interestingly, some of the melody from the song 'Her Mother Should Have Told Her', a short song cut from the production on Broadway, is repurposed in the number.

The remainder of the first Act continues as it did in 1988 – with Miss Gardner and Carrie's uplifting duet 'Unsuspecting Hearts' and a somewhat more restrained edition of 'Do Me a Favor' (in which Tommy's agreement to invite Carrie to the Prom feels significantly more considered). A short scene in which Margaret is summoned to the school for a meeting with Carrie's teachers was included after this number, but cut early in previews.

The Act rounds off with Margaret's explosive 'I Remember How Those Boys Could Dance', performed with vigour by Mazzie. After terrifying her mother with a display of her powers, Carrie calmly sits down at the dinner table to eat her dessert, leaving Margaret cowering in fear.

After intermission, gone is the dancing, leather-clad, pig-hunting mob of the original.

Gore   We ended up replacing 'Out for Blood' with a wholly different kind of number called 'A Night You'll Never Forget', an Ensemble-driven song that combined plot and storytelling in an up-tempo companion piece to the excitement and energy of Act One's opening number 'In'. It comes around again as the interwoven musical theme for the Prom sequence. This helped to rejigger the score so that it all now felt more of an integrated piece.

Miss Gardner, suspicious of Sue and Tommy's motivation for asking Carrie to the Prom, warns them sternly not to hurt her in any way. In the position previously reserved for Sue's brooding solo, a new song, 'You Shine', gave the writers the opportunity to explore Sue and Tommy's relationship in more depth and add poignancy to their story:

If you could see
The way that you look to me
I bet that you'd be amazed at the sight
You'd see a heart that's fearless and true
From my point of view, oh, you shine
No doubts, no more fears

I see you shine and the dark disappears
I'll be your mirror and you can be mine
Look to me and you'll see just how you shine

At its conclusion, Tommy declares that he loves Sue. Turning to the audience in her 'interrogation space' she reveals that, despite everything that happened, this moment is the one she remembers most clearly about the day of the destruction.

Soon, Carrie determinedly sings 'Why Not Me?' as she prepares for Prom. Fans of the floating hairbrush and self-tapping shoes from the original production's 'I'm Not Alone' might be disappointed to find they have been abandoned in favour of some self-motivation:

I'm gonna talk above a whisper
I'm gonna walk in three-inch heels
I'm gonna fight the urge to turn around and flee!
And then I will feel the magic
I'm told anyone can feel
When the stars align
And life is filled with possibility
And if everybody feels that way then why
Why not me?

Pitchford   She used to sing 'I'm not alone anymore . . .' It suggested that her heart was going 'pitter-patter' and a Prince Charming was going to show up at the door to take her away. No! Carrie's smart and she stands up for herself, and she stands up to her mother. She is not under any misapprehension that Tommy is going to fall in love with her, or that he'll sweep her off her feet and make her life whole. She's not going to be made complete by the captain of the football team. In its place is a song of affirmations. If everyone else can do this, why not me? She's pumping herself up, and it turns into a song of empowerment.

Gore   It was certainly an improvement over 'I'm Not Alone', losing its Disney-like quality and the display of her powers that we felt was tonally incorrect. Instead, it gave her a more positive take for her character.

Two familiar numbers follow: all set for her big night, Carrie brushes off her mother's plea to 'Stay Here Instead', leaving her mother alone to contemplate her fateful decision in 'When There's No One'.

And what of the story's iconic end sequence?

The bloodless *Carrie*

Arima   I always wanted to find a unique vocabulary for the blood moment in the production. The stage was so small that I didn't want to use prop 'blood' falling from the flies. The splash factor would definitely be an issue for the audience, and I was completely against the idea of offering *Carrie*-branded rain ponchos to the front row to protect their clothing . . . I was interested in exploring Carrie's emotional state during that precise moment, and how to translate it to the stage. At one point, I asked David Zinn, the set designer, if it would be possible to 'flood' the stage with 'blood', but he advised that the technical requirements for that effect could not happen at the Lortel due to its size. However, my idea of a 'flood' was translated – through the projection work of Sven Ortel – into a tsunami of blood that could be projected on the stage and the walls of the entire theatre, engulfing the audience in the effect.

Ortel   At the climax we see the shadow of the infamous bucket, as if cast by a spotlight. It tips and we see a hint of red liquid pour out and fall down towards Carrie. What follows is heightened and suggestive: at the moment the liquid would hit the floor an enormous roar builds up in sync with a giant wave of blood that rises from the floor to quickly encapsulate the entire space. When it collapses, Carrie is left devastated on the gym floor, standing in horror and bathed in red light. All the blood was imagined, or in the mind of Carrie. My hope was to highlight Carrie's horror by showing what she saw and experienced in her mind's eye at that moment.

Arima   To Carrie, the shame, the embarrassment, and the humiliation of being the brunt of a cruel joke is far greater, in her mind, than anything literal. De Palma used a similar technique in the movie with a kaleidoscope-like effect in which the students and faculty are uncontrollably laughing at Carrie. This shot takes the audience into Carrie's perceived reality, which is monumentally skewed. For our production, the geyser of blood produced by Ortel's animation, alongside the sound effects and lighting, were our way of using theatre tools to change the perspective of the blood moment and move into Carrie's headspace.

Williams   It was really fun to experiment with the sound effects. We searched and found just the right sort of metal ping where the bucket supposedly hits Tommy's head, and the echoing splash effect of the blood. For the final explosion we listened to, I don't know, 100 different possible explosions and then narrowed them down to twenty and then three and then one.

Ortel   I was able to very accurately choreograph how flames travelled along the set, the individual baseboards and mouldings, in time with the music. It was the first time I had mapped an entire set to such a level of detail and it opened up a whole new world of possibilities for visual storytelling.

Arima   After Carrie leaves the gymnasium, Molly changed into a blood-stained costume and was doused with 'blood'. She then re-entered the final scene to sing her closing number with her mother.

Cusack   On the first day of rehearsal, I remember Stafford having us sit in a circle on the floor as he explained his vision for *Carrie*. He seemed very adamant that he didn't want a drop of blood on the stage for this piece. I thought it was a brave move, but I wasn't convinced we could pull it off. Not sure that we did either. In the end, I still think the audience felt a little cheated that it wasn't a bloodbath. But, I'm not sure how we could have afforded it at the Lortel. I mean, the dry-cleaning bills alone would've been crazy! Rolling around on the floor, convulsing under Carrie's spell did allow me to conjure up all the visions I had of those Pentecostals I grew up with back in the day!

Adams   We all kind of accepted the idea of not doing the blood very quickly, I recall. It was just kind of the way it was. How do you dump blood on a costume? How do you clean that costume? How do you clean the stage? What do you do about blood that goes on the audience? What do you do for the rest of the show after the blood has fallen? And you have to do eight shows a week! No one in our meetings could really figure out how to overcome all those barriers.

Zinn   I think, mostly, they wanted the ability for the lights to come up for the final scenes after the Destruction and not have the space still splashed with blood, and maybe have more control over being able to suggest the scale of the Destruction. Was leaving blood out of *Carrie* a good idea? In retrospect, I would say no. I think there's a point where you realize it's not quite as exciting to have someone covered with red light and video blood as it is to actually cover them with 'real' blood.

Arima   The performance that Ben Brantley from the *New York Times* attended was the one at which the projection cue was not triggered, so he never had the opportunity to see the blood effect in action.

The creative decision was polarizing.

Arima   I'll always remember someone online with the username 'The Bloodless *Carrie*'. This person was vehemently upset that it was all done through technology instead of literally. Anyway, they ranted and ranted, and I was, at the time, mortified by that kind of reaction. Not necessarily hurt by it, but just like, wow ... you know? This individual wouldn't relent. It was endless. But then at the same time, there'd be somebody else who'd write about how thank goodness we didn't try to take a glob of paint and dump it on the actress and splatter it over the audience. There are two sides to everything.

The response

The show opened to the press on 1 March 2012. Special guests included Charlotte d'Amboise with her husband, the actor Terrence Mann, Rocco Landesman (of Jujamcyn Theatres, clearly having forgiven the sins of the original) and a host of other Broadway stars keen to find out how out how *Carrie* had been reinvented for a new generation.

Reaction to the new production – from fans, critics and casual theatregoers – was mixed.

Arima   There was a tremendous amount of very exciting, polarized responses. I think it was *Time* magazine that hailed the production and said something to the effect that it was very brave ['this *Carrie* has real weight and emotional conviction, and it engaged me more than a lot of musicals I've seen lately'].[11] Then there were others that, you know, hated it, and some that fell in between. There were others that could not help themselves but to compare the productions, whether it was Marin versus Betty, or it was that tone versus this tone, or the blood versus no blood.

Wachter   It was a little bit of a pressurized situation, because the show had such cult status. All eyes were on us; all of New York was wondering what this new *Carrie* was going to be like, and a lot of people were expecting to see the 'camp classic'. And then we did it, you know, rather seriously, and I think a lot of people responded to that positively, but some people were left kind of disappointed by it.

Altomare   There were people that were hoping that it was going to be just straight-up camp, and that's not what this show is about. This show is steeped in reality, these are real characters that are going through real things. Some people wanted it to be this super over-the-top, crazy thing, and it's just not that story.

While the production was praised by some reviewers for fixing many of the perceived problems of the original – 'the musical as a whole has cleaned up remarkably nice',[12] said Adam Feldman in *Time Out* – many still felt that the source

---

[11]Richard Zoglin, 'Carrie is Back: The Resurrection and the Life', *Time*, 5 March 2012, available online: https://entertainment.time.com/2012/03/05/carrie-is-back-the-resurrection-and-the-life/ (accessed 18 September 2022).

[12]Adam Feldman, 'Review: *Carrie*', *Time Out New York*, 2 March 2012, available online: http://newyork.timeout.com/arts-culture/theater/2745077/review-carrie (accessed 18 September 2022).

material was fundamentally unstageable or that the anti-bullying message infused the show with the feeling of a corny 'after show special'. An overarching consensus was that the production – though generally more coherent in terms of plot and cohesive in tone – felt too cautious and earnest in its approach; that the writers had been so nervous about the show being mocked again that any humour – even the dark humour laced throughout the novel and the movie – had been suppressed in order to stifle audience laughter and force them to take it more seriously this time around. 'Okay, everybody, please remember that we're on our very best behavior tonight,' opened Ben Brantley's eagerly awaited *New York Times* review of the 'much anticipated, exceedingly sober' revival, in a ribald parody of something Miss Gardner herself might say. 'There'll be no hooting, no teasing, no smart-aleck remarks. We will not – I repeat not – make fun of the girl with the really bad reputation.'[13]

Adams   Those characters are fun, right? It's not all dark. I really tried to make a case for that. I'd say, you know, 'People are really coming here to have fun, you know, it's okay to have them laugh *with* the show. That's not laughing *at* the show.' And they would not allow that.

'In stripping the story of its camp value Arima and his team have also robbed it of any sense of fun,' declared *Entertainment Weekly*. '*Carrie* takes itself very, very seriously, as if trying to elevate the material to the status of Greek tragedy. At times, director Stafford Arima seems to think he's doing *Medea* the Musical. It's not.'[14] The irony of the references was surely not lost.

Arima   The job of the critics is to put a lens on the production the best way that they feel they can. And that's okay. But we didn't make it for the critics. We all focused on telling a story that had the potential to entertain, to engage, to enlighten and to educate, meaning that if the piece could be used on some level as a tool regarding bullying, then that's a great thing. And the piece then can move outside of a quote-unquote 'flop' category and move into something brand new.

Betty Buckley, who saw the show and told the *New York Times* that she had enjoyed it, expressed a desire to see the show take more risks. 'I would love this production to be more dangerous. I think that's what we had going on that made it [the 1988 production] resonate for all these years,' she said. 'It's not about adding camp to this production, but about adding even more truth.'[15]

---

[13]Ben Brantley, 'Prom Night, Bloody Prom Night', *New York Times*, 1 March 2012, available online: https://www.nytimes.com/2012/03/02/theater/reviews/mccs-carrie-the-musical-at-the-lucille-lortel.html (accessed 20 September 2022).

[14]Thom Geier, '"Carrie"', review, *Entertainment Weekly*, 9 March 2012, available online: https://ew.com/article/2012/03/09/carrie/ (accessed 18 September 2022).

[15]Patrick Healy, 'Betty Buckley Weighs in on New "Carrie" Musical', *New York Times*, 13 February 2012, available online: https://artsbeat.blogs.nytimes.com/2012/02/13/betty-buckley-weighs-in-on-new-carrie-musical/ (accessed 18 September 2022).

Closure

Despite a middle-of-the-road response from critics to the production, the reviews were – on the whole – more balanced than those received by the original.

The production was nominated for five Drama Desk Awards, as well as winning the Off-Broadway Alliance Award for Best Musical Revival. It was also, finally, filmed by the Lincoln Center Library for the Performing Arts for preservation in their archives.

The show's original scheduled run was extended by three weeks before it opened, but that extension was cut down to just one week, and the new *Carrie* closed after thirty-four previews and forty-six regular performances. It was a respectable run for an off-Broadway show – and certainly longer than its original life on Broadway – but it meant that any possibility of a transfer to Broadway was scuppered.

> **Lupone**   We would love to have moved it, you know, and there was talk, but it didn't happen. You know, we can take it as far as we take it on my budget, and then the big boys have got to step in and play that game. We don't have the money for that, and so we had to close it. But yeah, there's that desire in every musical we do.

> **Telsey**   Yeah, there always are hopes. I think there were some more hopes in this particular case. The way the audiences were coming really gave you that impression that it could have moved. We had the pre-opening press, the articles, the features, you know, but like anything, you know, if you don't get the [*New York Times*] review, it's hard to move a show.

The writers were more sanguine: they had finally been able to find some closure.

> **Pitchford**   I did not realize what a deep wound the show had created in the 1980s. I had to put it in a box and lock it and put it on the shelf and not look at it. When we finally took that box down, we opened it up and we let the ghost out, and we let it go. Working with Stafford was a joy and the production was wonderful. Working with the cast that we had in New York, Marin and Molly, they were just astonishing talents. We had been given a chance to write another chapter in the *Carrie* saga, and it was a happy chapter.

And finally, *Carrie* was recorded for posterity with the release of an official cast recording on the Ghostlight Records label. Indeed, the album – which has received millions of streams online since its release in September 2012 – is the first introduction to the show for many new fans.

> **De Waal**   For someone who grew up loving musical theatre, recording the album was a total dream come true.

> **Klena**   That was the first cast album that I got to record. To have a solo on the album and to have featured moments on it was incredible. A lot of people

first fall in love with a musical through its album, so to be the voice people are listening to . . . that's what you work your whole life to do, and I had that opportunity right off the bat, right? It was really cool to see our work being stamped in history like that.

Arima   I feel very honoured and very blessed to be a part of the journey of *Carrie*. It's incredibly humbling. You know, I'm a kid from Toronto and I moved to New York. Never in a million years did I ever expect that I would direct a revival of this infamous musical! So, I always tell people that dreams can happen. Michael and Larry and Dean continued to believe in their show. They created a show that was incredibly well intentioned, but through a force of creative nuances and differences, it became what it became all those years ago. But a second life came in 2012. And perhaps another one will come again.

Another life for *Carrie* did come, with a much shorter gap. The off-Broadway revival had created a springboard for professional producers and directors to put their own stamp on a show they had obsessed about for decades. And in 2018, *Carrie* would get its biggest platform yet.

9 BACK FROM THE DEAD: *CARRIE*'S BIG COMEBACK

After twenty-four years, *Carrie*'s reappearance off-Broadway was the catalyst for new productions of the show around the world, with directors finally offered the chance to put their own unique stamp on the show.

Brady Schwind (Director La Mirada/Los Angeles, 2015) I had seen the 2012 production and I had my own opinions about it. Stafford Arima, who's the most warm, Zen person, created a safe environment for the writers to revisit the material. They had the wise idea to shrink the material down to its bare bones, so it could always be blown back up again. It gave them a chance to make sure that the script itself was what they wanted it to be. He [Arima] was able to kind of ground it in a realism. But I was interested in exploring the piece in a more grandly operatic, theatrical way. I understand the approach of saying, 'Let's do *Carrie* without blood and special effects so that we can focus on the script and the score,' but I come from the brand of theatre where 'more is more'. To me, the minute you put Carrie and Margaret in a super-realistic space, it feels silly. There's a theatricality to the piece. It is operatic. I think *Carrie* needs that scale. It has to ride this very careful divide of being absolutely real, and having a larger-than-life theatricality.

Schwind approached the writers with an idea.

Schwind   I said I'd be interested in exploring this as an immersive theatre piece. The brilliance of *Carrie* is that everyone has had a high school experience, and, by and large, it's the most terrifying experience of all our lives. I thought that if you could tap into that fear, and make the events of the show seem very real, you could create a very visceral experience for an audience. That was appealing to me.

Once again, Pitchford, Gore and Cohen opened themselves up to further exploration of *Carrie*.

Schwind They have spent so much time ruminating on *Carrie* that anything you can question you can possibly think of, they have an answer to. They've gone over it all a zillion times: why this is there, why that is there. Then, I came along and said, 'I want to do a third iteration of the show that incorporates what you have created, but it also has some new stuff as well.' When I began describing what I wanted, Larry and Michael – as they were recounting what drew them to musicalize *Carrie* in the first place – talked about these visual moments they had imagined: a lightbulb exploding over an audience, things like that. They realized that they had always imagined an immersive theatre piece in the back of their minds, but that wasn't really a thing back then.

Originally staged at the La Mirada Theatre for the Performing Arts south-east of Los Angeles, Schwind's production was subtitled 'the Killer Musical Experience', the first time the show had actively marketed itself in a way that emphasized the show's fear factor. Producers at the 1,200-seat venue had been considering a small-scale production of *Carrie* in which the audience would be seated around and inside the action on their large stage. Hearing of the plans, the writers put the venue in touch with Schwind, who proposed an 'immersive' production with a unique spin.

Schwind The audience sat on wooden bleachers on two sides of the playing space, and then the sort of 'theatrical coup' of our production was that the bleachers were rolled around throughout the performance, and the space was reconfigured for each scene.

Dean Pitchford (Lyricist) It was a stroke of genius which added an aspect of an amusement park ride to the show, and gave audiences a visceral experience of our story that they'd never get sitting in a theatre seat fixed in one place.

After its critically praised and sold-out run at La Mirada, commercial producers stepped in to transfer the production to the 2,000-seat Los Angeles Theatre, a shuttered, 1930s downtown movie palace. Built in the French Baroque style, it featured an enormous central staircase, lobbies on each of its three levels, twisting hallways and a warren of meeting and party rooms which were dressed as locations featured in the show, and which the audience could explore before the main action commenced on the theatre's stage.

Kayla Parker ('Sue Snell', La Mirada/Los Angeles, 2015) So, you walked into a room and it would be the locker room, and there were tampons all over the floor and 'Carrie White Eats Shit' written on the walls, and then you walk into another room and you're surrounded by the dead pigs at the farm . . .

Emily Lopez ('Carrie White', La Mirada/Los Angeles, 2015) We took one of the dead pigs home to our apartment and it stayed there until we moved out![1]

---

[1]Parker and Lopez bonded so much as Sue and Carrie that they became roommates for several years afterwards.

Schwind was particularly keen to explore the relationship between the characters of Carrie and Sue.

Schwind   I think that maybe one of the gifts our production gave is that we really looked at Sue's material. There was a really important moment, I thought, that had never been in the show before, where you see Sue get invited to the Prom by Tommy and understand how important that was to her. That she wasn't just giving it away because she didn't mind not going to the Prom, but that it was a self-sacrifice. We found a way to cut away from 'Evening Prayers' to work in a scene featuring Sue and Tommy to show that. In fact, when we were exploring doing this as an immersive theatre piece, there was one version that the authors and I discussed that would have been a true *Sleep No More*-style[2] experience where the show would have had parallel tracks. On one, you'd see the story from the point of view of Sue, and the other, from the point of view of Carrie, and at a point in the middle of the show, they would switch.

This production was notable for its staging of 'The Destruction', employing pyrotechnics, video walls and even a terrifying aerial stunt for the performer playing Chris.

Lopez   She was rigged to wires which – in a split-second – snapped her backward, flipping over the audience's heads until she disappeared in the darkness of the upper balcony!

Schwind   When you go back to Stephen King's book, it was so visceral. I decided, particularly because the audience was so close, we were going to have water in the showers, there was going to be nudity, there was going to be blood. There was going to be everything that makes this an uncomfortable experience for the audience as well as entertaining. I just thought that we had to fully commit, and luckily, I had actors that would do it.

Parker   That's the only way to make *Carrie* happen. Just dive into the nightmare and just go deeper and deeper into the depths!

Lopez   That word 'uncomfortable' encompasses so much of what that whole experience was like. But it had to be that way to work.

Schwind   I would go through the script line by line and say, you need to trust me, it's okay for her to say the line about the 'dirty pillows'![3] You know, the audience expects it, and their laughter is a natural response. They want it, and the release of that allows them to go into the next moment with these

---

[2] A long-running immersive show by the British theatre company Punchdrunk in which audiences are left to explore an immersive space in their own time and invited to decipher a story as it unfolds.
[3] Margaret's term, in the novel and movie, for her daughter's breasts.

characters. You can only care about a character if they're fully drawn, if they are funny and ridiculous and tragic and just very real.

Schwind added a coda to the show to suggest there was more to Carrie and Sue's connection.

Schwind   As the show began, Sue was already on stage, sitting in a chair in the middle of the stage in a pool of light. A few feet in front of her, in a separate pool of light on the floor, was Carrie's tiara. It instantly set up a relationship between them. By the end of the show, she was back in the chair and the tiara was on the floor. She reached out her hands and the tiara began moving across the floor towards her, and then it flew up into her hand, and she caught it. Blackout! Is Sue becoming Carrie? Is this a transference of power? Is it in her mind or is it simply that the essence of Carrie is so firmly a part of her now that she's literally becoming psychic, that she will always inhabit her, is she quite literally going to be haunted by her? It was an interesting moment, and I kind of liked it because the audience never quite knew exactly what it meant.

Parker   This show struck a chord with people. People remember it. It's funny that years later, people still share their videos and photos from the theatre. I'd never had that experience of walking into an audition afterwards and having someone look at my resumé and going 'Oh, my God. *Carrie*! You were in *that Carrie*!'

Schwind   We discovered a lot of things about the challenges of performing the show. No-one had ever performed it long enough to know how difficult it is to play the role of *Carrie* for months and months. If there's ever an open-ended production, she has to have an alternate. It's just too difficult a role. It's not even just the singing, it was the screaming and the crying and all of that.

Lopez   There's nothing like it. I'll never do another show like *Carrie*. Nothing will ever be as hard as *Carrie* was, or the process so insane.

Carrie's creators had seen their show make a comeback in New York, and they had now had the chance to explore something closer to their grandly operatic, original vision of it.

In 2015, the show returned to the UK for the first time since its infamous Stratford-upon-Avon run, at the intimate Southwark Playhouse, a tiny, 200-seat black box studio theatre in South London.

Gary Lloyd (Director and Choreographer, London, 2015)   It's actually the thing that I'm most proud of. It sold out before we even lifted a finger. It was, from beginning to end, just wonderful. I loved it.

A fan of the show from a young age, Lloyd was well aware of the show's notoriety.

Lloyd   It's the most famous flop in theatre history . . . how do you even start approaching that? I worked very closely with Larry and Michael, particularly, and we got into this groove where we had lots of meetings and phone calls. We'd workshop stuff in the day and I'd go back to them in the evening on American time and we'd go through it. They were really open and very generous with it all. I'd gone to them at the beginning of the process and said, 'Look, you know I love what you've done with the revamp off-Broadway, but how about we look at it a little bit more?'

The tiny space necessitated some creative thinking in terms of staging.

Lloyd   Southwark Playhouse had built a name for itself producing new and interesting musicals. We had lots of different ideas for staging it, but we ended up with an almost in-the-round version, so a lot of the elements of the show were visible all the way through. The audience was on three sides, and we designed the set around the audience. The closet was actually at the back of the auditorium, so at the end of 'And Eve was Weak', I had Kim [Criswell – Margaret] dragging Evie [Hoskins – Carrie] up a staircase in the middle of the auditorium and flinging her into what was basically a box behind the seats. It felt very immersive in that respect, especially when we got to the blood. The first two rows on all sides got completely splattered.

Evelyn 'Evie' Hoskins ('Carrie White', London, 2015)[4]   Oh, my God. It was deceptively physical. One of the reviews mentioned my bruised body. After being thrown in the trap door, I would have to crawl under the seating with a Stage Manager holding a torch. It was intense, but so worth it. I remember one night being dragged up the aisle of the seating, and Rowan Atkinson was sitting there! I had to die on the steps at the end of the show – spoiler – and then – because I was so into it, I guess – I would go so limp that my body would slide down the steps. I was covered in sticky stage blood, and I'd be stuck in this weird position for the last bit of the show just trying not to move. Someone fainted once whilst I was dying, because there was so much blood.

Lloyd had been firm on one matter . . .

Lloyd   I said, 'If we're going to do this, we're doing the blood! We're not doing lighting. We're not doing confetti! We are doing the blood!' We did lots of experiments with poor Evie, who was stuck under many bucketloads. Apart from one, I think we got her every time!

Hoskins   I got to a point in the run where I'd look forward to it. The challenge for me was to keep that unexpected moment of when it hit. Because

---

[4]Hoskins was perhaps destined to play Carrie: as the curtain went up on the opening night of the Broadway production on 12 May 1988, she was being born on the other side of the Atlantic . . .

everyone knows how the story goes, and they're waiting for that iconic moment. Some nights, I'd wake up and my pillow would have stage blood on it because it had gone in my ear or something.

Kim Criswell ('Margaret White', London, 2015)[5]   Listen, you need to make sure you have lots of washing machines because, my God, the wash up after that show! When we first opened, we were kind of, like, 'Well, what do we do with all this blood all over us at the end of the show? We'll drip it everywhere!' I said, 'Look, just get a great big tin wash basin, you know, just a big tub and put it in the wings and fill it with water so we can just kind of hose ourselves down!' And so that's what they did.

Lloyd   It was a big tick off Kim's bucket list to play Margaret. She really worked hard. Not that she had to work *that* hard, because she's a phenomenal actress, but she really put the hours into the audition and certainly in the rehearsal room. It was really rewarding to work with her and Evie on all of their scenes.

Criswell   You think it's a silly little teen horror movie musical? It's not. It's got a lot more depth, and classical roots, and the characters are fascinating. Margaret White is fascinating. She thinks she has been entrusted with the job of saving the world from evil. Everything that she does, she thinks she is doing it as a bit of divine instruction. She's being told she must do this, and she's the only one who can do it. So that's why 'When There's No One' is just so gut-wrenching. The realization: I have to do this. God is telling me I have to do this. There's no other way around it. I have to kill her. That's horrifying! Can you imagine if you really were in that situation? That you were very, very sure that you had to kill your own child because you had birthed the Antichrist? So, I mean, it's not silly! It's genuinely a heart-wrenching drama. I needed to be able to just be left in my own little bubble to get into the state I needed to be in emotionally to go out and do these things every night.

Lloyd   We changed the end of 'Why Not Me?' There was a bit of resistance, I remember, but I really wanted to interrupt the end of that song with a shadow of Margaret suddenly looming over the set, because I knew the space and I wanted to scare the crap out of everybody. You've got this jubilant song, where Carrie is getting ready and she feels like a princess for the first time in her life, and then suddenly we're reminded of the twisted world that she is living in.

Hoskins   I just adored singing those songs night after night, especially those duets with Kim. They were phenomenal to perform. 'Evening Prayers' . . . those harmonies are just stunning, and getting to do them with Kim was amazing.

---

[5]You may recall that Criswell was asked to audition as a potential replacement for Barbara Cook in 1988.

As the first production on British soil in nearly thirty years, the audience was filled with a mixture of long-term fans of the show – desperate to see it live for the first-time – and curious newcomers.

Hoskins   I remember the press leading up to the show focussing on the fact that it had been such a flop the first time around. I didn't get really affected by that sort of thing, so it wasn't a worry.

Lloyd   We all took it very seriously and we wanted to put on a serious piece of theatre. We weren't putting on a camp horror flick, we were putting on a serious story about a girl being bullied at home and at school, she just happens to have these incredible telekinetic powers. I think people came expecting to have a bit of a laugh, and to walk away being able to write something scathing and scoffing about a show they thought would be comical. They were surprised, and they all wrote really lovely things about what we did.

Hoskins   For me, honestly, it is probably the highlight of my career so far. It was a dream. It really was. It's just such a great role.

With the show now in close proximity to some of the original British cast members, several made trips to see it for the first time.

Linzi Hateley ('Carrie White', Stratford and Broadway, 1988)   I've got to be absolutely honest. When the revival was first talked about, I really wasn't comfortable with it. I'm not proud to say it, but I didn't want someone or something to be successful when it had caused me so much pain. I'm not proud about that, but that's how I felt. Why should someone else get the glory out of something that actually had scarred me? But I realized, I had to face it now, I knew people wanted my opinion on it. So, I went to see the London production, and actually it was really cathartic. It was the most useful experience that could have happened to me, it was very different and yet still so familiar, and Evie [Hoskins] was wonderful playing her version of Carrie. Actually, since then, it's sort of allowed me to move on and celebrate the show in a way I never thought possible.

Suzanne 'Squeeze' Thomas (Ensemble, Stratford and Broadway)   A few of us dancers went together and, I'm embarrassed to say this, we could hardly stop laughing all the way through. I felt so bad! Not because of the production, which was great, but because of the memories. When the music was playing, the memories just flooded over us. We were just remembering all this crazy stuff that had happened. It was just the funniest thing. We were hiding in the back, you know, because we didn't want them to think we were laughing, but we just couldn't contain ourselves. We were sweating, trying not to laugh.

Hateley and Sally Ann Triplett joined Hoskins and Lloyd for a post-show discussion, and were grilled by delighted fans about their experiences.

Lloyd   I was really nervous that night! They stayed and had a chat with everybody at the end. They were laughing and crying. They loved it. Like I said, the show is one of my proudest moments. I remember the cassette bootlegs that I had when I was seventeen or eighteen. I can still see them. I've probably got them in the loft. I remember just listening to them on loop and thinking, 'I know how good this is – I really want to direct this,' so to actually come full circle and be part of turning the flop thing around is huge for me.

Stage to screen

Soon, a new twist in the tale of *Carrie*'s journey would expose the story, characters and songs to its biggest audience yet.

Michelle 'Shelley' Hodgson (Ensemble, Stratford and Broadway, 1988)   My daughter started singing something from *Carrie*, and I freaked out. I burst into her room and said, 'What are you singing?!' I was shocked. I was talking gibberish. 'What?! Wha-wha-wha?!' She just said, 'It's on *Riverdale*!' She's singing the songs one after the other. I felt like I was in a parallel universe!

The film noir-style teen mystery drama *Riverdale*, based on the classic Archie Comics universe, featured a musical episode called *A Night to Remember* in its second season, with the songs of *Carrie* at the centre of its plot. Parallels are drawn between its high school-based characters and those of the musical, as the students stage their own version of the show. For example, the character Betty Cooper (played by Lili Reinhart) says to fellow student Veronica Lodge (Camila Mendes): 'You are the literal embodiment of Chris. Never has a role been so perfectly cast . . . I mean, think about it. Spoiled rich girl? Check. Major daddy issues? Check. Bad to the bone? Trying to control everyone around her, including her boyfriend and best friend? Check, check, check!'

Hodgson   I watched the episode, just on my own, then I had to connect with some of the others [cast members] because it was such a surreal moment. You know, 'Hang on a minute. This is from thirty odd years ago. . . . what is going on?!'

The episode attracted immediate viewership of over 1.1 million on the CW Network,[6] but was later globally syndicated on Netflix – though the streaming service does not release viewing figures, it is likely that millions more became acquainted with the songs and characters there. The episode led to a sudden upsurge in Google searches from young fans desperate for more *Carrie* in their

---

[6]Rick Porter, '"Empire" and "The Voice" Adjust Up', *TV by the Numbers*, 19 April 2019, available online: https://web.archive.org/web/20180419224607/http://tvbythenumbers.zap2it.com/daily-ratings/wednesday-final-ratings-april-18-2018/ (accessed 19 November 2022).

lives,[7] which in turn led to further exposure for the stars of the various high-profile productions.

Keaton Whittaker starred as Carrie in a professional production in Seattle, but her social media videos of songs from the show spiked in popularity after the release of the *Riverdale* episode.

Keaton Whittaker ('Carrie White', Seattle, 2016)   So many people see my videos after watching *Riverdale*. I've done bigger things in my career, but that show is the one thing that has followed me the whole time that I've been in theatre. One kid came up to me at a party and said, 'This is so weird, so niche, but you look like this girl Keaton Whittaker who does *Carrie* on TikTok!' I am her! That is me! I think it's cool, honestly. These kids that might never be exposed to musical theatre see it on these enormous platforms. You know, if you're Googling it and learning more about it, that's awesome.

The increased awareness of the show driven by professional productions, a readily available cast recording and the worldwide distribution of *Riverdale* have all been factors in the popularity of the show amongst amateur and college-based theatre groups, who can now acquire the rights to perform the show in their own communities.

Cohen   One especially heartening aspect of doing the show in 2012 was that Ted Chapin, an old friend of Michael's and mine, and then president of the Rodgers and Hammerstein Organization – came downtown to see the show. He phoned the next day to say that R&H would like to acquire the rights to license the show.

Hundreds of productions of *Carrie* have sprung up throughout the United States as well as worldwide in the United Kingdom, Australia, New Zealand, Spain, Germany, the Philippines, the Netherlands, Russia, Brazil and Mexico.

Stafford Arima (Director, off-Broadway, 2012)   What really brings me – and I know the authors – a tremendous amount of joy is the fact that other groups can do the show now.

Christy Altomare ('Sue Snell', off-Broadway, 2012)   *Carrie* has had this incredible resurgence and life outside of New York City. I teach acting and I can't tell you how many times people have said, 'Oh, my school's doing *Carrie*!' and sometimes someone will say, 'I'm playing Sue', and I'll say, 'Oh, it's hard, isn't it?' and they'll say, 'Yeah, it's really hard!'

---

[7]Google Trends, tracking search terms used since 2004, shows a distinct uptick in searches for '*Carrie* the Musical' in April 2018, when the episode aired.

It is not hard to see the appeal of the show for theatre companies, whether professional, student or amateur. *Carrie* offers several powerful lead roles for females – often lacking in many shows – and a flexibly sized, youthful ensemble. For a cast, its score is challenging yet rewarding, and the supernatural elements of the plot encourage inventiveness and resourcefulness from any creative team. Interestingly, the licensed edition of the score includes a polite warning on 'tone' in the introductory 'Authors' Notes' for any director contemplating the reintroduction of the colour-coded unitards or enormous metaphorical staircases of days gone by: 'We were never interested in seeing our show done in a campy or kitschy style; we've been offered that opportunity, and have never chosen to go down that road … Carrie and the stage musical that bears her name deserve to be treated with respect and dignity.'[8]

Although the writers probably never imagined such an outcome in 1988, *Carrie* has turned into a global phenomenon. Whereas the original production of *Carrie* faced the daunting prospect of surviving on a Broadway that squarely rejected shows about young people and their lives, a new generation of theatre makers have laced their youthful shows with the essence of *Carrie*.

Hateley I went to see *Heathers*, I was, like, 'It's *Carrie*!' It's all there. There are so many elements of it in different shows. It was a first of its kind, and actually, it was ahead of its time!

---

[8]Licensed edition of the 2012 libretto.

10 EPILOGUE: WHEN DID EVERYBODY DECIDE I'M THE ONE WHO'S THE FLOP?

The *Carrie* fandom continues to grow. Social media brings fans closer to cast members. No longer are they distant smudges on a blurry VHS recording; the most dedicated Friends of *Carrie* are delighted to see their love of the show validated with likes and shares from Hateley, Buckley and the gang on Instagram and Twitter. A live two-hour online reunion of the show's original cast and creatives, hosted by Broadway personality Seth Rudetsky during the Covid-19 lockdown, was watched by tens of thousands of people.[1] The *Out for Blood* podcast attracted 100,000 streams in its first year. *Carrie* has its own dedicated Reddit, Facebook and Discord channels, populated by digital natives discovering the show for the first time and discussing its intricacies, just as others have done in the preceding decades. Performers, directors, composers and other creatives continue to draw inspiration from it, and can stage their own interpretations. That a short lived 'flop' from 1988 can still generate such an enthusiastic response is undeniably impressive.

During the final weeks of writing this book, I had the chance to direct a production of *Carrie* at the intimate Bridewell Theatre in central London. I leapt at the opportunity – not only because I had always wanted to – but because I knew it would provide a deeper understanding of the show's plot, characters and structure, and allow me to explore the work from a different perspective. Though it meant that every spare hour of my day was suddenly filled with versions of *Carrie* past, present and future, I'm glad that I took on the challenge.

Something struck me midway through rehearsals, as the actors threw themselves into a vigorous run-through of 'The Destruction': though they had a vague notion

---

[1] In it, tributes were paid to Gene Anthony Ray (Billy Nolan), who died in 2003, aged forty-one, and fellow principal cast member Paul Gyngell (Tommy Ross), who died in 2010, aged fifty-one.

of the show's previous life (most of them, alarmingly, weren't even born in 1988) there was no concern from anyone that they were appearing in a notorious 'flop'. The show's chaotic back story was rarely mentioned. In fact, they were thrilled by the chance to appear in an unconventional, challenging musical that felt very different from most of the licensed works usually available to amateur groups, and one which they knew mostly from the off-Broadway cast recording. The wider creative team relished the opportunity to find innovative ways to present the epic finale, the Musical Director and band found the score thrilling to teach and play, and the Choreographer found a unique balance of realistic and abstract movement to tell the story, inspired by the stylized movement of the 2012 production. I resisted the temptation to add various nods to the doomed original, but one character may have briefly worn a *Grease* T-shirt.

In production meetings, I found myself surprised to be facing many of the exact challenges I had heard the 1988 team describe in their interviews for this book: how do you 'do the blood' night after night (especially on a tight budget)? How do you bring Carrie's powers to life?[2] How do you divide up rehearsals to work on the story's two distinct worlds whilst maintaining a cohesive aesthetic and approach? On more than one occasion, I found myself sympathizing with the difficult decisions faced by Hands, Allen et al. back in 1988.

IMAGE 10.1 Sadie Kempner as Carrie in the author's production of the show. Adrian Hau (photographer).

[2]Spurred on by the writers' encouragement to find imaginative ways to stage Carrie's 'power', we added an extra 'character' – literally called 'The Power' – a talented contemporary dancer who appeared alongside Carrie to physicalize the telekinetic effects and dispatch her classmates in dramatic, creative ways . . .

The members of our troupe threw themselves into the challenges that *Carrie* presented, and we had a lot of fun doing so. It was one of the fastest-selling musicals in the society's long history. And there in the audience, to our delight, was Linzi Hateley and two of her former cast-mates, Kenny Linden and Shelley Hodgson. To our company, their presence was like royalty.

I am sure that young Linzi would have never predicted – on that dark day in May 1988 when her Broadway dream was snatched away – that nearly thirty-five years later she would be guest of honour at a humble but heartfelt revival of the show declared to be the one of the biggest disasters in theatre history. These experiences – meeting the original cast, directing the show, researching this book – reminded me that behind every piece of art, success or flop, is an army of people who poured their heart and soul into making it work, all with their own personal stories about the journey they have undertaken.

Carrie's legacy

So, before this tale wraps up, perhaps it is worth a look at how the experience of being part of the original production, its reputation and its legacy impacted some of its key players. We have heard about the journey of redemption of the show itself, and the emotional journey of its creators, but what happened next for everyone else?

Soon after the sudden closure of *Carrie*, Friedrich Kurz opened a custom-built theatre in Bochum, Germany, to house his transfer of *Starlight Express*.[3] As of writing, it is still playing there, having been seen by over 17 million audience members. In his autobiography, he talks candidly about his involvement with *Carrie* and expresses sadness about the way it ended. 'My name went around the world as that of the man who had launched the biggest flop in theater history,' he said. '*Carrie* and the top-notch artists who brought it to the stage didn't deserve that disaster.'[4]

In the unlikeliest of twists, Kurz and Hands once again partnered on a new musical in 1993. The *New York Times* announced that the Berlin production of *Where Have All the Flowers Gone?*, a show about the life of Marlene Dietrich, would be 'the country's first home-grown mega musical.'[5] In all-too-familiar scenes, the show was soured by poor reviews and various crises (including a leading lady replaced at the last minute), and alienated its German audiences by

---

[3]Kurz had taken Pitchford, Cohen and Gore on a flying visit to see the theatre under construction during one of their early casting trips to London.
[4]Kurz, *Der Musical-Mann*, 9.
[5]Stephen Kinzer, 'Show about the Eternal Dietrich Attracts Germans from All Over', *New York Times*, 12 April 1993.

lacing the story with heavy-handed messages 'causing the audience to squirm in its seat as it faces ugly truths about Germany's past and present'.[6] The show, which was originally planned to run at least seven years and open in replica productions around the world, closed soon after.

Carrie was Kurz's only attempt to break into the American market. In 2014, he 'discovered the Word of Jesus Christ and began to see the world through completely new eyes', commenting that, from this transformed perspective, he would not have produced the show. 'I'm happy that *Carrie* wasn't successful,' he concluded in his memoir: 'It's a show with an occult atmosphere, full of lies and religious madness. That alone wouldn't have been terrible, if the whole thing had been resolved conclusively. But the overall message of the show is sinister, the malevolent scenes can lead to lasting disturbances for some viewers. There are better plays with messages that reach an audience much more positively on a deeper level.'[7]

Terry Hands directed more productions at the RSC than any other director in its history, but the high-profile failure of *Carrie* would always linger over his tenure. He retired from the company in 1991, twenty-five years to the day after joining. His departure – despite his last years being 'exceptional'[8] – was marked in a *Guardian* exit interview (headlined *Cash and Carrie*) describing his time at the company as 'notorious for two things – money trouble and a musical of a Stephen King story'. Hands was belligerent, as ever: 'Why should there be such *Schadenfreude* about what was, after all, a musical mounted in our Stratford winter season and one which earned us enough money, a quarter of a million, to programme trilogies of Bond and Barker plays?'[9] According to Colin Chambers in *Inside the Royal Shakespeare Company*, *Carrie* 'did irredeemably tarnish Hands's reputation and severely damage the RSC's standing'.[10]

Linzi Hateley ('Carrie White', Stratford and Broadway)   I used to get quite upset by how hard a time Terry got, because I think that, as a director, musical theatre wasn't his forte. That clearly wasn't where he was comfortable. But I do think that, visually, he had a concept in his mind, and I commend what he was trying to do. I think that it was a brave choice, but it wasn't the right time for it. I think the reason why the show is still talked about is because of its extreme creative choices.

Sadly, *Carrie* also damaged one of Hands' particularly long-standing collaborations:

---

[6]Christine Toomey, 'Dietrich Musical Hits a Bitter Note in Germany', *Sunday Times*, 18 April 1993, 21.
[7]Kurz, *Der Musical-Mann*, 21.
[8]Trowbridge, *Rise and Fall*, 107.
[9]Billington, 'Cash and Carrie'.
[10]Colin Chambers, *Inside the Royal Shakespeare Company* (London: Routledge, 2004), 94.

Mark Bailey (assistant to Ralph Koltai)   It completely ended the relationship between Ralph and Terry, both professionally – they never worked together again – and personally – they hardly ever spoke again.

Regardless of *Carrie*'s legacy, Hands was credited with leaving the RSC in a better state than he found it, 'radiating the de-mob serenity of someone who has bags of work lined up, a new sense of directorial confidence and the knowledge that two years of intense politicking has restored the RSC's finances'.[11] After a period of freelance work, he later became the Artistic Director of Wales' Theatre Clwyd, where his work was well regarded. He died in February 2020. His obituary in the *New York Times* led with the headline, 'Terry Hands, Known for Hits and *Carrie*, Dies at 79', and continued with, 'While at the Royal Shakespeare Company He Took Several Shows to Broadway. One . . . Didn't Go so Well.'[12]

Despite the warnings of the British press, *Carrie* did not sound the death knell of the RSC. Occasionally, the company will stage something deemed 'gimmicky' or beyond its classical wheelhouse, and the same debate about public funding will be rehashed in the press. The company had little further success with musical theatre until *Matilda* – ironically, another story about a telekinetic young girl – which premiered in 2010 and continues to play in London's West End, having enjoyed lengthy runs on Broadway and around the world.

The writers Dean Pitchford, Michael Gore and Lawrence D. Cohen – who, as we have learned, gained much joy from the resurrection of *Carrie* – still occasionally assist and advise directors about their productions of their show. All three continue to fill their schedules with other writing projects.

While some of the original cast have stepped away from performing to enjoy other occupations, many continue to enjoy successful stage careers or work in the industry as choreographers, directors or teachers on both sides of the Atlantic.

Linzi Hateley recently reprised another early and much-loved role – the Narrator in *Joseph and the Amazing Technicolor Dreamcoat* – three decades after her first appearance in the show. In 2021, she sang 'When There's No One' from *Carrie* as part of an online concert, but encouragement from keen fans for a plucky producer to cast her as Margaret White in a full production of the show has, so far, been fruitless.

Hateley kept in touch with Barbara Cook – in August 1988, Cook returned to London for a concert at the Barbican, 'and there was Carrie [Hateley] herself in the balcony enjoying the recital.'[13] Cook continued to perform her cabaret shows until the end of her life. She died in 2017, aged eighty-nine.

---

[11]Billington, 'Cash and Carrie'.
[12]Neil Genzlinger, 'Terry Hands, Director Known for Hits and *Carrie* Dies at 79', *New York Times*, 10 February 2020), available online: https://www.nytimes.com/2020/02/10/arts/terry-hands-dead.html (accessed 3 October 2022).
[13]Sidney Vauncez, 'Barbara Cook', review, *The Stage*, 11 August 1988, 5.

Betty Buckley continues to teach acting and perform extensively on stage and screen, releasing a series of albums throughout the 1990s and 2000s.

Hateley   My connection with Betty has remained over the years because we went on a very personal journey together that no one else went on. We had our own very strange – but also wonderful – experience together.

Dean Pitchford (Lyricist)   My relationship with Betty kind of went into a hibernation. I never knew what to say about it, and neither did she. I'm a lyricist, and I had no words! But when we came back to it, our friendship was as strong as ever. I had a birthday recently, and the doorbell rang: an enormous bouquet of roses with a card reading, 'Love, Betty Lynn.' My husband and I came over to see her when she was in London doing *Dear World*, and we had arranged to have dinner with her afterwards. To our surprise, she invited Linzi to join us. We closed that place. We were there late, late, late, talking about the wild journey we had all been on. It was just fantastic.

Charlotte d'Amboise can still be seen regularly appearing on Broadway, regularly revisiting her high-kicking performance as Roxie Hart in *Chicago*.

D'Amboise   I would be in a million shows and I would go out and sign autographs, and there were tons of people with *Carrie* programmes. Or 'Would you sign my bootleg of *Carrie*? I'm a *Carrie* fan!' I'm proud of the work that we did and I'm proud of a lot of the show. I feel so thrilled that I got to do it.

Other cast members have met with similarly passionate responses from *Carrie* fans.

Michelle 'Shelley' Hodgson (Ensemble, Stratford and Broadway)   When we came back and did auditions, people would stop us and say, 'Can you tell me about *Carrie*? Was it true about the pig's blood . . .?' I'm so, so proud. It could have just disappeared in the annals of time. But it hasn't, and there's a reason for that. It was an interesting, tough journey. But at the same time, what a learning curve.

Mark Santoro (Ensemble, Stratford and Broadway)   Having it listed on my resumé intrigued people. Did it change my life? Of course. I made new friends, made history appearing in one of the biggest flops ever to hit Broadway. And it made me think twice about the projects I would audition for in the future!

Eric Gilliom (Ensemble, Stratford and Broadway)   It carries a lot of weight, especially in the theatre community, and it will forever. It was exhilarating. It was traumatizing. I think we collectively went through such a range of emotions. It is something that I will certainly cherish for the rest of my life.

Rosemary Jackson (Ensemble/understudy 'Carrie White', Stratford and Broadway)   It gave me a career. It set the standard for me. It sounds crazy, but as much as can be said about *Carrie*, the standard was always really, really high. Everybody had this really high expectation of how you were going to show up in the room. And if you're going to be a part of a flop, you go big![14]

Suzanne 'Squeeze' Thomas (Ensemble, Stratford and Broadway)   If I'm ever in New York and I meet somebody new on Broadway, even someone really young, if we've had a few drinks, I'll say, 'Oh, I was in the original cast of *Carrie*!' They'll be twenty-two years old and they'll know exactly what I'm talking about!

Sally Ann Triplett ('Sue Snell', Stratford and Broadway)   When my daughter was at school, she came back one day, and she started playing me songs from *Carrie*. She said, 'Mum,. . . my friends were showing me videos of *Carrie*! You were in it, and they couldn't believe it!' In the past, people have sent me bootlegs but I'd never really given it the time it needed. But when my daughter started listening to it, you know, it made it more special. Whenever I bump into another cast member, we can't help but just instantly go back to that time. It feels like we're twenty-year-olds again.

Someday, someone will know my name

Lawrence D. Cohen (Book writer)   Looking back to 1988, the saga of our musical's off-stage drama actually threatened, at times, to eclipse the production onstage, and had a profound effect on the three authors. But finally, in the years leading up to 2012, we were ready – at long last – to take a very deep breath and try to overcome our fears. We proceeded to revamp the show from top to bottom, circling back and returning to where we'd started out at a time when everything seemed possible. That decision led to so many great things: the first official cast recording of the off-Broadway, the worldwide licensing of our show, the *Riverdale* episode exposing it to hundreds of thousands of people, and so much more. The 2012 'revisal' allowed us, for the first time, to see a version of our show that resembled what was in our minds when we began working on it all those years ago. Best of all, its existence subsequently allowed hundreds and hundreds of other theatre-makers to be able to now bring the story of King's timely and timeless fable to musical life for audiences around the world – a dream come true, and one beyond our wildest expectations.

---

[14]Though Darlene Love's *Carrie* experience was apparently not one she relished – her autobiography contains only a brief (albeit, erroneous) paragraph about her time in the show, in which she suggests the show 'closed on the first night' – she does talk about the close bond she formed with Rosemary Jackson. Love says she was astonished by Jackson's dance skills and the pair hit it off right away. They remain close friends, and Jackson is still Love's go-to choreographer.

Carrie almost never was. Stephen King's tossed-aside manuscript led to a classic novel, a beloved movie and eventually a strange, legendary musical, a show whose mythos has prevailed precisely because of its dichotomies: American culture and British sensibility. Soaring, operatic songs one moment, frothy, bubblegum pop the next. *Grease* and Greece. High concept, multimillion-pound set design with doors that jammed closed. The leafy town of Stratford and bright lights of Broadway. High school kids in leather bondage gear and gym togas. Horror and humour. An epic finale with the most anti-climactic moment of the season. Crowds booing one moment, and cheering the next. A chaotic 'failure' which found redemption on a global scale.

Somehow, Carrie White's story is the story of *Carrie* itself. It was the underdog of Broadway. It dreamed big but didn't fit in, and – in its own special way – it pulled off an act of revenge on everyone who had mocked it.

> **Hateley**   Had it not been as brilliant and bonkers and awful and fabulous as it was, it would simply not still be talked about. You know, the brilliant bits were just so brilliant and the bad bits were so bad that it just created this phenomenon that won't go away.

> **Betty Buckley** ('Margaret White', Stratford and Broadway)   People who saw that original Broadway production saw something the likes of which they had never seen or never will see again. I was really proud of the work we did on the show. I think it was very provocative and ahead of its time. I have no regrets about *Carrie*. I learn from every role I play. I formed a life-long friendship with Linzi and I look back on working with her with great fondness.

> **Joey McKneely** (Ensemble, Stratford and Broadway)   I think theatre is forgetful when it's boring. We were not boring. Whether it was Linzi's phenomenal talent, or what Betty did with her acting scenes, or the audacity of the choreography, there was just so much that people could talk about.

> **Stephen Purdy** (author, *Flop Musicals of the Twenty-First Century*)   I can name dozens of musicals that were just so bland that if it had been a cookie, you would have said, 'No, this isn't worth the calories.' But I think *Carrie* had some really strong elements, notably the score, and that combined with the folklore and audacity and blood onstage led to its infamy.

The electric performances of its leading ladies – in particular Hateley ('the rock that held us all together',[15] according to Cook) – have gone down in history, adding a level of kudos to the production and aiding the endurance of its legacy.

---

[15]Cook, *Then and Now*, 208.

Jackson   There was a crapload of talent on that stage. Betty was phenomenal. Linzi was phenomenal.

Kenny Linden (Ensemble, Stratford and Broadway)   To have the privilege of seeing Betty and Linzi working together: that alone was worth the price of an entry ticket. I think you could have cut all of us, and just put them up there on stage, and you'd have got your money's worth.

Hateley   I like to think of it now as 'the most successful flop on Broadway', because actually, thirty-five years later, here we are still talking about it. It's nice that we are at the point where it can be celebrated for what it was. It was groundbreaking. Of course, it wasn't all right, but I think that the choices that were made were brave ones and I think that's why it's withstood the test of time, and has become such a talked-about show. I have absolutely no regrets about being Carrie. In fact, now, I'm very proud of her! But it's been a journey that'll stay with me for life!

Carrie. There's never been a musical like her.

BIBLIOGRAPHY AND OTHER SOURCES

Books

Backemeyer, Sylvia, ed. (2003), *Ralph Koltai: Designer for The Stage*, rev. edn, London: Nick Hern Books.

Beahm, George (1998), *Stephen King from A to Z*, Kansas City, KS: Andrews McMeel Publishing.

Beahm, George, ed. (1989), *The Stephen King Companion*, London: Macdonald.

Behr, Edward (1989), *The Complete Book of* Les Misérables, New York: Arcade.

Chambers, Colin (2004), *Inside the Royal Shakespeare Company*, London: Routledge.

Cook, Barbara (2016), *Then and Now: A Memoir*, New York: HarperCollins.

Duffett, Mark (2013), *Understanding Fandom: An Introduction to the Study of Media Fan Culture*, London: Bloomsbury.

Goodwin, John, ed. (1998), *British Theatre Design: The Modern Age*, rev. edn, London: Orion.

Kantor, Michael and Laurence Maslon (2004), *Broadway: The American Musical*, New York: Bulfinch Press.

King, Stephen (1974), *Carrie*, 19th edn, London: New English Library.

Kurz, Friedrich (2010), *Der Musical-Mann*, Munich: GarthMedien. The *Carrie* chapter was translated from German for this project by Jon Putnam.

Love, Darlene (2013), *My Name is Love*, New York: William Morrow.

Mandelbaum, Ken (1991), *Not Since Carrie: 40 Years of Broadway Musical Flops*, New York: St Martin's Press.

Mitchell, Neil (2013), *Devil's Advocates: Carrie*, Leighton Buzzard: Auteur.

Purdy, Stephen (2020), *Flop Musicals of the Twenty-First Century*, Abingdon: Routledge.

Rich, Frank (1998), *Hot Seat: Theater Criticism for* The New York Times*, 1980–1993*, New York: Random House.

Riedel, Michael (2016), *Razzle Dazzle: The Battle for Broadway*, New York: Simon & Schuster.

Royal Shakespeare Company (RSC) (1988), *Annual Report 1987/8*, Stratford-upon-Avon: Royal Shakespeare Company.

Shapiro, Eddie (2014), *Nothing Like a Dame: Conversations with the Great Women of Musical Theater*, Oxford: Oxford University Press.

Sontag, Susan (2018), *Notes on Camp*, London: Penguin.

Sternfeld, Jessica (2006), *The Megamusical*, Bloomington, IN: University of Indiana Press.

Trowbridge, Simon (2013), *The Rise and Fall of the Royal Shakespeare Company*, Oxford: Editions Albert Creed.

Vincent, Bev (2022), *Stephen King: A Complete Exploration of His Work, Life, and Influences*, New York: Epic Ink.

Articles

As well as the articles and reviews cited below, I am grateful for three invaluable audio-tape recordings of interviews with Terry Hands (recorded 30 December 1987 and 17 January 1988), Alexander Reid (recorded 13 January 1988) and Ralph Koltai (recorded 6 January 1988) for *Theatre Craft* magazine conducted by journalist Adam Pirani, now located in the British Film Institute archives. Pirani also generously supplied the draft of his article, which was never published. These are referenced in the text as '*Theatre Craft*/Pirani interview tapes' and '*Theatre Craft*/Pirani interview draft'.

'A Carrie on Over Music at the RSC' (1988), *Daily Mail*, 30 January.
Apone, Carl (1984), 'Maureen McGovern has Big Heart for CLO', *The Pittsburgh Press*, 12 August, 93.
Ball, Ian (1988), 'RSC Musical £3.7m Flop on Broadway', *Daily Telegraph*, 18 May.
Bamigboye, Baz (1988), 'I Just Can't Carrie on Like This, Says Star', *Daily Mail*, 23 February.
Bamigboye, Baz (1988), 'Debbie Causes a Carrie On', *Daily Mail*, 1 March, 20.
'Barbara Cook' (1988), in 'On Stage' column, *New York Times*, 16 February, 58.
Barker, Felix (1988), 'A Horror Glory', *Sunday Express*, 21 February.
Barnes, Clive (1988), 'Musical "Carrie" Soars on Blood, Guts and Gore', *New York Post*, 13 May, 19.
Beck, Marilyn (1988), '"Carrie" On', in 'Extra Entertainment' column, *Daily News*, 4 March, 60.
Benedict, David (2019), 'West End Review: Andrew Lloyd Webber's *Stephen Ward*', *Variety*, 19 December. Available online: https://variety.com/2013/legit/reviews/west-end-review-andrew-lloyd-webbers-stephen-ward-1200977286/ (accessed 9 November 2022).
Billington, Michael (1991), 'Cash and Carrie', *The Guardian*, 4 July, 24.
Bisson, P. A. (y), 'Show Should Go On – For Us', Letters, *Birmingham Evening Mail*, 22 February.
Blank, Ed (1988), 'Reviewing Broadway', *Pittsburgh Press*, 8 May, 99.
'Blood and Guts in High School' (1988), *The Face*, February.
Bonner, Hilary (1987), 'Carrie on Linzi!', *Daily Mirror*, 2 November, 1.
Brantley, Ben (2012), 'Prom Night, Bloody Prom Night', *New York Times*, 1 March. Available online: https://www.nytimes.com/2012/03/02/theater/reviews/mccs-carrie-the-musical-at-the-lucille-lortel.html (accessed 20 September 2022).
Brierley, David (1988), '"Carrie" a Money Spinner', Letters page, *Stratford Herald*, 19 February.
'Broadway Knives are Out for *Carrie*' (1988), *Daily Mail*, 14 May.
'Broadway "Saved by the British"' (1988), *Walsall Express & Star* (syndicated), 14 June.
Brook, Danae (1988), '"Leroy" is Just Streets Ahead', *Sunday Express*, 21 February.
'Carrie on Playing' (1987), *The Stage*, 1 October, 12.
'Cast Ignore Glitch and Carrie on Regardless' (1988), *The Stage*, 18 February, 1.
'Chit Chat' (1987), column, *The Stage*, 1 October, 12.
Citron, Peter (1988), '"Carrie" Faces Final Broadway Curtain', *Omaha World-Herald*, 17 May.
Clearfield, Andy (1984), 'Maureen McGovern has a "Morning After"', *Camden New Jersey Courier-Post*, 26 October, 51.

Clines, Francis X. (1988), '"Carrie" Churns towards U.S.', *The New York Times*, 2 March, 67.

Collis, Clark (2012), 'Carrie: Broadway's Bloodiest Flop', *Entertainment Weekly*, 10 March. Available online: https://ew.com/article/2012/02/10/carrie-broadways-bloodiest-flop/ (accessed 12 September 2022).

Coveney, Michael (1988), 'a', *Financial Times*, 22 February, 19.

Coveney, Michael (2013), 'West End Poster Boy Russ Remembered in a Muse of Fire', *WhatsOnStage*, 28 October. Available online: https://www.whatsonstage.com/london-theatre/news/michael-coveney-west-end-poster-boy-russ-remembere_32445.html (accessed 19 September 2022).

Daily Mail comment piece (1988), 21 February.

De Jongh, Nicholas (1988), 'Will to Solvency', *The Guardian*, 16 January, 12.

De Jongh, Nicholas (1988), 'Carrie on', *The Guardian*, 20 February, 16.

Edwardes, Jane (1988), 'Carrie' review, *Time Out*, 24 February, 23.

Evans, Gerard (1988), 'Shakespeare Stars in Record Broadway Flop', *Today*, 18 May.

Feldman, Adam (2012), 'Review: *Carrie*', *Time Out New York*, 2 March. Available online: http://newyork.timeout.com/arts-culture/theater/2745077/review-carrie (accessed 18 September 2022).

Fetherston, Drew (1988), 'Broadway Goes for Blood', *Newsday*, 8 May, 72.

Finn, Philip (1988), 'Musical Carrie is $4.5m U.S. Flop', *Daily Express*, 18 May.

'Finer Feelings and Finance in Conflict' (1988), *The Stage*, 25 February, 14.

Fisher, Sue (1988), 'Star Survivor of a Stage Disaster', *Tamworth Herald*, 20 May.

Freedman, Samuel G. (1986), 'Putting it Together: A Producer's Week on Broadway', *New York Times*, 6 April, 93.

Geier, Thom (2012), 'Carrie' review, *Entertainment Weekly*, 9 March. Available online: https://ew.com/article/2012/03/09/carrie/ (accessed 18 September 2022).

Genzlinger, Neil (2020), 'Terry Hands, Director Known for Hits and *Carrie* Dies at 79', *New York Times*, 10 February. Available online: https://www.nytimes.com/2020/02/10/arts/terry-hands-dead.html (accessed 3 October 2022).

Gerard, Jeremy (1987), 'Drowsy Broadway about to Be Stirred', *New York Times*, 7 December, 69.

Gerrie, Anthea (1988), 'Linzi Flies Home: The Only Good Thing to Come out of *Carrie*', *Daily Mail*, 21 May.

Goldfarb, Michael (1988), 'From the Shakespeareans, a Carrie for Broadway', *Washington Post*, 21 February, 23.

Gordon, George (1988), 'RSC Horror as Broadway Curtain Falls on Carrie', *Daily Mail*, 18 May.

Gouveia, Georgette (1988), '"Carrie"'s Musical Mother', *Rockland County NY Journal-News*, 16 May.

Grant, Peter (1987), 'Carrie On Linzi. She is Going Places', *Liverpool Echo*, 30 December, 8.

Gussow, Mel (1985), 'Chilling "Carrie" in Vengeful Return – As a Musical', *New York Times*, 29 November, 62.

'Hands Carries the Can for Rocky Drama' (1988), *Evening Standard*, 11 March.

Handy, Bruce (1994), 'Kitty Litter', *New York Times*, 6 March, 86.

Harper, Timothy (1988), 'STAGE: Horrors! The Royal Shakespeare Stages "Carrie"', *Los Angeles Times*, 27 March, 51.

Healy, Patrick (2012a), 'An Outsider Gets a Nicer Date for the Prom', *New York Times*, 5 February. Available online: https://www.nytimes.com/2012/02/05/theater/carrie-a-huge-stage-flop-is-reinvented-by-mcc-theater.html (accessed 18 September 2022).

Healy, Patrick (2012b), 'Betty Buckley Weighs in on New "Carrie" Musical', *New York Times*, 13 February. Available online: https://artsbeat.blogs.nytimes.com/2012/02/13/betty-buckley-weighs-in-on-new-carrie-musical/ (accessed 18 September 2022).

Helbing, Terry (1988), 'Darlene Love is Here to Stay', *TheaterWeek*, 23 May, 16.

Hemley, Matthew (2019), 'RSC Begins Crunch Talks with Cameron Mackintosh over *Les Misérables* Royalties', *The Stage*, 16 January. Available online: https://www.thestage.co.uk/news/rsc-begins-crunch-talks-with-cameron-mackintosh-over-les-miserables-royalties (accessed 2 August 2022).

Henry III, William A (1988), 'Theater: Getting All Fired Up over Nothing', *Time*, 23 May. Available online: https://content.time.com/time/subscriber/article/0,33009,967445,00.html (accessed 5 May 2022).

Henry III, William A. (1988), 'Theater: The Biggest All-Time Flop Ever', *Time*, 30 May. Available online: http://content.time.com/time/magazine/article/0,9171,967517,00.html.

Hepple, Peter (1986), 'Barbara is the toast of London', *The Stage*, 25 September, 5.

Hepple, Peter (1988), 'Post-Menstrual Tension – Bad Blood at the RSC', *The Stage*, 25 February, 15.

Hetrick, Adam (2012), 'Tony Award Winner Betty Buckley Looks Back at Carrie on Stage and Screen', *Playbill*, 8 March. Available online: https://www.playbill.com/article/tony-award-winner-betty-buckley-looks-back-at-carrie-on-stage-and-screen-com-188293 (accessed 18 September 2022).

Hiley, Jim (1988), 'Couldn't Scare Less', *The Listener*, 25 February.

Hummler, Richard (1988), 'Weisslers, Zollo in On "Carrie" for Percentage of Gross, Profits', *Variety*, 11 May, 129, 136.

Hurren, Kenneth (1988), 'A Rocky Horror Show', *The Sunday Times*, 21 February.

Jehu, Jeremy (1987), 'Equity Backs Hands across the Water Deal', *The Stage*, 15 October, 1.

Joffee, Linda (1988), 'Why "Carrie" Didn't Scare Hands', *Christian Science Monitor*, 23 May.

Kerensky, Oleg (1988), 'Carrie' Broadway review, *The Stage*, 2 June, 11.

King, Francis (1988), 'Blood and Bucks', *The Sunday Telegraph*, 21 February.

Kinzer, Stephen (1993), 'Show about the Eternal Dietrich Attracts Germans from All Over', *New York Times*, 12 April.

Kissel, Howard (1988), 'Don't "Carrie" Me Back to Ol' Virginny', *Daily News*, 13 May, 59.

Kramer, Mimi (1988), 'Bloody Awful', *The New Yorker*, 15 May, 85.

Kuchwara, Michael and William B. Collins (1988), 'Broadway Musical "Carrie" isn't Bad Enough to be Good', *Associated Press*, 17 May.

Lawson, Mark (1988), 'Hands on His Knees', *The Independent*, 27 May.

Lawson, Mark (2021), 'What's it Like to Star in a Flop?', *The Guardian*, 16 December.

le Sourd, Jacques (1988), '"Carrie" Fires Up Audience with Gothic Fun', *The Daily Times* (Mamaroneck, New York), 13 May, 65.

Ledford, Larry S. (1988), 'Linzi Hateley's Date with Broadway', *TheaterWeek*, 23 May, 10.

Madge, Tim (1988), 'What a Carrie-On Up at the Good old RSC', *The Guardian*, 17 February, 38.

Mahoney, Elizabeth (2004), 'Oscar Wilde', review, *The Guardian*, 21 October. Available online: https://www.theguardian.com/stage/2004/oct/21/theatre (accessed 15 October 2022).

Mandelbaum, Ken (1999), 'Stage Views', column, *Playbill*, exact date unknown.

McGarry, Peter (1988), 'Public Given the Cold Shoulder', *Coventry Evening Telegraph*, 19 February.

Morley, Sheridan (1988), 'Teen-Pulp at Stratford', 24 February.

Morley, Sheridan (1988), 'Carrie on Regardless', *Punch*, 4 March.

Murdin, Lynda (1987), 'RSC Gives Star Role to Teenager', *The Times*, 30 October, 16.

Nachman, Gerald (1989), '*Showbiz*' column, *San Francisco Examiner*, 21 May, 17.

Nemy, Enid (1986), 'Broadway' column, *New York Times*, 26 December, 58.

Nemy, Enid (1987), 'Good News from the Rumor Mill', in 'On Stage' column, *New York Times*, 20 November, 66.

Nemy, Enid (1989), 'Possible Disk for "Carrie"', in 'On Stage' column, *New York Times*, 5 May, 62.

Nunn, Trevor (1988), 'The Nunn's Tale', *The Stage*, 29 September, 14.

Owen, Michael (1988), 'Carrie on Terry'/'Two in Tune', *Evening Standard*, 8 January, 24.

Paton, Maureen (1988), 'What a Carrie on', *Daily Express*, 19 February.

Petrucelli, Alan W. (1985), 'Hot Line' column, *The News Tribune*, 5 May, 70.

Porter, Rick (2019), '"Empire" and "The Voice" Adjust Up', *TV By The Numbers*, 19 April. Available online: https://web.archive.org/web/20180419224607/http://tvbythenumbers. zap2it.com/daily-ratings/wednesday-final-ratings-april-18-2018/ (accessed 19 November 2022).

Radin, Victoria (1988), 'Blood Money', *New Statesman*, 4 March, 31.

Ratcliffe, Michael (1988), 'Strutting their stuff', *The Observer*, 21 February, 24.

Rhodes, Peter (1988), 'Terrific Linzi Carries off an Epic Triumph', *Birmingham Express and Star*, 4 March.

Rich, Frank (1988), 'The Telekinetic "Carrie", with Music', *New York Times*, 13 May, 63.

Richards, David (1988), 'N.Y.'s hairy "Carrie"', *The Washington Post*, 13 May. Available online: https://www.washingtonpost.com/archive/lifestyle/1988/05/13/nys-hairy-carrie/cb4fe984-9a9e-4be4-8322-a194fa373489/ (accessed 5 May 2022).

Riedel, Michael (2009), 'Carrie, Unburied', *New York Post*, 10 October. Available online: https://nypost.com/2009/10/28/carrie-unburied/ (accessed 18 September 2022).

Rothstein, Mervyn (1988), 'After Seven Years and $7 Million, "Carrie" is a Kinetic Memory', *New York Times*, 17 May, 61.

Rothstein, Mervyn (1989), 'On Broadway, Spectacle Raises the Stakes', *New York Times*, 8 January.

Schaeffer, Martin (1988), 'Theatre Reviews', *Back Stage*, 20 May, 30A.

Schulman, Michael (2012), 'Is "Carrie" the Worst Musical of All Time?', *The New Yorker*, 27 January. Available online: https://www.newyorker.com/culture/culture-desk/is-carrie-the-worst-musical-of-all-time (accessed 5 May 2022).

Sherwin, Andy (2013), 'Viva Forever? Not Exactly – Spice Girls Musical Closes after Six Months Leaving Backers with £5m Loss', *The Independent*, 2 May. Available online: https://www.independent.co.uk/arts-entertainment/theatre-dance/news/viva-forever-not-exactly-spice-girls-musical-closes-after-six-months-leaving-backers-with-ps5m-loss-8600424.html (accessed 15 October 2022).

'Shock Treatment' (1988), *Coventry Evening Telegraph*, 19 February.

'Show Didn't Go On' (1988), *Stratford Herald*, 19 February.

Shulman, Milton (1988), 'Carrie with Rock is a No Horror Show', *Evening Standard*, 19 February, 10.

Simon, John (1988), 'Blood and No Guts', *New York*, 23 May.

Slatin, Peter (1995), 'A Broadway Showplace Returns to the Renaissance', *New York Times*, 22 January, 250.

Smurthwaite, Nick (1988), '"Carrie" from Behind the Scenes', *The Listener*, 11 February.

Spencer, Charles (1988), 'A Tragedy for the RSC', *Daily Telegraph*, 20 February.

Staff writer (1988), '"Carrie" Dies on Broadway', *The Cincinnati Enquirer*, 17 May, 21.

Staff writer (2011), 'Post-Mortem on the Bloody Mess that was "Carrie"', *Variety*, 4 Auugust. Available online: https://variety.com/2011/film/news/post-mortem-on-the-bloody-mess-that-was-carrie-1118040857/ (accessed 5 May 2022).

'Stephen King's "Carrie" Lands on London Stage' (1988), *Associated Press reproduced in Standard-Speaker*, 24 February, 8.

Steyn, Mark (1988), 'Period Pains', *The Independent*, 20 February.

Thorncroft, Antony (1988), 'Carried Away by the Cash', *Financial Times*, 6 February.

Tinker, Jack (1988), 'Oh Dear, Girls, What a Dreadful Carrie On', *Daily Mail*, 19 February.

Tookey, Christopher (1988), 'Flop!', *Telegraph* magazine, 3 December, 16.

Toomey, Christine (1993), 'Dietrich Musical Hits a Bitter Note in Germany', *Sunday Times*, 18 April, 21.

Trilling, Ossia (1985), Peter Hall profile, *The Stage*, 16 May, 10.

Trucco, Terry (1988), '"Carrie" Ghost Haunts Stage of Thatcher Britain', *Wall Street Journal*, 20 May.

Vauncez, Sidney (1988), 'Barbara Cook', review, *The Stage*, 11 August, 5.

Vellela, Tony (1988), 'A New Role for Debbie Allen', *TheaterWeek*, 21 May, 24.

Vidal, John (1988), 'The Selection of the Fittest', *The Guardian*, 7 April, 33.

Vincentelli, Elizabeth (2010), 'A Chat with Orchestrator Harold Wheeler', *New York Post*, 19 April. Available online: https://nypost.com/2010/04/19/a-chat-with-orchestrator-harold-wheeler/ (accessed 15 October 2022).

Wardle, Irving (1988), 'What a Carrie on . . .', *The Times*, 20 February.

Winer, Linda (1988), '"Carrie": Staging a Horror on Broadway', *Newsday*, 13 May, 221.

Wolf, Matthew (1988), 'The Horror of "Carrie" was Getting it Staged', *The Chicago Tribune*, 26 February, 51.

Wolf, Matt (1988), 'Carrie on Equity', *Drama*, May.

Young, Gregory (1998), 'Noises Off', column, *Entertainment Weekly*, 4 July.

Zoglin, Richard (2012), '*Carrie* is Back: The Resurrection and the Life', *Time*, 5 March. Available online: https://entertainment.time.com/2012/03/05/carrie-is-back-the-resurrection-and-the-life/ (accessed 18 September 2022).

Scripts, Libretti and Ephemera

There are no officially published scripts of the 1988 production. The following documents were consulted when quoting stage directions and excerpts. Lyrics are quoted with permission of Dean Pitchford.

2012 licensed edition of the score.

'Broadway score' (undated), possibly fan-produced using recordings, via archive.org.

'UK score' (March 1988), produced during the Stratford run, via archive.org.

'Working draft' (October 1987), produced for rehearsals, located in Royal Shakespeare Company Archives.

The RSC programme for the show is available online via https://archive.org/details/CarrieTheMusical1988Program (accessed 13 December 2022).

Videos

Carrie and associated special features (1976), DVD, Brian De Palma, United Artists.
Howard (2018), Disney+, Don Hahn, Stone Circle Pictures.

Footage of the musical

YouTube has a plethora of 'official' and 'bootleg' video and audio recordings of various productions of the show (which come and go), as well as associated films, including news footage, backstage and rehearsal footage and two seemingly abandoned 'making of' documentaries – a twenty-one-minute-long, fully edited one commissioned by Friedrich Kurz, referred to in this text as the 'Kurz documentary', and a shorter nine-minute-long, roughly edited film apparently commissioned by the RSC, possibly for media syndication, referred to in this text as the 'RSC documentary'. For Chapters 5 and 6, I have attempted to describe the show as clearly as possible based on the existing audio and video recordings, but there are so many variations in lyrics, script, structure and orchestration across the show's lifetime that it would be near impossible to describe every quirk. I encourage you to delve into the bootleg archives and explore!

INDEX

Dates of performances are shown in brackets after titles. Illustrations are shown in *italic* figures. Character names are entered directly – Carrie White will be found under C.